POWER OF UNDERSTANDING

POWER OF UNDERSTANDING

Essays in honour of Veikko Tähkä

Editor

Aira Laine

KARNAC

LONDON   NEW YORK

First published in 2004 by
H. Karnac (Books) Ltd.
6 Pembroke Buildings, London NW10 6RE

British Library Cataloguing in Publication Data

A C.I.P. for this book is available from the British Library

ISBN 1 85575 3952

Designed, typeset and produced by The Studio Publishing Services Ltd, Exeter EX4 8JN

Printed in Great Britain

10 9 8 7 6 5 4 3 2 1

www.karnacbooks.com

CONTENTS

ACKNOWLEDGEMENTS   ix

CONTRIBUTORS   xi

FOREWORD   xv

CHAPTER ONE
Psychoanalytic understanding and psychoanalytic therapy: 1
Veikko Tähkä's contributions
  Robert S. Wallerstein

CHAPTER TWO
A Festschrift for Veikko Tähkä—2003   29
  Pearl King

CHAPTER THREE
"Dissidence" in psychoanalysis: a psychoanalytic reflection 55
  Otto F. Kernberg

CHAPTER FOUR
Illusion and reality in the psychoanalytic relationship   73
  Riitta Tähkä

v

CHAPTER FIVE
On transference: an historical and present-day perspective   101
    Eero Rechardt

CHAPTER SIX
Actualized unconscious fantasies and "therapeutic play"   119
in adults' analyses: further study of these concepts
    Vamik D. Volkan

CHAPTER SEVEN
The past in the present: a case vignette   143
    Anne-Marie Sandler

CHAPTER EIGHT
Sexualities and neosexualities   157
    Joyce McDougall

CHAPTER NINE
Father makes a difference.
    The development of the son   175
    Leena Klockars

CHAPTER TEN
Dreams in the therapeutic relationship   199
    Terttu Eskelinen and Pere Folch

CHAPTER ELEVEN
A brief inquiry into the value of man   217
    Pentti Ikonen

CHAPTER TWELVE
The religions of health and beauty   225
    Mikael Enckell

CHAPTER THIRTEEN
Descartes' *cogito* as a model of reality   235
  Johannes Lehtonen

CHAPTER FOURTEEN
The conceptual space of psychoanalysis   251
  Simo Salonen

CHAPTER FIFTEEN
On the conditions of understanding.
  Reflections from the patient's point of view   261
    Henrik Enckell

CHAPTER SIXTEEN
On the idea of a new developmental object in   277
psychoanalytic treatment
  Jukka Välimäki

CHAPTER SEVENTEEN
When mother wasn't there to be left
  From functional to developmental object: a case report   301
    Aira Laine

SCIENTIFIC BIBLIOGRAPHY: *Veikko Tähkä, M.D.*   317

INDEX   329

ACKNOWLEDGEMENTS

I feel deep gratitude to the contributors and want to thank them warmly for their articles and pleasant collaboration. This book was made possible by you.

I want to thank from my heart Leena Häkkinen, Publishing Manager, for well-functioning cooperation which could even be conducted in Finnish, and I also want to thank H. Karnac Books for their interest in this project.

Aira Laine
Editor

CONTRIBUTORS

Henrik Enckell, M.D. Psychoanalyst, Finnish Psychoanalytical Society. Editor of *The Scandinavian Psychoanalytic Review* 1998–2002. His doctoral dissertation *Metaphor and the Psychodynamic Functions of the Mind* was published in 2002, and he has a private practice.

Mikael Enckell, M.D. is a training psychoanalyst, Finnish Psychoanalytical Society, and the author of several books on literature (most notably about the works of Marcel Proust, Friedrich Hölderlin, and Rabbe Enckell) His interests include cinema and Judaism. He has been a Member of the Swedish Psychoanalytical Society since 1967, and operates a private practice.

Terttu Eskelinen, Lic.Psych. is a training psychoanalyst, Spanish Psychoanalytical Society, a former editor of the *European Psychoanalytical Federation Bulletin,* former President of the European Psychoanalytical Federation, and former Vice-President of the International Psychoanalytical Association (2000–2002).

Pere Folch, M.D. is a training psychoanalyst, Spanish Psychoanalytical Society, a Member of the Swiss Psychoanalytical Society, and a former lecturer at the Sorbonne and Barcelona Universities. He is currently interested in organizing psychological assistance in public institutions.

Pentti Ikonen, MSc. (Psych.). Honorary Member, training psycho-analyst, former President of the Finnish Psychoanalytical Society, and former Chairman of the Training Committee. He has published on the theory and method of psychoanalysis in the international journals, and has been a member of the Swedish Psychoanalytical Society since 1956.

Otto F. Kernberg, M.D. is the Director of the Personality Disorders Institute, New York Presbyterian Hospital Westchester Division; Professor of Psychiatry, Weill Medical College of Cornell University; Training and Supervising Psychoanalyst, Columbia University Center for Psychoanalytic Training and Research. He is a former President of the International Psychoanalytical Association (1997–2001).

Pearl King, MSc. (Psych.). Honorary Member, training and super-vising psychoanalyst, former President of the British Psycho-analytical Society and Honorary Secretary of the International Psychoanalytical Association. Secretary to the Sponsoring Com-mittee of the Finnish Study Group (with Donald Winnicott as Chairman) and Honorary Member of the Finnish Psychoanalytical Society. Co-editor with Riccardo Steiner of *The Freud/Klein Contro-versies 1941–1945* and editor and compiler of *No Ordinary Psycho-analyst: The Exceptional Contributions of John Rickman*. She received the Sigourney award in 1992 for her contributions to psychoanalysis.

Leena Klockars, Lic.Psych. is a training psychoanalyst in adult, adolescent and child analysis, Vice-President of the Finnish Psychoanalytical Society, and is also in private practice.

Aira Laine, Lic.Psych. is a training psychoanalyst and former President of the Finnish Psychoanalytical Society, a former Secretary of the Eastern European Committee of the European Psychoanalytical Federation, and Associate Director of the Training Section of the IPA-EPF Han Groen-Prakken Psychoanalytic Institute for Eastern Europe (PIEE). She is also in private practice.

Johannes Lehtonen, M.D. is Professor of Psychiatry and Medical Director, Department of Psychiatry, University Hospital and the University of Kuopio, Finland. He is a Member of the Finnish Psychoanalytical Society, and a former President of the Finnish Psychiatric Association (1996–1999) and the Joint Nordic Committee of Psychiatric Associations (1994–1997). His research interests lie in the clinical, developmental, and theoretical aspects of the body ego.

Joyce McDougall, D.Ed. Honorary Training and Supervising Psychoanalyst, Paris Psychoanalytical Institute and Society. Author of *Dialogue with Sammy; Plea for a Measure of Abnormality; Theatres of the Mind: Illusion and Truth on the Psychoanalytic Stage; Theatres of the Body: A Psychoanalytic Approach to Psychosomatic Illness;* and *The Many Faces of Eros*—all translated into many languages. She is also in private practice.

Eero Rechardt, M.D. Docent in Psychiatry, University of Helsinki, Honorary Member, Training Psychoanalyst and former President of the Finnish Psychoanalytical Society, former Chairman of the Training Committee, Vice-President of the International Psychoanalytical Association (1981–1983) and former Chairman of the East European Committee of the European Psychoanalytical Federation. He has been a Member of the Swedish Psychoanalytical Society since 1960.

Simo Salonen, M.D. Docent in Psychiatry, University of Turku, Training Psychoanalyst, former President of the Finnish Psychoanalytical Society and former Chairman of the Training Committee. His scientific work deals with the foundations of psychic functioning and the traumatic states with special reference to psychotic disorders. He also operates a private practice.

Anne-Marie Sandler, Lic.es Scs. is a training and supervising psychoanalyst for adults and children, former assistant to Jean Piaget, former President of the British Psychoanalytical Society and of the European Psychoanalytical Federation, and a past Director of the Anna Freud Centre, London.

Riitta Tähkä, MSc. (Psych.). is a Training Psychoanalyst, Finnish Psychoanalytical Society, and is also in private practice.

Robert S. Wallerstein, M.D. is Emeritus Professor and former Chair, Department of Psychiatry, University of California, San Fransisco School of Medicine, and Emeritus Training and Supervising Psychoanalyst, San Fransisco Psychoanalytic Institute. Former President of the American Psychoanalytic Association (1971–1972) and former President of the International Psychoanalytical Association (1985–1989).

Vamik D.Volkan, M.D. is Emeritus Professor of Psychiatry and Founder of the Center for the Study of Mind and Human Interaction at the University of Virginia, Charlottesville, Virginia; Training and Supervising Psychoanalyst, Washington Psychoanalytic Institute, Washington, DC; Erik H. Erikson Scholar, The Austen Riggs Center, Stockbridge, Massachusetts.

Jukka Välimäki, M.D. is a training psychoanalyst, former President of the Finnish Psychoanalytical Society, former Chairman of the Training Committee, and also runs a private practice.

FOREWORD

This book has been published in honour of Veikko Tähkä, M.D., the prime founder of the Finnish Psychoanalytical Society and a central pioneer in psychoanalysis and psychoanalytic psychotherapy in Finland. The book celebrates his life-work and his eightieth birthday.

Veikko Tähkä was born on 13 August 1923 in Noormarkku, a rural community where his father worked as a country doctor. When he was eight years old the family moved to the city of Turku and, seven years later, to Helsinki, where his father had a leading position in the National Medical Board.

Having graduated from school and participated in the Second World War at the Finnish front in Karelia against the Soviet Union (1941–1944), Veikko Tähkä enrolled in medical studies at the University of Helsinki and received his M.D. in 1950.

There were no psychoanalysts at that time in Finland, and psychiatry was predominantly descriptive and heredity-orientated. However, during those post-war years there developed an increasing interest in psychoanalytic and psychodynamic thoughts among several young graduates and students of medicine and psychology. The general cultural climate in Finland was favourable for such a development and there were no strong prejudices against psycho-analysis in academic circles. A "Society for the Advancement of Psychoanalysis in Finland" was founded and some of the most motivated people decided to go abroad for psychoanalytic training.

Veikko Tähkä was among the first to leave. In the spring of 1953 he moved to Stockholm with his wife and three pre-school children. After an economically difficult but professionally rewarding four years in Sweden he returned with his family to Finland in 1957 as an associate member of the Swedish Psychoanalytical Society. He completed his residency at the Psychiatric University Clinic in Helsinki and received the speciality in psychiatry and neurology in 1958. Simultaneously he had a part-time psychoanalytic practice and became a full member of the Swedish Society in 1958 by a case presentation of a schizophrenic girl´s treatment.

Having become acquainted with the works of Erik H.Erikson and David Rapaport and encouraged by his Swedish colleague Börje Löfgren, who at that time was working at the Austen Riggs Center in Stockbridge, USA, Veikko Tähkä started corresponding with Robert P. Knight, the medical director of the Center, which resulted in his moving with his family to work at Riggs for two years (1959–1961). Veikko Tähkä has described these two years at Riggs, a period that coincided with a time when Knight, Erikson, Rapaport, David Shapiro, and several other dedicated people belonged to its staff, as extremely stimulating and rewarding, both professionally and socially. When, after the two years, he was offered a permanent position on the staff, he faced a difficult deci-sion. However, a number of private family and loyalty reasons made him choose to return to his home country.

Back in Finland Veikko Tähkä received the status of training and supervising analyst in the Swedish Society. At that time there still were only two other analysts in Finland and as the only training analyst Tähkä filled his schedule with motivated professionals. When, after two years, five more analysts had returned from train-ing abroad, Veikko Tähkä began negotiations with the International Psychoanalytical Association about the possibility of starting a Finnish Study Group.

This was followed by a rapid development during which the Finnish Sudy Group was established (1964) and a Sponsoring Committee was founded with Donald Winnicott as the chairman and Pearl King as the secretary. Four more training analysts were appointed and the first seven candidates started their seminars in the autumn of 1965. The Finnish Study Group became a Provisional Society of International Association in 1967 and a Component Society in 1969.

Veikko Tähkä presided over all those successive organizations through the pioneering years between 1964 and 1971. The Finnish Psychoanalytical Society has been, and still is, an active society both clinically and scientifically, with regular meetings every other week and frequent visitors from foreign societies; in 1981 the Finnish Society arranged the International Psychoanalytic Congress in Helsinki. Today there are about 190 members in the Finnish Society and about forty candidates in training. Veikko Tähkä was elected an honorary member in 1977.

When the European Psychoanalytic Federation was founded in 1966 Veikko Tähkä became a member of its Committee of Scientific Exchange and served as a vice-president of the Federation during the years of 1970–1979. He has also served for several years as a member of the Research Advisory Board of the International Psychoanalytical Association.

Veikko Tähkä´s first published book, entitled *The Alcholic Personality* (1966), was his doctoral thesis based on the interviews with and projective tests on a sample of fifty Swedish male alcoholics. After his dissertation in 1966 Veikko Tähkä was nominated as assistant professor at the University of Helsinki. As an academic teacher he was a central figure in introducing psychoanalytic thinking and psychoanalytic psychotherapy into Finnish psychiatry. He worked as a senior psychiatrist at the Psychiatric University Clinic in Helsinki (1964–1971), while at the same time having his own psychoanalytic practice. Besides lecturing to students of medicine and psychology and teaching psychoanalytic psychotherapy to residents, he also set up in one ward of the clinic Finland´s first therapeutic community, run in accordance with the principles applied at the Austen Riggs Center. It was the first psychiatric ward in Finland where the wearing of uniforms by the personnel was abandoned.

As the chairman of the psychotherapy section of the Finnish Psychiatric Society, Veikko Tähkä started to arrange with his colleagues regular training courses in psychoanalytic psychotherapy for psychiatrists and other interested physicians. The courses, with

40–50 participants, lasted from three to four years and trained psychoanalysts as teachers and supervisors. This programme has been continued right up to the present day, although now with smaller groups. To meet the growing need for a Finnish textbook of psychoanalytic psychiatry, Veikko Tähkä published his first major work *Psykoterapian perusteet* (*Basic Principles of Psychotherapy*) in 1970. With some revision this book has been the basic textbook in the most training programmes of psychoanalytic psychotherapy in Finland for over thirty years. Its Danish, Swedish and, lately, also Estonian and Lithuanian editions have also been widely used in the neighbouring countries. Veikko Tähkä was the president of the Finnish Psychiatric Society 1968–1970 and became an honorary member in 1983.

In 1971 Veikko Tähkä was invited to take the position of associate professor at the University of Turku, where he worked for five years. Besides teaching residents and developing a therapeutic community at the Psychiatric University Clinic, his territory included teaching the patient–doctor relationship to medical students. This being a novel branch of study in Finland, in 1977 Veikko Tähkä wrote, with the support of the Finnish Medical Association, his second textbook *Potilas-lääkärisuhde* (*The Patient–Doctor Relationship*). This book became required reading in Finnish medical faculties and was later translated into English and Portuguese. During his stay in Turku Veikko Tähkä also had in training analysis some people who later became the core of a steadily growing group of psychoanalysts.

In 1976 Veikko Tähkä became professor of psychiatry at the University of Kuopio and the head of the Psychiatric University Clinic. During his stay there the Psychiatric University Clinic was structured and organized with training programmes for residents and several scientific projects, especially in psychosomatic problems and various levels of therapeutic relatedness and interaction in both somatic medicine and psychotherapy. The "Eastern Finland Psychotherapy Association" was established, with a psychotherapeutic training programme of its own. As in Turku, Veikko Tähkä had in training analysis people who later became members of the Finnish Psychoanalytical Society.

Veikko Tähkä´s first wife died of breast cancer in 1980. When, in 1987, after retiring from his professorship, he returned to the

Austen Riggs Center as the Erik H. Erikson Scholar and continued his stay with another year as a Visiting Scholar, his second wife Riitta, a psychoanalyst, followed him to work at Riggs also as a Visiting Scholar. These two years gave Veikko Tähkä an opportunity to concentrate on preliminary preparation of his main work *Mind and Its Treatment: A Psychoanalytic Approach*. This book, which represents the synthesis of his thinking based on more than forty years' experience as a clinician, researcher, teacher, and supervisor, was first published in English 1993, in Finnish in 1996, and in Russian in 2001.

Having finished this vast undertaking after his return to Finland, Veikko Tähkä moved to the neighbourhood of Helsinki, where he and his wife opened private practices in Espoo in 1991. In addition to that he has continued to be active as a dedicated teacher and supervisor whose enthusiasm, clarity, and thorough knowledge of the field has been available to several generations of Finnish analysts and psychotherapists. He has held many positions of trust and continues with his writing. In the register of Finnish physicians he lists as his special interests visual arts, literature, and the essence of the experiential world. His favourite place is his small island in the Baltic Sea.

Veikko Tähkä's main work, *Mind and Its Treatment: A Psychoanalytic Approach*, consists of three parts: *On the Formation of the Mind; The Nature and Elements of Psychoanalytic Understanding*; and *Therapeutic Use of Psychoanalytic Understanding*. Together they form an original and innovative overall theory of the development of the human mind, the arrests and disturbances of that development and the phase-specific encountering of the latter.

Although stressing dynamic, developmental, and object relational points of view, VeikkoTähkä's theoretical framework does not belong to any particular psychoanalytic school of today. In his work the whole spectrum of psychic disturbances has been taken as a challenge for psychoanalytic treatment. In his own words:

> During the last thirty to forty years our knowledge has increased substantially both regarding the early development of the mind and the structure and dynamics of psychoses and borderline states. Simultaneously, our understanding of the analytic instrument as well as of the phase-specific ways of activating and assisting

belated mental structure building in pathologic conditions more severe than neurosis have greatly improved. It seems that these developments are sufficient for justifying attempts, already referred to by Freud, at integrating the present-day psychoanalytic knowledge of normal and pathological development and the current clinical expertise into a unified theory that would allow the development of psychoanalytic treatment into a phase-specific approach, applicable in principle to all levels of disturbed and arrested mental development. An attempt in this direction is made in the present book. [Tähkä, 1993, p. 1]

The achievement of a goal of this magnitude requires important reassessments of theories about normal and disturbed developments of the mind, as well as major enlargements and specifications in current theories of the goals and curative factors of psychoanalytic treatment. Veikko Tähkä´s magnum opus represents an impressive step on the road, still less travelled, towards a general psychoanalytic theory of the human mind and its treatment.

In Veikko Tähkä's clinical theory *understanding*—its origins, nature, and interactive sharing—emerges as the key concept. The analyst's sharing with his patient as accurately as possible his individual and phase-specific understanding of the patient´s way of experiencing himself and the object world is considered both as the general goal of psychoanalysis and the means that motivates the analyst's becoming represented as a new developmental object for the patient, thus motivating a new start for his arrested structural development. This view of the role of shared understanding as the principal curative element in the analytic process is clearly expressed in the choice of the title of the present book.

Aira Laine and Jukka Välimäki

Psychoanalytic understanding and psychoanalytic therapy: Veikko Tähkä's contributions

Robert S. Wallerstein

From its inception, psychoanalysis has always been concerned to delineate its dimensions, its therapeutic reach and limitations, and the arc of the psychopathological spectrum amenable to its deployment. For Sigmund Freud, who almost single-handedly created psychoanalysis as a theory of mental life and a systematic therapy for the disorders of mental life, these concerns were not problematic. He developed psychoanalysis as a purified product out of the congeries of therapeutic approaches in vogue in his time, or experimentally introduced by him and his first co-worker, Josef Breuer—electrical stimulation, rest cures, hypnotic suggestion, forced associations on command—and it soon became the scientific psychology and the etiologically-based therapy.

By as early as 1905, Freud had already set down, in his paper "On psychotherapy", his criteria for analysability, i.e., amenability to this rationally understood and powerful new tool for mental therapy. The criteria there stated are those that have always marked our conception of the "good analytic patient"—one who suffers from a chronic neurosis of the kind classically designated (by Freud) as a transference neurosis—who has "a reasonable degree of education . . . [and] a fairly reliable character" (1905, p. 263), who is well motivated ("driven to seek treatment by their own sufferings", *ibid.*), who is beyond adolescence but still in the prime of adulthood, is not in any situation of emergency, and who possesses a "normal mental condition" (*ibid.*, p. 264) (Eissler's [1953] "normal ego"[1]), that is, is not suffering, in Freud's language, from psychosis, states of confusion, or deeply rooted depression. By implication—and in contrast—psychoanalysts had little or nothing to offer to patients not suited to the classical analytic method, beyond the same varieties of suggestive and hypnotic techniques that their non-analytically informed confrères employed.

It is this view, that proper psychoanalysis ("classical psychoanalysis") directed at the amenable classically psychoneurotic patients (those suffering from hysterias, phobic states, or obsessional disorders) was the only truly scientific and curative psychotherapy available, that pervaded the period extending over most of Freud's working lifetime. And it was reinforced by a number of articles, especially by Ernest Jones (1910) and Edward Glover (1931, 1954), which drew even more sharply the distinctions between psychoanalysis as an etiologically-directed and curative therapy and all other psychotherapeutic interventions, dismissed as but various species of outmoded suggestion. This viewpoint was carried to its furthermost by Glover as late as the 1954 article. He said then: "A further case exists: should the analyst's interpretations be consistently inaccurate then quite clearly he is practicing a form of suggestion, whatever else he himself may call it. It follows then that when analysts differ radically as to the aetiology or structure of a case—as they nowadays do with increasing frequency—one side or the other must be practicing suggestion" (1954, p. 394). But Glover had earlier softened the blow: "bad analysis may conceivably be good suggestion" (1931, p. 407).

We all know of course that Freud's fervent efforts to maintain his psychoanalysis as a theoretically coherent and unitary understanding of mental functioning, and a clinically unified vehicle for ameliorating the disorders of mental functioning, were not sustained, even in his lifetime, despite his creation in 1910, together with his followers, of the International Psychoanalytical Association (IPA), established at the second International Psychoanalytical Congress, held that year in Nuremberg,[2] and the creation two years later, in 1912, of the "Secret Committee" of the seven ring-holders;

both of these moves being efforts to guarantee the stability of his central psychoanalytic doctrines against fractious divisiveness from within, and against diluting or hostile pressures from without. In this way, Freud and his continuing closest adherents sought to ensure the enduring capacity and loyalty to their reigning conceptions of all those who carried the psychoanalytic imprimatur.

The developments that undid Freud's efforts to maintain this bounded unitary and unified theory and technique of psychoanalysis took place in two directions, distinct, but also complexly interrelated; (1) the rise, beginning with the Kleinian movement, even in Freud's lifetime, of alternative metapsychologies, posing differing visions of the essential theoretical structure of psychoanalysis with then differing technical applications, unto today's widely acknowledged diversity (or pluralism, as we call it) of theoretical perspectives; and (2) the derivation, out of psychoanalytic understanding, of modified and altered techniques—called expressive and supportive psychoanalytic psychotherapies—adapted to the clinical exigencies of the vast spectrum of mental patients not amenable to the "classical" psychoanalytic techniques devised by Freud, i.e., "sicker" or beyond the traditionally psychoneurotic.

I have written about both these developmental directions at length, in a sequence of articles (Wallerstein, 1988, 1989, 1990, 2002), and in two books (1992, 1995). Here I will trace, very briefly, relevant aspects of one of these developments, the historical growth and unfolding of psychoanalytically informed psychotherapy based on the psychoanalytical theoretical understanding of mental functioning, but with the modified and altered techniques necessary to bring the wider spectrum of psychopathological disorders, not amenable to proper psychoanalysis, within our therapeutic orbit.[3] It is in this framework that I can then place the signal contribution to psychoanalysis propounded by Veikko Tähkä, to whom this volume is dedicated, in a sequence of articles and then developed most fully in his masterful volume, *Mind and its Treatment: A Psychoanalytic Approach* (1993).

Actually, psychoanalytic psychotherapy as we have come to know it was, at the start, a distinctively American development.[4] For various reasons of historical and social context, which I have spelled out in detail elsewhere (Wallerstein, 1974, 1980), and with whatever degree of credit or blame we wish to attribute to the defensive responses of Freud and his followers, or to the hostile reactions of an unreceptive academic and intellectual milieu fearful of the Freudian idea, however we wish to parcel out the responsibility for the developing state of affairs, the fact is that psychoanalysis grew up in its European heartland essentially outside psychiatry, medicine, and academia—a major intellectual–educational enterprise run as a private night school carried on the tired energies of part-time men and women after working days spent in full-time clinical practice.

This was precisely the fate that the American psychoanalysts, swollen by the tide of Hitler refugee analysts in the 1930s which propelled America into the majority centre of organized psychoanalysis in the world, sought successfully to avoid. And in the post-Second World War decades of the 1950s and 1960s, this quest succeeded brilliantly; as the prior generation of Adolf Meyer-trained "psychobiological" psychiatrist[5] chairs of departments of psychiatry in the nation's medical schools came to retirement, full-time academic psychoanalysts were avidly sought to replace them, with the expectation of ensconcing psychoanalytic theory as the prevailing psychology of psychiatry, and applied psychoanalytic techniques as the prevailing therapeutic. But in this setting the psychoanalyst department chairs, and the supporting psychoanalysts brought in as teachers and supervisors, were confronted with the patient populations of the medical schools' psychiatric hospitals and out-patient clinics, a more diverse and a sicker population than the out-patient psychoneurotic patients in the European analysts' consulting rooms around whom the technical precepts of classical psychoanalysis had been originally elaborated by Freud and his colleagues.

It is in the adaptation of psychoanalytic understandings to the clinical exigencies of this new, sicker patient population, ranging all the way to the hospitalized overtly psychotic, that the principles of the psychoanalytic psychotherapies, in all their more expressive and more supportive forms, were elaborated. This in itself is a long and complicated developmental unfolding, which I have chronicled at length elsewhere (Wallerstein, 1989, 1995), in which some of the central names were, first, Robert Knight, Leo Stone, Merton Gill, Leo Rangell, Franz Alexander, Frieda Fromm-Reichmann, Edward Bibring, and Anna Freud, and then shortly after, Hans Loewald,

Elizabeth Zetzel, and Ralph Greenson, to be followed then by the generation of Heinz Kohut, Otto Kernberg, and John Gedo, among many others. It is of note that in this listing of the major figures in the development of a distinctive psychoanalytic psychotherapy, linked to, and derived from, psychoanalysis proper, only Anna Freud, who was of course closely linked, theoretically and clinically, to the ego psychology metapsychological paradigm architected by Hartmann and his collaborators in America, did not work in the United States.[6]

Very briefly, I can summarize this large volume of work—many contributors over a several-decade time span—under two temporal time frames, the earlier, centring around three panel discussions held sequentially at the meetings of the American Psychoanalytic Association, and all published together in one issue of the *Journal of the American Psychoanalytic Association* in 1954, which I have described in detail elsewhere (Wallerstein, 1989, 1995) under the rubric, "the era of consensus", and the second time period, encompassing work during the 1970s and 1980s (also in Wallerstein, 1989, 1995), in what I have called "the era of fragmented consensus". It is during that second period that Veikko Tähkä emerged as a central protagonist with a distinctive hierarchical and developmental model of the nature of mind and the treatment of the disorders of mind, in which the parameters of psychoanalysis proper as conceptualized for classically neurotic patients have been modified and extended "beyond interpretation" in order to encompass sicker and more disorganized patients within the purview of psychoanalytic understanding, where it becomes a matter of arbitrary choice as to where along this spectrum one wishes, for conceptual or heuristic reasons, to state that one has crossed the border into the realm of psychoanalytic psychotherapy. In fact, with Tähkä's scheme, the designation psychoanalysis or psychotherapy hardly seems to matter—the entire theoretical conceptualization is indubitably psychoanalytic. More about that in explicit detail later.

First, some words about the preceding "era of consensus" out of which the work of Tähkä and all the other diverging directions emerged. In the earlier period—the 1940s and 1950s, starting with the pioneering papers of Robert Knight[7]—the aim was to clearly delineate psychoanalytic psychotherapy from the psychoanalysis from which it derived, as a distinctive technical modification of classical psychoanalytic therapy, geared to the clinical exigencies of those patients who were "sicker", that is, beyond amenability to psychoanalysis proper, and/or also those patients whose life difficulties could be ameliorated without the need for the full psychoanalytic unravelling of the total life experience back to the early infantile oedipal configurations.

The first of these two groups, in the words of Merton Gill (1954) the "sicker" patients, would be candidates for a more supportive psychoanalytic psychotherapy, and the second group, "weller" patients (with more situationally based neurotic difficulties) would be candidates for a more expressive psychoanalytic psychotherapy. And with all of these, the effort would be to demarcate the distinctive characteristics of the three separable treatment modalities, psychoanalysis proper, expressive psychoanalytic psychotherapy, and supportive psychoanalytic psychotherapy, to clarify their similarities and their differences, and to specify their distinctive (and different) aims, technical implementations, and expected outcomes. That was essentially the majority consensus in the 1950s, based on the sharpening of distinctions. There was at the time a distinct minority, Franz Alexander and his followers, and Frieda Fromm-Reichmann (1950) and her followers, who were intent on blurring these distinctions, but they were essentially marginalized within the prevailing ego psychology metapsychological paradigm, monolithically regnant in American psychoanalysis at the time—when the Americans still represented the majority of the institutionally organized psychoanalytic world.

But it was also this majority consensus that fragmented over the succeeding twenty-five years, partly out of the growing preoccupation with categories of patients not encompassed within the classical psychoanalytic tradition (Kohut's work with the narcissistic personality disorders, Kernberg's work with the borderline personality organizations, etc.), and partly out of the growing recognition within American psychoanalysis of the theoretical diversity or pluralism that had come to characterize worldwide psychoanalysis, beginning with the Kleinian movement in Britain, and followed by the growth of the British object relational school (based on Fairbairn and Balint and Winnicott and Bowlby and many others), the Bionian extension of Klein, the Lacanian and, even in America, the creation of Kohut's self psychology and Mahler's developmental perspectives, as well as the particular hermeneutic emphases of Ricoeur in France and Habermas in Germany, and others as well.

And within the fragmenting of the earlier (American) consensus on the nature of the relationship between psychoanalysis and the related and derived psychoanalytic psychotherapies, one of the major voices that emerged, articulating an integrated hierarchical and developmental overview, bringing the therapeutics of the whole range of technical approaches across the entire psychopathological spectrum from the highest function, classically psychoneurotic patients all the way to the disorganized psychotic patients, within an overall psychoanalytically understood and conceived framework, was the Finnish psychoanalytic leader, Veikko Tähkä. A member of the first generation, pioneering psychoanalytic community in his native land, and deservedly the first president of the Finnish Psychoanalytic Society, Tähkä's various writings, and especially his already mentioned 1993 book, propelled him into an internationally recognized orbit as among the powerful voices redefining the relationship of psychoanalysis to the derived psychoanalytic psychotherapies in the era I have called that of the "fragmented consensus" (roughly, the 1970s and 1980s).

I had come to know Veikko Tähkä somewhere along the line, perhaps from reading his earlier work in the *Scandinavian Psychoanalytic Review* (published in English), perhaps during one of his two periods of sojourn in America, at the Austen Riggs Center (where Robert Knight had been the Director), in Stockbridge, Massachusetts. Out of our acquaintance and our shared deep interest in these issues—theoretical, clinical, technical—in psychoanalysis *vis-à-vis* psychoanalytic psychotherapy, Veikko asked if I would write the Foreword for his impressive 1993 book, an assignment that I accepted with pleasure, and which indeed gave me the opportunity to study in detail and to comment upon his masterful synthesis of a professional lifetime of creative and insightful thought on these very important psychoanalytic issues of such concern to both of us.

And I have thought that I can best carry out the assignment I have undertaken in contributing to this Festschrift in Veikko Tähkä's honour, in celebration of his eightieth birthday, by providing my overview of his major contribution to this field of joint concern and of signal importance—drawn in very significant ways by direct quotations from his writing—and setting it then into the context of present-day discourse on these issues that have centrally concerned our discipline for over half a century now; that is, over the whole of both our professional lifetimes.

Actually, the main thrust of Veikko Tähkä's book was presaged in a 1979 article published in the *Scandinavian Psychoanalytic Review*. There he carried his views distinctively beyond Freud's original conceptualization—which I have outlined at the beginning of this chapter—of the nature of our psychoanalytic enterprise and its therapeutic applications. By jumping ahead to Tähkä's own articulation of Freud's conception, I quote from his 1993 book:

> Freud was explicit in his definition of psychoanalysis as "a method for the treatment of neurotic disorders. . . ." The technique often referred to as "classical" analysis was specifically developed by him for the treatment of neurotic patients, and he never recommended its use in treating other patient categories. On the contrary, he excluded from the indications of psychoanalysis all those patients who were not capable of developing analyzable transference neuroses. . . . This was fully consistent with the established body of psychoanalytic knowledge at that time. Freud never developed a theory of preoedipal development and its failures, that would have allowed a structural and dynamic understanding of the pathogenic conditions underlying psychotic and borderline levels of psychopathology. In the absence of such theory and understanding, no specific psychoanalytic approach for their treatment could be developed either. [Tähkä, 1993, p. 161]

By contrast, and going back to his earlier 1979 paper, Tähkä developed a concept of

> psychotherapy [i.e., analytic psychotherapy] as a phase-specific interaction in which the curative factors change in accordance with the changes in the level of the patient's relatedness to his therapist. What in the classical analyses are defined as "parameters"[8] of the technique appear to be curative factors of prime importance when dealing with patients whose disturbances are more severe than neuroses. [Tähkä, 1979, p. 113]

To put this a little differently and even more clearly, he also wrote

There are therapeutic applications of the psychoanalytic theory not only for the treatment of neurosis but also for the more severe levels of pathology. This does not mean "widening" the scope[9] of application of the classical technique to the treatment of personality disturbances for which it has not been developed. What it does mean is the application of psychoanalytic knowledge to patients who represent earlier and more extensive disturbances of personality development than neurotic patients do and who therefore also benefit from other aspects of the therapeutic interaction. [ibid., pp. 115–116).

In this context, Tähkä advanced his concept that repetition is not always transference, and this concept in turn undergirded all his recommendations for technique. He put it thus:

Pathogenic object relations from the past regularly repeat themselves in the patient's relationship to his therapist. . . . It is important to realize that this repetition is not always that which we call transference . . . that the term transference is also used to describe repetitions of disturbed developmental interactions from levels other than neurotic easily leads to erroneous conclusions about the nature of these repetitions and a tendency towards treating them as neurotic transferences. [ibid., p. 118].

And here Tähkä clearly distinguished the psychotherapeutic from the psychoanalytic process: "Prestructural disturbances in object relations may be treatable but it is very questionable whether they are analyzable" (1979, p. 119).

Tähkä made his developmental distinctions in terms of three levels, not the five specified in parallel work during the same time period by two American workers, John Gedo and Arnold Goldberg (Gedo & Goldberg, 1973; Gedo, 1979),[10] Tähkä's three corresponding to the familiar psychopathological categories of the psychotic, the borderline, and the neurotic. In the overtly psychotic,

the patient's regression has then reached an objectless period, and this makes it impossible for the interactional disturbance to repeat itself in transference which, by definition, is an object relationship. [Täkhä, 1979, p. 119]

In this sense, he adhered to Freud's original conception that psychotics do not form transferences in the true sense. Then what is the nature of the therapist–patient relationship in such cases?

> If our basic assumption is . . . that this pathogenic disturbance repeats itself in a phase-specific way in the patient's relationship to his therapist, then the therapist, at least to some extent, has a position analogous to that of the primary object at the time of the original disturbance. The therapist's becoming a phase-specific object to the patient also gives him an opportunity in a new interaction to try to repair or ameliorate the consequences of the once disturbed interaction between the patient and his primary objects [ibid., p. 121]

This proffered interaction with the psychotic, Tähkä called the experiences of gratification:

> The analysts who have studied the early development of personality quite unanimously emphasize the importance of the experiences of gratification as the central precondition for those early internalizations which lead to differentiation of self and object. . . . The therapist should, therefore, act in a way which leads to the formation of a good object image in the patient's representational world. . . . The key word is gratification and a kind of gratification in which the therapist has, by the help of his complementary reactions, correctly grasped the patient's need and an acceptable form and time for its gratification. . . . A central problem in offering gratification to psychotic patients is that the infant–mother analogy cannot be carried too far. . . . The experiences of gratification should therefore usually be offered in indirect and symbolic ways, for which the therapist's phase-specifically tuned presence provides the foundation.[11] [ibid., pp. 123–124).

Next are the borderline states, defined by Tähkä more broadly than usual:

> Borderline states represent that level of pathology which, in addition to the "regular" borderline states, includes the so-called narcissistic personality disorders (Kohut), most addictions and perversions, and a considerable fraction of various character disorders (Kernberg). . . . The specific developmental disturbance of the borderline pathology is thought to consist of disturbances of those internalization processes which normally create the basic structure

of the ego. Differentiation between the self and the object ha been sufficiently reached, which protects the patient against psychotic breakdown, but the interaction between his primary objects and himself has failed in its phase-specific task of promoting internalization and structuralization of the personality. . . . The individual's ability to secure drive satisfaction, control anxiety and maintain an inner balance remains deficient and dependent on outside sources [*ibid.*, p. 126]

Therefore,

the . . . goal with a borderline patient seems to be to help him build that inner equipment which is the precondition of his autonomy, identity, and ability to love and hate real people. This goal can also be expressed in Mahler's terminology as the resolution of the separation–individuation crisis, in Hartmann's as the attainment of object-constancy, in Kohut's as the transformation of a prestructural object into a poststructural one, or in Kernberg's terminology as the integration of the good and bad representations. [*ibid.*, p. 127]

And finally, "As the key word in the treatment of psychoses is gratification, in the case of borderline states it seems to be identification" (*ibid.*, p. 127).

With the neurotic, the key words are "interpretation" and "insight". Interpretation, it is to be understood, means different things at the different phase-levels:

If interpretations mean to a psychotic patient oral gifts from the therapist, to a borderline patient their effects seem to depend primarily on their suitability for identification models. [*ibid.*, p. 128]

Insight, too, is qualified: "Insight does not create structures—it mainly changes the economic and dynamic relationships between already established structures" (*ibid.*, p. 128). Further,

The analyst's task in this phase-specific repetition [of the transference neurosis] is to liberate the patient from his unconscious ties to his parents, whom he no longer needs as developmental adjuvants. The analyst refuses to assume the role offered to him by the patient and, instead, reveals to the patient the existence and origins of his transference. There is little doubt that the analyst's main instrument in this work is interpretation, and that insight is the specifically curative factor in the treatment of neurotic pathology. [*ibid.*, p. 129]

Tähkä concluded:

If psychosis is considered a condition in which the differentiation between self- and object-representations has been lost, the therapist's phase-specific task is to become a good object in the patient's inner world by adequately providing him with experiences of gratification. If borderline states are thought to be the conditions in which the disturbance in the formation of ego structures is specific, the therapist's function, analogous to that of the primary object, is to provide the patient with useful identification models for a belated ego building. If neurosis is regarded as the pathology of an already structured personality, in which repressed oedipal love and hate problems are specific, the therapist's task is to help the patient to become conscious of them and resolve them by providing him with insight through interpretation and working through. [*ibid.*, p. 130]

And then, even more tersely, and very epigrammatically,

For the psychotic patient we have to become an object, for the borderline patient we have to act as an object and, finally, the neurotic patient we have to liberate from an object which has become superfluous. (*ibid.*, p. 131]

Thus were laid out, by 1979, the main outlines of Tähkä's hierarchical and developmental model of mind and its disorders, and their psychoanalytically guided treatment, encompassing the entire spectrum of psychopathological disorders, from the classical neuroses for whom Tähkä clearly was recommending a traditional psychoanalysis quite within the American ego psychological model dominant at the time—at least in America—and ranging then through the various categories of borderline into the overt psychoses, with extensive technical modifications of basic psychoanalytic treatment approaches, the kinds of modifications that other contributors to the ongoing dialogue at the time concerning the proper relationship between psychoanalysis and the derived and linked psychoanalytic psychotherapies were designating as varieties of expressive and supportive psychoanalytic psychotherapies.

Tähkä's was certainly a carefully conceptualized and thoroughly integrated schema which, sadly from my point of view, was not published in a journal readily accessed by American readers and therefore did not become widely known within the American psychoanalytic audience where this debate re psychoanalysis *vis-à-vis* psychotherapy was of such central interest. The very similar five-level conceptual schema being elaborated over this same time period by John Gedo (Gedo & Goldberg, 1973; Gedo, 1979) was much more visible in America, and it could indeed have led to useful refinements and clarifications if both these models had comparable visibility and could have been readily compared side by side for their convergences and possible divergences.

Veikko Tähkä, of course, continued in his own directions, which included a second period in America, again at the Austen Riggs Center in Stockbridge, Massachusetts, this time from 1987 to 1989, and he brought his thinking on these issues to full-fledged fruition in his most impressive book of 1993, *Mind and Its Treatment: A Psychoanalytic Approach* (published in Finnish in 1996), for which I was privileged to write the Foreword. I began my Foreword with the statement that it was part of our parochialism in America that we were insufficiently conversant with the psychoanalytic traditions and developments in other regions of psychoanalytic activity, and this was of course especially so when combined with different language areas than our own—though this latter should have been less of a handicap with the writings from very small language groups (like Finnish), where so many of the contributors made the effort to also write in English, as Veikko Tähkä did with the 1979 article that I have quoted at such length. In my Foreword, I called it part of the true internationalization of organized international psychoanalysis that this hiatus was at the time of my writing—1993—clearly being overcome, and that important contributions from other regions and nations, even small ones like Finland, were being brought prominently within the American and anglophone orbit, and that this volume by Veikko Tähkä, the distillate of more than forty years of scholarly reflection as psychoanalytic researcher, clinician, and teacher in Finland, was a happy and excellent example of this.

I said in that Foreword that actually this was not one, but rather two, books, as indicated by the implicit split in its title. First, it was a book about the development of the mind, the dynamic mental developmental process from its earliest beginnings until the achievement of personal autonomy and emancipation, that is, adulthood, with all of the possibilities along the way for inadequate, distorted, and deflected development, or rather maldevelopment, and the consequent emergence along the way of the array of mental disorders across the psychopathological spectrum: the frankly psychotic, the variously borderline, and the typically neurotic.

Second, this was a book about the treatment, the psychoanalytic therapeutics of this psychopathological array, treatment grounded in, and derived from, the theory of development that Tähkä propounded, and that sought then to offer a psychoanalytically conceived therapy specifically relevant to the psychopathological disturbances of each level of developmental fixation and distortion, without getting caught in the thicket of the limitations, semantic or substantial, of the various designations of proper, or "classical" psychoanalysis, *vis-à-vis* psychoanalytic or psychoanalytically-orientated psychotherapy or psychotherapies.

In his book, Tähkä begins to elaborate his theory of the development of mind with a number of guiding principles, actually few and simple. His is an uncompromisingly mentalist approach with mind being all (but also only) that which can be experienced and represented in the language of mental representations. It is, additionally, a dynamic approach that essays to establish a meaningful and motivated basis for each developmental step in the increasingly complex and layered hierarchical organization of the mind, as against a more purely genetic (and descriptive) approach focused more on the "what" and the "how" than the "why" of the normal and abnormal maturational and growth process. And it is set in the language of self and of self-experience, as the mind develops a capacity for self-reflective awareness, while avoiding the conceptual abstractions of ego and id, or libido and cathexis, or forces and mechanisms, as too experience-distant, not elements of the experiencing self, the sentient mind that is Tähkä's unwavering focus.

Within these parameters, Tähkä creates an increasingly complex model of the mind, in its overall conceptualization neither unfamiliar nor uncongenial to those reared within Freud's structural theory and the ego psychological metapsychology paradigm that for so long represented the American psychoanalytic mainstream. There are, too, clear-cut roots in—and linkages to—conceptualizations and formulations of Jacobson, Mahler, Winnicott, Kohut, and Kernberg, and yet the whole is a distinctive ensemble that is uniquely Tähkä's and not at all the eclectic mélange that a less original or creative mind might have made of the effort at melding elements from such distinct and different streams.

Along the way, Tähkä proposes a considerable number of novel concepts, or at least of provocatively (and evocatively) new semantics. To list the more striking: the primary mental state of undifferentiation and the regressive threats of undifferentiation at subsequent developmental levels; dedifferentiation anxiety, in preference to either the more familiar annihilation anxiety or separation anxiety; the primary ideal state of the self; protective dichotomies; the functional object and functional object-relatedness, with many echoes here of Kohut's self-object and self-object relatedness, and the transcending of such functional relatedness via the process of functional selective identifications; defensive operations of the self, in preference to ego mechanisms of defence, deployed to preserve the self-experience as close to the ideal state of the self as possible; judgmentally selective identifications, a higher developmental achievement than functional selective identifications, where characteristics rather than functions of the ideal paragon are introjected and identified with; and alongside those, informative identifications, the basis of object love, of empathy, and of all varieties of loving attachment; as elaborations of this, of comparative and of creative empathy; self-ideal (instead of ego-ideal) and its counterpart, object-ideal; functional object (and object relationship) and individual object (and object relationship), again somewhat analogous to Kohut's self-object and true object; and remembrance formation, the third and highest kind of internalization when conflicted (oedipal) object ties are resolved by interpretation, their constraint upon present functioning overcome, and their being consigned then to the status of historic remembrance, no longer a dynamically active presence in the present. Through all of this, the guiding threads are varieties of structuralization, at levels of ever increasingly nuanced complexity, via internalization processes, of introjections and identifications, and, with ultimately "ideal" resolutions of remembrance formations.

How Tähkä gives distinct meaning to these new phrases embodying his particular conceptions of the developmental dynamic, and then, out of it all, weaves the fabric of a coherent (mental) theory of mental development can emerge only in the full reading of his closely packed, at times densely written, but somehow always eminently readable, book. The phrases I have quoted can only hint at the particular meanings with which Tähkä invests his concepts, and develops the distinctive, though at no time discordant or jarring, theory of development that he propounds, and which truly bears his particular imprint.

But all that is only half the book. The other half is a much expanded exposition of Veikko Tähkä's derived psychoanalytic therapeutic as outlined in the 1979 predecessor article, the articulated array of phase-specific psychoanalytic approaches, differentially applied to patients at the varying levels of mental structuralization and object-relatedness. The basic considerations here stem from the complex variety of interlocking and interacting relationships embedded in every therapeutic situation; the analyst as a contemporary object for the patient, the basis for the vital working alliance; the analyst as a past (or transferential) object with whom the whole history of past and buried object relationships is revived and repeated; the analyst as a new (or developmental) object (reminiscent here of Loewald) with whom is realized a new vision of the possibilities for transcending transferential re-enactments into new ways of relating, freed from the bondage to the past, with then the transition from the working alliance to a truly therapeutic alliance (one of Tähkä's distinctions); and the counterpart of all of these, the patient as a contemporary object for the analyst (the so-called real relationship); the (adult) patient as a "child", both the transference "child" that he is, and the developing "child" that he is being helped to become; and also, of course, inevitably, the patient as the analyst's counter-transference object. In all the vicissitudes of the psychoanalytic treatment process at every psychopathological level, the issue, as Tähkä puts it, is to meet the patient's psychic needs and to foster the developmental process, within the fullest possible understanding of the complex interactions of all these ongoing relationship modes.

This is done via a variety of phase-specific therapeutic strategies—specified and elaborated far beyond the 1979 article—all called psychoanalytic, however much they depart from the usual parameters of the classical psychoanalytic encounter, and here I can again present them best in detailed citations of Tähkä's own words from his 1993 book. Starting again at the level of the meaning and place of gratifications *vis-à-vis* interpretations in the therapy of the overtly psychotic, he stated

> It seems to be of the utmost importance to realize that providing experiences of gratification is the only way to approach an undifferentiated mind, in order to enter into it as a structure-building and thus development-promoting element. Gratification is the only language received and accepted prior to the emergence of a self experience. . . . Thus, adequate gratification of a patient reiterating his symbiotic failure in a regression to undifferentiation seems to be very different from if not diametrically opposite to gratification of a neurotic patient's transference expectations [1993, p. 275][12]

Of so-called interpretations with the psychotic, Tähkä said

> It seems inevitable that as long as interpretations are offered to a patient who has regressively lost his self-experience, any signs indicating that the analyst's words have reached and influenced the patient's structure-building representational processes are due to the positive affective attributes of the analyst's words as "things" instead of being results of a new "insight" due to the abstract content of the interpretation. What was meant to be effective as an increase of self-knowledge may thus turn out to be effective more in the manner of a lullaby. [*ibid.*, p. 281]

Then how best to describe the gratifications that are stated to be the proper therapeutic approach to the psychotic?

> Since the useful introjects represent soothing, tension-regulating, and security-inducing functional presences in the mind of a developing individual, the creation and maintenance of a generally safe "holding" atmosphere in the interaction between him and his developmental object is necessary for offering such experiential models for introjection. In the treatment of newly differentiated schizophrenic patients this includes the stability and relative unchangeability of the therapeutic setting, regular and predictable treatment sessions, as well as full availability and interest from the analyst, whose demeanor could ideally be kind but not intrusive, genuine but not courting, firm but not disciplinary. [*ibid.*, p. 288]

Where this is reasonably successful,

> when there has developed an analyst-derived, quantitatively and qualitatively sufficient, security-inducing introjective structure in the patient's mind to ensure differentiation and to counteract "all-bad" introjects that become mobilized by frustrations, the schizophrenic patient may feel safe enough to attempt the first functionally selective identification with some of the analyst's introjected functions. [*ibid.*, p. 294]

—that is, he has advanced at that moment to the borderline level of functioning.

With the borderline,

> I have ... tried to demonstrate that the decisive and essential structure-building process, and thus the crucial curative factor, ... is ... the patient's *functionally selective identifications* with his analyst (*ibid.*, p. 313, my italics).

Accomplishing this is a very different task than with the psychotic:

> The analyst tends to become accepted and idealized as a new developmental object for a borderline patient specifically through his function as a provider of interest in the patient's subjective way of experiencing, rather than a provider of concern for his staying mentally alive, as is just as specifically the case with psychotic patients. [*ibid.*, p. 341]

Further,

> the specific way for the analyst to enter into a borderline patient's world of experience as a new developmental object, as well as to provide the latter with models for functionally selective identifications, is for the analyst to catch the patient's subjective way of experiencing through *transient informative identifications, and to forward the resulting empathic understanding to the patient.* [*ibid.*, p. 349, my italics).

Again, where it is reasonably successful, "structure building through identification in the treatment of borderline patients ... means a gradual loss of the experiential presence of a functional object" (*ibid.*, p. 395).

And last, with the neurotic,

> transference interpretations will be the communications of the analyst that specifically confront the patient with the illusory and anachronistic nature of his analyst-directed expectations, thus building a bridge between past and present, and initiating a gradual replacement of the transferential images by real or fantasied images of the oedipal parents, correctly located in time and space. This gradual giving up of the images of oedipal objects as existing in the present, with simultaneously emerging recollections of them as belonging in the past, is analogous to the "classical" sector of mourning work . . . that comprises the gradual "letting die" of the lost object as an individual, through a painful comparison of the recalled and actual realities, accompanied by a simultaneous rebuilding of the object's image in the mourner's mind as a remembrance of a past object. [*ibid.*, pp. 426–427]

This is an evocative restatement, in Tähkä's idiom of the classical (i.e. Freud's) conceptualization of the mode of operation of traditional psychoanalysis proper, an allegiance which has been one of the bedrocks from which Tähkä took off and upon which he built.

Tähkä then concluded,

> As a rule, the content and form of interpretations do not correspond with the experiencing and receiving conditions of a borderline or psychotic patient. Functional experiencing, as well as a partly or fully undifferentiated world of experience, cannot be understood, and that understanding communicated in the form of an interpretation. Instead the functional experiencing, characteristic of borderline patients, can be understood as something that can be empathically described to the patient. The psychotic experiencing, with its partial or total loss of differentiation, will be phase-specifically understood mostly as an unarticulated and thwarted neediness. This understanding can only be communicated by the analyst's letting himself and the treatment setting become a holding atmosphere, impregnated by generative complementarity, that it is hoped will be accepted by the patient as a new developmental agency, leading to a resumed dialogue between him and the object world. Thus, the nature of understanding and its conveyance depend entirely on the respective level of the patient's mental structuralization and relatedness. While an interpretative understanding

mostly seems to be phase-specifically appropriate for a neurotic patient, a describing understanding appears to be similarly adequate for a borderline patient. Finally, the analyst's complementarily tuned-in presence understanding seems to represent the most elementary and basic form of phase-specific understanding, necessary in the work with psychotic patients. [*ibid.*, p. 372]

Put succinctly, the ameliorative agents are

symbolic gratifications of a psychotic patient's symbiotic needs, empathic descriptions of a borderline patient's inner experience, or empathically caught and formulated interpretations of a neurotic patient's dissociated mental contents. [1993, p. 352]

Tähkä considers all these treatment approaches psychoanalytic, even if not psychoanalysis proper as deployed with classically psychoneurotic patients, and does not designate any of them as "only" psychotherapy—although of course other workers in the same conceptual vineyard would separate off the work Tähkä describes with the borderline and the psychotic as very appropriate exemplars of the range of psychoanalytic psychotherapies.

Tähkä described his own preferred designations as follows:

If by psychoanalytic treatment is meant those applications of established psychoanalytic knowledge that strive to promote maximally a belated growth of the patient's personality, it is obvious that techniques founded in psychoanalytic developmental psychology and proved as phase-specifically adequate and effective should be included under the general heading of psychoanalytic treatment. ... Many therapeutic interactions and techniques discussed may customarily be regarded as belonging to psychotherapy and not to psychoanalysis. I do propose, however that when used in cases in which they have proved to be growth-promoting and phase-specifically founded in the developmental theory of psychoanalysis, they should be regarded as important elements of the entirety of psychoanalytic treatment, in which the classical technique stands as an advanced and well-established segment for the treatment of predominantly neurotic patients. [*ibid.*, p. 165]

All this is, of course, a highly condensed synopsis of the integrative achievement and integrated edifice created by Veikko Tähkä—the assemblage of an overall account of mental development, largely familiar enough and yet with novel and intriguing emphases propounded via the kinds of new phrases and altered formulations that I have enumerated, leading then to a derived therapeutic, phase-specifically linked to the developmental needs of the broad categories of patients, the psychotic, the borderline, and the neurotic, each with its particular central therapeutic approach; concern and symbolic need gratification for the psychotic, empathic description for the borderline, and interpretation for the neurotic, each of these uniquely adapted to lead the patient to the next higher developmental level of structuralization (via internalizations) and more mature object relationships.

But that is not all. Along the way, as already indicated, Tähkä has given his unique perspective upon familiar enough concepts. I will cite just two examples. For example, he urges a separateness of the conceptions of the working and therapeutic alliances—something already alluded to—and propounds a sequential and consequential nature of their (potential) relationship. He put it thus:

I propose to restrict the term working alliance to refer primarily to the contemporary aspects of the analytic relationship that are based on the patient's preexisting capacity for emotionally meaningful age-appropriate collaboration between individuals. Once the developing transference has given the analyst the position and authority of a developmental object, it depends on the patient's remaining developmental urges, as well as on the analyst's ability and willingness to present himself as a new developmental object for the patient, whether a newly motivated and reactivated developmental interaction will ensue. Provided that this will be the case, and that the established relationship between the patient and the analyst as a new developmental object will be adequately allied with the contemporary aspects of the relationship, the working relationship has been expanded to a therapeutic alliance proper, (ibid., p. 230]

In this conception, the therapeutic alliance becomes a developmentally higher form, that, as a consequence of proper psychoanalytic work, has evolved out of the working alliance—again, Tähkä's signature developmental emphasis that is so remindful of the profoundly influential thrust of Hans Loewald's contributions.

And this close affinity with Loewald's overall perspective comes through clearly in the second example I cite, Tähkä's comments on the once very popular—and always very controversial—conception of Franz Alexander of the "corrective emotional experience." This is discussed as follows:

> Provided that the analyst has received the position of a past parental object for the patient, an obvious requirement for his becoming a new developmental object is that he behaves in an unexpected way from the patient's point of view. Objects, behaving in an expected way are familiar objects, with whom the patients, without being aware of it, expect to repeat or continue relationships that are determined by their repressed or continually actualized past. The new and unexpected ways of the analyst to approach his patients in his role or function as a new developmental object, could be regarded as providing the patient with a corrective experience, although not in the original Alexandrian . . . sense of the term. Unlike the latter, the analyst's becoming a new developmental object for the patient has nothing to do with purposeful role playing, regarded as opposite to the patient's prevailing transference expectations. Instead, the analyst's approach as a new object is, or ought to be, based on his empathic and/or complementary recognition of the patient's frustrated and arrested developmental needs and potentials, that are present alongside of the repetition and continuation of his failed developmental interactions in the analytic relationship. (*ibid.*, p. 231)

—truly a Loewaldian recasting of a basic Alexandrian tenet.

Clearly, with his 1993 book, capping a forty-year-long professional lifetime as a psychoanalytic scholar, Veikko Tähkä, prior to that too little known outside his native land and region, established himself as a major contributor to the central corpus of psychoanalytic theorizing and praxis in the always problematic realm of the theory and practice of psychoanalysis *vis-à-vis* the psychoanalytic psychotherapies based upon it and derived from it, as the psychoanalytic idea has transcended the narrower psychoanalytic universe within which Sigmund Freud originally brought it into being. This is true despite however much each individual reader finds Tähkä's perspectives on the evolution of mind and its disorders, and their psychoanalytically guided amelioration, persuasive in terms of its resonances with his or her own particular clinical experience and theoretical stance in this ever-evolving dialogue. For my part, I have felt privileged to have been asked to contribute to this Festschrift in Veikko Tähkä's honour, and fortunate to have been able to present my particular assessment of the signal place of this colleague within the arena of our shared interest.

Notes

1. Eissler (1953) put it this way:

   The basic model technique, without emendations, can be applied to those patients whose neurotic symptomatology is borne by an ego not modified to any noteworthy degree ... [an ego that] has preserved its integrity. [p. 116]

   And in a footnote to this same passage he said: "I will pursue this problem further in connection with Freud's concept of the hypothetically normal ego" (p. 116).

2. In "On the history of the psychoanalytic movement", Freud wrote:

   I considered it necessary to form an official association because I feared the abuses to which psycho-analysis would be subjected as soon as it became popular. There should be some headquarters whose business it would be to declare: "All this nonsense is nothing to do with analysis; this is not psycho-analysis." [1914, p. 43]

3. Actually, the other theoretical perspectives (alternative metapsychologies) that arose in psychoanalysis other than Freud's structural theory "mainstream", like the Kleinian, for example, were from the start willing to treat in psychoanalysis—as they conceptualized it—sicker patients whom the Freudians (especially in America), with few exceptions (like Frieda Fromm-Reichmann, 1950) declared to be beyond the capacity of proper psychoanalysis, and consigned to varieties of psychoanalytic psychotherapy. See in this regard the work of the prominent British Kleinian, Herbert Rosenfeld (1965) and the Argentine Kleinian, David Rosenfeld (1992). But all this is a line of discussion beyond the scope of this paper.

4. Psychoanalytic (or "dynamic") psychotherapy is indeed the one distinctively American contribution to modern day psychiatric therapeusis, albeit a glorious one. Psychoanalysis was created by Freud in Austria; the descriptive nosology of the major mental disorders was the work of Kraepelin and his school in Germany;

electroconvulsive therapy was inaugurated by Cerletti and Bini in Italy; insulin coma by Sakel (a Hungarian) in Vienna; the ill-starred lobotomy operation by Egas Moniz in Portugal; the concept of the therapeutic community was developed by Maxwell Jones in England; the modern psychoactive drug era was inaugurated in Switzerland with Largactil, later brought to America as Thorazine; and lithium was first successfully employed by Cade in Australia.

5. This is an entirely different meaning of the word "psychobiologist" than the current usage which denotes modern-day biological psychiatry and its clinical application in psychopharmacology. In Adolf Meyer's day, the word connoted an integrated biopsychosocial approach to the understanding of the unfolded life history and illness picture but without the psychoanalytic conceptions of the dynamic unconscious, and of the transference.

6. It states matters too starkly to claim that dynamic (or psychoanalytic) psychotherapy had no roots or independent beginnings in other countries than the United States. Henry Dicks's book, *Fifty Years of the Tavistock Clinic* (1970), covers the years 1920 to 1970 and recounts the particular role of the Tavistock, situated between the fiercely anti-psychoanalytic psychiatric establishment in Britain on the one hand, and the psychoanalytic establishment (the British Psycho-Analytical Society) on the other, in providing a receptive meeting ground for psychiatrists and psychoanalysts alike who were interested in the development of a British dynamic psychotherapy, more heavily orientated, of course, to the object-relational, and, in later years the Kleinian, perspective, than its American ego psychological counterpart. This differing theoretic emphasis has indeed persisted to the present day. Similar separate developments of a psychoanalytic psychotherapy, distinct from, but quite clearly derived from, and related to, psychoanalysis itself, no doubt also took place elsewhere, I would say especially in Germany, Holland, and Scandinavia.

7. Among Knight's signal contributions was solidly implanting the conception of the borderline patient (1953), which has become a seemingly indispensable diagnostic categorization within psychoanalytic theorizing ever since.

8. A reference to Kurt Eissler's (1953) benchmark article outlining the defined dimensions of technically proper psychoanalytic work within the confines of the then regnant ego psychology paradigm in America.

9. A reference to Leo Stone's (1954) paper on the tendency to treat psychoanalytically a "wider scope" of patients than the classically neurotic for whom psychoanalysis was devised, for example, the psychosomatic, the addicted, the delinquent, the sexually disordered, etc.

10. Gedo and Goldberg in America, over essentially the same time span, were developing their own conceptually very similar hierarchical and developmental model of mental functioning, and of the therapeutic measures designed to ameliorate the disorders of mental functioning, as manifest differently at each of five levels. Their conceptualization (developed further by Gedo in a series of successor books) consisted of a hierarchy of modes of psychic functioning in five stages, each with characteristic dangers, defences, and anxieties, and each with its central treatment strategy. They are—in ascending order—(1) traumatic states to be treated by pacification, (2) psychotic disintegration to be treated by unification, (3) narcissistic personality disorders to be treated by optimal disillusionment, (4) neurotic character disorders to be treated by interpretation, and (5) expectable adult functioning to be dealt with by introspection—each of these in turn defined, specified, and illustrated in detail in their 1973 volume. What is striking is that Gedo and Goldberg in America and Tähkä in Finland developed such strikingly similar models of the working of the mind and the treatment of its disorders with no indication on either side of any awareness of the work of the other. All of Gedo's books contain very numerous references, but I could not find any reference to Tähkä in either the indices or the cited references; similarly in Tähkä's book—not published until 1993—there is no reference to Gedo in either the index or the cited references.

11. Sometimes such a need-gratifying approach has to become endless:

> A progressive process of internalization, which presupposes certain frustration tolerance, often cannot with psychotic patients be brought farther than to the formation of a good inner object, which must then be sustained with maintenance therapy. A continuous "psychic presence" of the therapist will then be a necessary condition for the patient's nonpsychotic existence. [1979, p. 125]

These are among the patients whom I have elsewhere called "therapeutic lifers" (Wallerstein, 1986, pp. 631–641).

12. And therefore the concept of analytic abstinence must be understood very differently with the psychotic and the psychoneurotic.
Tähkä put it this way:

> The problem of the analyst, trained to work with neurotic
> patients, is that he has been taught never to satisfy a
> patient's infantile needs. Analytic abstinence as one of
> the cornerstones of the classical technique seems to be seri-
> ously threatened by any suggestion that the analyst might,
> or even should, gratify an undifferentiated patient's
> symbiotic needs. However, as I hope to show, this is a
> misunderstanding based on an erroneous equation of the
> psychotic patient's developmental arrest with that of a
> neurotic patient. [1993, p. 272]

References

Dicks, H. V. (1970). *Fifty Years of the Tavistock Clinic*. London, Routledge and Kegan Paul.

Eissler, K. R. (1953). The effect of the structure of the ego on psychoan-alytic technique. *Journal of the American Psychoanalytical Association*, 1: 104-143.

Freud, S. (1905) [1953]. On psychotherapy. *S.E.,7*: 255-268. London: Hogarth.

Freud, S. (1914) [1957]. On the history of the psycho-analytic move-ment. *S.E.,14*: 1-66. London: Hogarth.

Fromm-Reichmann, F. (1950). *Principles of Intensive Psychotherapy*. Chicago & London: University of Chicago Press.

Gedo, J. E. (1979). *Beyond Interpretation: Toward a Revised Theory for Psychoanalysis*. New York: International Universities Press.

Gedo, J. E., & Goldberg, A. (1973). *Models of the Mind: A Psychoanalytic Theory*. Chicago & London: University of Chicago Press.

Gill, M. M. (1954). Psychoanalysis and exploratory psychotherapy. *Journal of the American Psychoanalytical Association*, 2: 771-797.

Glover, E. (1931). *The Therapeutic Effect of Inexact Interpretation: A Contribution to the Theory of Suggestion. International Journal of Psycho-Analysis*, 12: 397-411.

Glover, E. (1954). The indications for psycho-analysis. *Journal of Mental Science*, 100: 393-401.

Jones, E. (1910) [1918]. The action of suggestion in psychotherapy. In: *Papers on Psychoanalysis by Ernest Jones*, (pp. 318-359). New York: William Wood & Co.

Knight, R. P. (1953). Borderline states. *Bulletin of the Menninger Clinic*, 17: 1-12. Reprinted in: S. C. Miller (Ed.), *Clinician and Therapist: Selected Papers of Robert P. Knight*, (pp. 208-223). New York: Basic Books, 1972.

Panels (1954). The widening scope of indications for psychoanalysis; The traditional psychoanalytic technique and its variations; Psychoanalysis and dynamic psychotherapy: similarities and differences. *Journal of the American Psychoanalytical Association*, 2: 565-797.

Rosenfeld, D. (1992). *The Psychotic Aspects of the Personality*. London & New York: Karnac Books.

Rosenfeld, H. A. (1965). *Psychotic States: A Psycho-Analytical Approach*. New York: International Universities Press.

Stone, L. (1954). The widening scope of indications for psychoanalysis. *Journal of the American Psychoanalytical Association*, 2: 567-594.

Tähkä, V. (1979). Psychotherapy as phase-specific interaction: towards a general psychoanalytic theory of psychotherapy. *Scandinavian Psychoanalytical Review*, 2: 113-132.

Tähkä, V. (1993). *Mind and Its Treatment: A Psychoanalytic Approach*. Madison, CT: International Universities Press.

Tähkä, V. (1996). *Mielen Rakentuminen ja Psykoanalyyttinen Hoitaminen* (*Mind and its Treatment*, Finnish edn). Helsinki: Werner Söderstrom Osakeyhtiö.

Wallerstein, R. S. (1974). Herbert S. Gaskill and the history of American psychoanalysis in American psychiatry. *The Denver Psychoanalytic Society Newsletter*, 1(3): 1-9.

Wallerstein, R. S. (1980). Psychoanalysis and academic psychiatry-bridges. *Psychoanalytical Study of the Child*, 35: 419-448.

Wallerstein, R. S. (1986). *Forty-Two Lives in Treatment: A Study of Psychoanalysis and Psychotherapy*. New York: Guilford Press.

Wallerstein, R. S. (1988). One psychoanalysis or many? *International Journal of Psycho-Analysis*, 69: 5-21.

Wallerstein, R. S. (1989). Psychoanalysis and psychotherapy: an historical perspective. *International Journal of Psycho-Analysis*, 70: 563-591.

Wallerstein, R. S. (1990). Psychoanalysis: the common ground. *International Journal of Psycho-Analysis*, 71: 3-20.

Wallerstein, R. S. (Ed.) (1992). *The Common Ground of Psychoanalysis*. Northvale, NJ & London: Jason Aronson.

Wallerstein, R. S. (1995). *The Talking Cures: The Psychoanalyses and the Psychotherapies*. New Haven and London: Yale University Press.
Wallerstein, R. S. (2002). The trajectory of psychoanalysis: a prognostication. *International Journal of Psycho-Analysis*, *83*: 1247-1267.

CHAPTER TWO

A Festschrift for Veikko Tähkä—2003

Pearl King

"And as the evening twilight fades away
The sky is filled with stars, invisible by day"

(Longfellow)

I t is a privilege for me to write a paper for inclusion in the Festschrift in honour of Veikko Tähkä's eightieth birthday. I remember first meeting Veikko in 1964, after he and his colleagues in the Finnish Society had been permitted to form a Study Group of the International Psychoanalytical Association (IPA), in order that Finland could have its own Finnish Psychoanalytical Society that could train its own psychoanalysts, instead of their having to go abroad to Sweden and other countries to be trained. Veikko Tähkä was the leader of this Study Group. The Central Executive of the IPA then appointed Donald Winnicott as the Chairman of their Sponsoring Committee and I was appointed as its Honorary Secretary, and we were assisted by Dr Thorston Sjovall from the Swedish Society, Thorkil Vangaard from the Danish Society and Fanny Wride from the British Society, as members of the Sponsoring Committee.

We first met members of the study group and decided the principles on which we would work with them until the Society could take over its own training activities. We then met every member of the group and discussed how they could help us to help them. We agreed to form what we called a "Training Committee". It consisted of Dr Veikko Tähkä, Dr Stig Bjork, Dr Eero Rechardt, and the Sponsoring Committee. This Training Committee was responsible for receiving reports of the interviews which were carried out by Dr Thorston Sjovall and the three Finnish members of the Training Committee (Laine *et al.*, 1997).

That was how my relationship with Veikko Tähkä and his Finnish colleagues started in 1964. By June 1967, the Finnish Sponsoring Committee recommended to the IPA that the Finnish Study Group be given Provisional Society status of the International Psychoanalytical Association. We were very pleased with and proud of what we had achieved together. In 1987 the Finnish Society celebrated the first twenty years of their work together as a Society of the IPA; they invited me over to share their achievement with them and, much to my pleasure, they made me an Honorary Member of their Society. I was very pleased to join them in their celebrations. Now nearly forty years have passed since I first started working with Veikko Tähkä and his friends, and it gives me much pleasure to offer this paper for his Festschrift.

*   *   *

Over the past forty years I have become interested in the impact of the ageing process on human beings and have tried to consider what special difficulties confront people during the latter half of their lives or of the developmental cycle (as I prefer to think of it) and what new opportunities open up for them.

This particular line of interest has led me to consider, and to attempt to conceptualise, the impact of the ageing process on the capacity of patients suffering from different types of neuroses to cope with their illnesses. I have often wondered why there are so few case reports of elderly patients in psychoanalytic literature. I had assumed that this was so mainly because it was thought that the defences of such patients were so rigid and their need for instinctual gratification so reduced that sufficient motivation for change did not exist in them.

My own experience with patients in this age group, however, has led me to the conclusion that they can benefit a great deal from analysis, particularly between the ages of forty and sixty-five, although because of the generally held belief that psychoanalysis can be of little help to a patient over forty-five, only a limited number of such people find their way into analysis.

In a paper that I read at a European Conference some years ago on "Narcissism and sexuality" (King, 1972), I tried to raise some of these issues. Certain French colleagues expressed the opinion that one could not psychoanalyse anyone over forty. However, a number of people also came up to thank me for what I had said, as it had helped them to understand their elderly patients.

Since then I have talked to a number of my colleagues and several of them "confessed" that they have analysed patients in the second half of life with considerable success. I use the word "confessed" advisedly, because they were almost apologetic about it, as though they were breaking a taboo or going against the "book".

I decided to take up this challenge and to try to find out where this rigid attitude of some of my colleagues had come from and what reference there was to age in relation to the prognosis of psychoanalytic therapy in the twenty-three volumes of Freud. I found only three references, but they gave me a clue to the present state of affairs among these colleagues. When he was forty-two, Freud wrote in his paper "Sexual aetiology of the neuroses" (1898a),

> Psychoanalytic therapy is not at present applicable to all cases. It has, to my knowledge, the following limitations. It demands a certain degree of maturity and understanding in the patient and is therefore not suited for the young or for adults who are feeble-minded or uneducated. It also fails with people who are very advanced in years, because, owing to the accumulation of material in them, it would take up so much time that by the end of the treatment they would have reached a period of life in which value is no longer attached to nervous health ... [Freud, 1898a]

Here, Freud is referring to patients of "very advanced years'; that is, who are at quite a distance in time from his own age. However, he had had relatively little experience with the psychoanalytical method by then and he does use the words "at present', thus leaving open the question of extending the age limits of the usefulness of psychoanalysis later.

When he was forty-nine, Freud wrote in his 1905 paper "On psychotherapy",

> The age of patients has this much importance in determining their fitness for psychoanalytic treatment, that, on the one hand, near or above the age of fifty the elasticity of the mental processes, on which the treatment depends, is as a rule lacking—old people are no longer educable—and, on the other hand, the mass of material to be dealt with would prolong the duration of the treatment indefinitely. [Freud, 1905a]

Strachey, commenting on this paper, sums up Freud's opinion at the time more succinctly:

> If the patient's age is in the neighbourhood of the fifties the conditions for psychoanalysis become unfavourable. The mass of psychical material is then no longer manageable; the time required for recovery is too long; and the ability to undo psychical processes begins to grow weaker. [Strachey, 1953]

What amazes me about Freud's comments is that he is referring to people of his own age—near or above the age of fifty—and yet his own experience of himself must have shown him that his mental processes were still elastic and he was, to some extent, able to learn from experience. Perhaps it indicates how difficult it is to accept that we ourselves grow old as well as other people.

In 1912, when he was considering the aetiology of various neurotic conditions in his paper "Types of onset of the neuroses", he discusses seriously the possibility that developmental biological processes may produce an alteration in the equilibrium of the psychic processes, thus producing neurotic breakdowns at key phases of the life-cycle at puberty and the menopause. I think he must by then have had to deal with neuroses linked with the menopause, for when he was fifty-six he writes:

> It is well known that more or less sudden increases of libido of this kind are habitually associated with puberty and the menopause—with the attainment of a certain age in women; in some people they may in addition be manifested in periodicities that are still unknown . . . [Freud, 1912c]

Now it seems to me that Freud is touching on the possibility of developmental crises in the course of the life-cycle that are still unknown to him. He does not, however, seem to go on to the next step and reconsider the possibility of new factors emerging that would facilitate the psychoanalysing of older patients.

The first person to challenge Freud's position in relation to the psychoanalysis of patients in the second half of life was Karl Abraham in 1919 in a paper, "The applicability of psycho-analytic treatment to patients at an advanced age". Abraham wrote,

Freud (1898) has expressed the opinion that psychoanalysis loses its effectiveness if the patient is too advanced in years. There is no doubt about the general correctness of this view. It was only to be expected that at the commencement of physical and psychical involution a person should be less inclined to part with a neuroses which he has had most of his life. Daily psychoanalytical experience, however, shows that we must not expect mental processes to be too uniform. It warns us against approaching the investigation or treatment of nervous conditions with *a priori* theories. For instance, has it not been shown that certain mental diseases which psychiatric medicine has pronounced to be quite intractable are accessible to psychoanalytic methods? It would seem therefore incorrect to deny a priori the possibility of exercising a curative influence upon the neuroses in the period of involution. It is rather the task of psychoanalysis as a scientific procedure to inquire into precisely this question as to whether, and under what conditions, the method of treatment can attain results in patients in the later years of life. [*ibid.*]

Abraham continued

In my psychoanalytical practice I have treated a number of chronic neuroses in persons over forty and even fifty years of age. At first it was only after some hesitation that I undertook cases of this kind. But I was more than once urged to make the attempt by patients themselves who had been treated unsuccessfully elsewhere. And I was more confident that if I could not cure the patients I could at least give them a deeper and better understanding of their trouble than a physician untrained in psychoanalysis could. To my surprise a considerable number of them reacted very favourably to the treatment. I might add that I count some of those cures as among my most successful results. [*ibid.*, pp. 312–313]

Abraham's findings were corroborated by a number of other psychoanalysts. Yet in his much quoted work on "The psychoanalytic theory of the neuroses", published in 1945, Fenichel could still consider age as a strong contra-indication for psychoanalytic treatment, although he is not so definite about it as Freud had been, and he allowed some degree of variation according to the total situation of the older patient. He writes: "The ideal age for the undertaking of an analysis lies between fifteen and forty. But certainly analysis is not impossible either earlier or later" (Fenichel, 1945, pp. 575–576).

It was now clearer to me where my French colleagues obtained support for their strongly expressed opinion that you could not offer analysis to anyone over forty years of age. This led me to wonder whether there were meta-psychological difficulties that made it difficult for some psychoanalysts to accept the possibility of analysing elderly patients.

I felt that there was a discrepancy between the conceptual framework and theories with which these analysts worked and the clinical experience that some analysts were reporting. It seemed to me that when these analysts have attempted to think about the possibility of conceptualizing their work with ageing patients, they use the same concepts and frames of reference that were applicable to the younger patients. I think that this arose, not only from a "theoretical fixation" on the first five years of life, but also from a failure to understand and conceptualize the inter-relation that continues through the whole life-cycle, between the socio-biological and psychodynamic processes within the individual. Concern with these seemed to stop after puberty. There was therefore no adequate conceptual framework for considering the possibility that later socio-biological changes would lead to psychological ones, and that changes imposed by ageing could be assimilated and integrated within the personality or that this process could lead to psychological growth.

Developments in psychoanalytic theory and research

Leading up to and following the Second World War, certain developments took place in psychoanalytic theory and research which I think opened up new possibilities for extensions of the conceptual frames of reference within which psychoanalysts work. I summarize them as follows under four main developments:

1. The understanding of the intrapsychic importance of *object relations* arising from the work of Melanie Klein (Klein, 1948, 1957) and her colleagues (Klein *et al.*, 1952, 1955), and also the work of Rickman (1957), Winnicott (1956, 1965), Jacobson (1965), Balint (1957) and Fairbairn (1952) who focused on the fate and function of internal objects in normal and pathological development within the context of two-person relationships.

2. The understanding of *the self* and the *development of the ego and autonomous ego functions* arising from the work of Hartmann (1958, 1964) and his colleagues, and the concept of *developmental lines* formulated by Anna Freud (1966).

3. The understanding of the importance of the mother–child matrix from which the young child emerges, the infant being seen as part of an interdependent unit with the mother, whose actual personality contributes to the situation, arising from the work of Winnicott (1957, 1960a), Khan (1963), Balint (1968), Greenacre (1953), Spitz (1950, 1956) and Escalona (1953). Bowlby (1969), following ethnological concepts, emphasized the importance of *critical periods* in relation to the developmental processes in the context of the child's attachment to the mother and the effect of separation at different ages.

4. Arising from the epigenetic approach of Erikson (1951, 1959) (see also Rapaport, 1959), the understanding of the importance of the capacity of the maturational processes of the child to fit appropriate cultural requirements and vice versa, and thus the significance of these being appropriate to the child's phase of development.

These significant advances in psychoanalytic thinking and research have increased our understanding of developmental processes in the area of ego functions and object relations, and the affective implications of these for mental health. They have provided additions to our conceptual frame of reference and this has encouraged some analysts to reconsider the possibility of analysing patients in older age groups. These include psychoanalysts in

Boston, Chicago, and London, among others, who have done pioneer work exploring the problems, limitations, and possibilities of treating the neurotic illnesses of elderly patients.

I think that I have been most influenced by Erikson (1959), who made a major contribution to our understanding of the impact of the experience of the life-cycle on the psychosocial development of individuals, when he formulated eight developmental stages in the life-cycle, which he related to phase-specific developmental and psychosocial tasks, which individuals could meet in a healthy, life-promoting way or in a neurotic, life-negating way. Thus, how the individual deals with the challenges and anxieties of one developmental phase will influence his capacity to cope with the crises associated with the next one; the way we meet the tasks and crises posed by middle age will influence how we are able to meet old age and the decades before death. It is Erikson's conceptual frame of reference that has made me most aware of the impact of the various stages of the life-cycle on my patients of different age groups and the anxieties and pressures that these can produce in patients suffering from different psychoneurotic conditions (King, 1974, 1980).

The relevance of Klein's work has also been important to me in understanding the vicissitudes of emotional responses in the course of ageing, particularly her work on the importance of the integrative processes that result from the acceptance of destructive impulses, as well as loving ones, towards the significant objects or people in our lives. It offers the possibility of working through the guilt and bitterness of life's failures and gaining enrichment thereby, and not just, as Fenichel put it, giving "the insight that life has been a failure without offering any opportunity to make up for it" (Fenichel, 1945).

With the help offered by these new ways of conceptualizing certain developmental processes and mechanisms, two important papers were published reporting the use of this approach to the analysis of patients in the context of ageing. One paper is by Hanna Segal (Segal, 1958) entitled "Fear of death: Notes on the analysis of an old man". It is a good example of the use of Kleinian concepts in relation to the problems of ageing and death. The other paper is by Elliott Jaques and is entitled "Death and the mid-life crisis" (Jaques, 1965). He deals with the crises that occur around the age of thirty-five, which he calls "the mid-life crises", and his patients are therefore within the "acceptable" age range of fifteen to forty.

But Jaques does more than illustrate the usefulness of Kleinian concepts in the analysis of patients concerned with ageing. He puts forward and delineates a new concept that integrates psychological processes with developmental and maturational ones and relates both to the socio-cultural activities of the individual. He sees the mid-life crisis as the first sign of middle age, when the individual is confronted not only with discrepancies between the demands of his ego-ideal and his reality achievements, but also with the fact of his eventual death. This confrontation, he feels, can lead either to a depressive breakdown or to a reappraisal of the appropriateness of the individual's current life pattern and system of values. It is, perhaps, during this process of reappraisal that individuals may become aware of the "senselessness and aimlessness of their lives", from which many analysts have described patients to be suffering in the second half of life.

What pressures bring middle-aged and elderly patients to seek analytic and therapeutic help?

I have analysed a number of middle-aged and elderly patients whose descriptions of their problems in early adulthood would lead one to classify them as typical narcissistic personalities. They exhibited narcissistic over-valuation of the self, inability to cathect their sexual partners with object-libido, and omnipotent needs to control their objects, which were cathected with narcissistic libido and treated as extensions of themselves, so that the needs of their objects were treated with indifference.

I had the feeling that unless they had needed analysis for professional purposes, they would have been unlikely to seek treatment earlier, since they were not aware of their ailment (Main, 1957). If anyone needed help it was their objects, who were narcissistically unsatisfactory to them. They themselves had not then experienced sufficient discomfort to be able to face the pain of changing.

The reasons these patients eventually came to analysis was that while they had achieved reasonably satisfactory positions in their professional lives, they had come to feel that their relationships were artificial and devoid of meaning; they suffered from feelings of futility, lack of satisfaction in their achievements, and an increasing feeling of alienation from themselves and others (King, 1968). The picture they presented of themselves was similar to the false-self personality often described by Winnicott (1960b) and Khan (1971). They had managed to develop a sufficient reality sense in the course of their lives so that part of their ego could transact relationships with external objects, and some degree of object cathexes had been achieved. But this had been achieved on the basis of identification with external requirements. A false self had developed, as an intermediary, whose task was to keep the balance between the narcissistic requirements of the individual and the demands of external objects. This gave the illusion that they were in control of their objects and that the environment was a narcissistic extension of the self. Hence, the boundary between the self and their objects could be denied. These patients had been able to use their professional roles and successes in work as supports to their impoverished or immature egos and this, together with their position in their friendship networks and in their families, where they were supported by the achievements of their spouses and children, had helped them to appear to function effectively over a considerable period of their lives. They had, therefore, met to some extent the demands of their ego-ideal and, as a result, they had been able to maintain a feeling of achievement and satisfaction which had counteracted their fear of failure, of narcissistic wounds, and consequent disintegration of their brittle, defensive ego-structure.

I asked myself what had changed in their situation that made it now possible for them to seek treatment. It seemed to me that an important reason for this change was their increasing awareness of the reality of the physical, psychological, and social affects of ageing on themselves, and this was a reality that they could no longer deny, and which, in turn, was undermining the effectiveness of their narcissistic equilibrium. The prospect of ageing was felt to threaten them with disintegration, and they had little notion of being able to adjust progressively to the changes demanded of them by the process of ageing.

I would now like to consider *some* of the pressures which seem to operate as sources of anxiety and concern during the second half of the life-cycle and which lead some neurotic individuals to seek psychotherapeutic help, when either they have managed without it up to that time, or their neurosis has been inadequately or partially helped at a younger age. I will summarize them:

(1)   the fear of the diminution or loss of sexual potency and the impact this would have on relationships;

(2)   the threat of redundancy or displacement in work roles by younger people and awareness of the possible failure of the effectiveness of their professional skills, linked with the fear that they would not be able to cope with retirement, and would lose their sense of identity and worth when they lost their professional or work role;

(3)   anxieties arising in marital relationships after children have left home, and parents can no longer use their children to mask problems arising in their relationship with each other;

(4)   the awareness of their own ageing, possible illness, and consequent dependence on others, and the anxiety this arouses in them;

(5)   the inevitability of their own death and the realization that they may not now be able to achieve the goals they set for themselves, and that what they can achieve and enjoy in life may be limited, with consequent feelings of depression or deprivation.

Psychoanalytic work with a middle-aged woman

As I described in a previous paper (King, 1980), the impact of these pressures on the analysis of a patient became clear to me early in my analytic career, when I was asked to analyse a woman of sixty-three, whom I will call Miss A, who was suffering from an acute anxiety state prior to retirement. She had been in charge of a children's home for many years and her job had become the main source of her own sense of worth, self-esteem and identity, so that her ego had become parasitical on her role due to narcissistic investment of the latter. She had no adequate image of herself apart from her role, and therefore no appropriate sense of ontological security. As one could predict, she had developed severe psychosomatic symptoms linked with her body boundary. (She was losing her hair and had developed a serious skin condition.) She had had some analysis thirty years earlier, and she was no stranger to the meaning of her condition, and suffered much shame as a result. She was very grateful, at first, that I had agreed to help her, and was aware that many psychoanalysts would have refused to do so.

She was the youngest of a large family and was brought up mainly by nannies and governesses. Her mother was unable to show any emotion or to respond to affection from her children. When her father was at home he was distant and aloof, but he spent much time away on business. The whole family treated her as "the baby", and while some elder siblings "mothered" her, she nevertheless felt isolated and of little worth, except when she was gaining the "perks" that went with her role as the family's baby. In fact, she looked young for her age and she still had a capacity for openness and excitement in discovering new things that one associates with young children, which must have helped her to be good at her job.

In her analysis it became clear that she suffered intense jealousy and envy of her older siblings, whom she felt had had a better time, and this was also experienced in relation to her younger colleagues who would take over her job, for she had been a pioneer in her field. These feelings were soon experienced towards me, as she felt me to be different figures from her past. She became resentful and angry at my youth, that I was an analyst, and yet afraid that I would give her up, not being able to stand either her physical condition, which was rather unpleasant, or her paranoid anxieties and resentful feelings. She was very aware that this was her last chance. During the early stages of the analysis much pre-genital material emerged and she developed an intense transference relationship to me. But as time went on, and we could work through her defensive stance of being the "baby" we came to her feelings of shame and depression that she had been a spinster all her life, and had never had children of her own. At first she tried to defend herself from awareness of her sexual deprivation and ageing by self-denigrating fantasies, but gradually these gave way to an acceptance of herself as she was and the depression changed to sadness about what she had missed in her life, and to a consideration of what was still possible for her. It was during this period that her psychosomatic symptoms cleared up and it seemed to me that considerable ego growth had taken place. She also managed to make plans for her retirement. She bought a cottage in the country and started exploring contacts in that area. When she retired she moved away from London and we terminated her analysis. She kept in touch with me and sent me occasional reports on how she was progressing. She has now had twenty-five years of creative and contented life since she came to me for analysis. When she left me I was unsure how she would manage. In retrospect, I realize that she had re-experienced during her analysis many of her adolescent problems that had made it difficult for her to pass from childhood to adulthood, but that with the analysis of her paranoid and depressive anxieties related to that stage of her life-cycle, ego growth and phase appropriate sublimation could take place.

Since then I have analysed a number of middle-aged and elderly patients, and I have noticed the parallels between the developmental and psychological tasks posed during adolescence and middle age. One reason for this may be that the middle-aged individual is having to face many of the same problems that he did in his adolescence, but this time in reverse, for it is a period of involution. At both phases of the life-cycle he has to adjust to sexual and biological changes in himself; awareness of these changes can arouse anxiety as basic sources of security are threatened. These are exacerbated by role changes and their socio-economic consequences; for example, possible lack of money following retirement, leading to conflicts about dependency and independence, which are also experienced during adolescence. During both periods he will probably have to face a change from a two-generational home to a one-generational household and the consequent need to make new relationships; old defences may break down as sociobiological and psychological pressures shift, often precipitating an identity crisis, in terms of self-perception and perception of the self by others, and necessitating changes in his self-image, accompanied by possible narcissistic trauma and wounds to self-esteem. I think that it is the existence of these parallels that often exacerbates the conflicts between parents and their adolescent children, and leads to their mutual scape-goating.

However, it has become progressively clear to me that for analysis to be successful for middle-aged and elderly patients, *the traumas* and *psychopathology of puberty* and *adolescence* must be re-experienced and worked through in the transference, whatever other early infantile material is also dealt with. Before I can continue I must discuss what I mean by this phrase "re-experienced and worked through in the transference". It is through the operation of the phenomenon of *transference* that we can become aware of and obtain access to the *context* of our patients' past traumas and the aetiology of their neuroses. This context is their *life-cycle*, within which they experienced their own development, maturation and ageing.

As I understand the concept, *transference is* the process by which a patient, as a result of the repetition compulsion, repeats and re-lives in the present of the psychoanalytic relationship, unconscious conflicts, traumas and pathological phantasies from his past, and re-experiences them, together with affects, expectations and wishes appropriate to those past *situations and relationships,* in relation to his analyst, who is *then* felt to be the person responsible for whatever distress he is re-experiencing. In this way, the symptoms of the patient's illness are given a new transference meaning and his neurosis is replaced by a

> transference-neurosis of which he can be cured by the therapeutic work. *The transference thus creates an intermediate region between illness and real life through which the transition from the one to the other is made.* [Freud, 1912c, p. 154, (my italics)].

When I have discussed the analysis of elderly patients with younger colleagues, they have sometimes expressed the opinion that they would be unable to treat older patients, as they thought the patients would be unwilling to trust someone obviously younger than themselves. But patients may well experience themselves, in terms of a psychological time-scale, as quite small and even helpless, and the analyst as older than they are. Thus, I find it important to remember that middle-aged and elderly patients may be functioning within a number of different time-scales. These may include a chronological time-scale, a psychological one, and a biological one, alongside the time-scale of unconscious processes, which are, paradoxically, timeless. An understanding of the time-scale within which an elderly patient is currently functioning in the analytic session gives the analyst an important key to the understanding of transference phenomena in such patients. The analyst can be experienced in the transference as any significant figure from the elderly patient's past, sometimes covering a span of five generations, and for any of these transference figures the roles may be reversed, so that the patient behaves to the analyst as he experienced them behaving to him, and he treats the analyst as he felt he was treated by them (King, 1978). But it has been my experience that the developmental phases that most often need to be worked through in the transference of middle-aged patients are those of puberty and adolescence, the analyst being experienced (whatever his or her actual age) as significant adults from those phases of the patients' life-cycle.

What can be achieved in the psychoanalysis of ageing patients

It has been my experience that the gradual awareness of the changes in the life situation of my middle-aged patients not only brings them into analysis, but the pressures arising from these changes tend to introduce a new dynamic and sense of urgency into their analysis, thus facilitating a more productive therapeutic alliance than one often manages to establish with similar but younger adult patients. They are usually conscious of the fact that this is their last chance to effect an alteration in their lives and relationships, before being faced with the reality of the physical, psychological, and social effects of ageing to themselves. The immediacy of their actual losses and depletions makes it less easy for them to deny paranoid and depressive anxieties, so that a process of mourning can more easily be initiated and blaming others can give way to sadness and forgiveness of themselves and others.

Furthermore, the lessening of the intensity of instinctual impulses that occurs with ageing reduces the need for the maintenance of the rigidity of their defence systems, so that as the archaic, parental imagoes and object representations become less terrifying, they are able to assimilate new objects into their psychic structure, thus facilitating new ego growth. *Along with these changes, the often impossible standards of their ego-ideal become modified and extended to incorporate achievable goals and value systems.* Thus, the feeling of alienation from themselves and others decreases as the dissociation in their egos is lessened, and they begin to experience a new sense of their own identity and the value of their own achievements and worth, which then no longer depends on their manipulation of captive objects.

This rediscovery of their own identity I link with a shift from living through their false self to living through their true self, which often runs parallel to, and is perhaps mediated by, the development of new forms of creativity and new ways of perceiving people, time, and the world around them. With some it is as though they have to learn to exist in a new key, or dimension of being, which they feel is very different from how they have lived before. It is as if the centre of their gravity moves from the edge of themselves to their own inner centre. They begin to experience a new sense of tranquillity that is not dependent on the continuity of an intact body, or on family relationships, or on a role in the community, although it may be enriched by these, but which is based on a sense of identity and of their own value and purpose in life. When elderly patients have achieved this, I find that they are then often able to get access to new forms of creativeness within themselves, which result in experiences of satisfaction quite different from any experiences during the first half of their lives. Marion Milner has very sensitively described this process in her book *The Hands of the Living God* (Milner, 1969).

What are the special problems for analysts and therapists working with elderly patients?

In asking that psychoanalysts consider the implications of ageing and the particular problems of patients in the second half of life, one is really suggesting that they look at themselves and what is happening to them as people. It is easy enough to work with people younger than you are because you have survived the problems of their age group. It is more difficult to work with those much older than you because they could be your parents (and you have to come to terms with your ambivalence towards them), but you can always comfort yourself with the idea that you will be different when you grow old. Most of the psychoanalysts who write papers, however, are middle-aged, between forty-five and sixty-five, and I think that writing about patients of this age group confronts them with their own problems in accepting ageing and the reappraisal of the satis-factoriness of their own lives as people.

I think this is difficult for us psychoanalysts because we have not yet worked out and shared an adequate conceptual frame of reference based on acceptance of the socio-biological facts of the life-cycle and their psychological concomitants, within which the changing functions of mental processes can be reassessed in rela-tion to the stage in the life-cycle reached by an individual.

Special transference and problems as they affect the psychoanalysts or psychotherapists of middle-aged and older patients

Finally, I would like to consider transference and counter-transfer-ence problems that can be encountered by psychoanalysts during the analysis of middle-aged and elderly patients. The transference itself may take various forms, and whatever is being re-experienced in the transference, *eroticized or psychotic affects* may be superim-posed on it as a result of the impact of unconscious phantasies. *But* the affects, whether positive or negative, that may accompany transference phenomena are often very intense with older patients, and they may arouse unacceptable feelings in the analyst towards his or her own ageing parents. It is therefore necessary for those undertaking the psychoanalysis of such patients to have come to terms with their feelings about their own parents and to have accepted in a healthy, self-integrative way, their own stage in their life-cycle and their own ageing process. They are then more able to make use of their affective responses to their patient's communica-tions to illumine the vicissitudes of his transference.

There are, however, certain reality problems which can influence the analyst's emotional responses to his middle-aged and elderly patients. He will be aware that there may be time limits within which he and his patient have to work, and this may impose both a strain on the work and an incentive. One such time limit may be set by financial considerations, when a patient is unable to continue analysis after retirement. But patients may behave as if they had the same span of time before them that they had in their adolescence, leaving their analyst to carry the urgency of their situation and denying their actual position in their life-cycle. This belief may be reinforced by acting out and behaviour more reminiscent of adolescence than middle age, which can endanger the continuation of treatment and the health of the patient. But while it is not easy to keep adolescents in psychoanalysis, it is often the opposite for middle-aged and elderly patients. It is difficult to terminate their analyses. They may, for example, develop a negative therapeutic reaction which is linked with the fantasy that by avoiding change or therapeutic improvement, they will be out of time and therefore avoid ageing and death. Unconsciously, they link mental health with being alive, and if they can manage not to be part of life, they will not die. This reaction from the middle-aged patient can be difficult for the analyst to deal with emotionally, because these patients also manage to convey the impression that analysis is keeping them alive. It is sometimes possible to work through this phase, when, for example, through the patient's transference it can be understood that the analyst is being made to carry his patient's guilt for having, as he felt, left his own parents to die. As ageing continues and is accompanied by physical illness and immobility more infantile phases of the life-cycle may be re-experienced.

I hope that what I have written will make sense to those who have to work with problems arising from the effect of ageing both on themselves and on their patients, and that they will have gained some new ways of thinking about ageing and the therapeutic process we evoke to deal with it. Ageing can be exciting when we can accept it as a challenge for further investigation and exploration of ourselves.

What are the special problems of an "ageing" psychoanalyst?

Recently, I wrote a paper entitled "On becoming an ageing psychoanalyst" (King, 2002). In it, I started to consider the professional life-cycles of myself and my colleagues and I decided that there were distinct phases that psychoanalysts has to pass through in the course of membership of their Professional Society, which involved changes in their roles. These include restrictions in what they can do and changes in their responsibilities or what their colleagues expect from them.

In 1976 the International Psychoanalytical Association held a Symposium at Haslemere on "The Identity of a Psychoanalyst", and I discussed these problems at some length in the published version of my contribution to the proceedings (King, 1983). Then I considered the impact of life events on the psychoanalyst's sense of identity and the consequent crises that could develop within that sense identity and worth.

I then went on to consider the various threats to their identity and view of themselves that confront psychoanalysts at different stages of their professional life. As we pass through our professional lives, we undergo various changes in our capacities. There are, for example, a number of critical phases in the professional life-cycle of psychoanalysts when they are faced with the need to reassess and accept changes in their own view of themselves, their identity, and the view of themselves taken by significant others, i.e. colleagues and members of their particular "reference group": Each of these phases is characterized by a transition from one stage of professional skill to another. They often involve a change in status from that which is known to that which is at least partially unknown, and the loss of a past role and the identity associated with it.

I list these changing roles as follows:

(1) being a student of psychoanalysis;
(2) being a newly qualified psychoanalyst;
(3) becoming a full member of a psychoanalytic organization;
(4) becoming a training analyst;
(5) becoming an ageing psychoanalyst.

Here, I am only interested in the fifth stage or phase. When I wrote about this I realised that the inclusion of the word "becoming" was important, because we often only gradually become aware of the changes in ourselves and the restriction of what we can do satisfactorily to ourselves or to others. When I wrote about this phase in a paper to honour Leo Rangell published in *The Psychoanalytic Core* (King, 1989), I described the situation of the ageing psychoanalyst as follows:

A fifth critical phase in the professional life-cycle of a psychoanalyst may occur when he becomes aware of his own ageing, the depletion of his skills, capacities and abilities and his possible retirement from professional work. Psychoanalysts tend to work much longer and to retire later than people in other professions with the possible exception of politics, the arts or religion. They often only reach their full potentiality as psychoanalysts in the second half of life when the long training and period of apprenticeship starts to bear fruit. So that they may attain positions of maximum professional responsibility at an age when their friends in other professions are preparing for retirement. Indeed many analysts do their most creative work between the ages of 45 and 65, creative work which earns for them the approval and gratitude of their colleagues. Attempts are made in some Societies to encourage psychoanalysts to retire, at least from training activities, at an agreed age ... But people are affected very differently by the ageing process and. in addition the process of ageing is also complicated by illnesses which exacerbate the depletion of abilities and undermine the capacities of an analyst prematurely.

Nevertheless, as it is very difficult to give a date to the onset of the process of ageing, every psychoanalyst is inevitably confronted with its impact on the view he takes of himself, his capabilities, his expectations of what is possible, for himself as a person and how he is therefore currently viewed by colleagues and close collaborators. He can discuss these issues with others, but he has to make up his own mind about himself.

But when psychoanalysts are over-dependent or even parasitical on their role as psychoanalysts, unconsciously using their patients and their professional activities as extensions of themselves, the main sources of their identity as a human being, then the process of retirement or withdrawal from over-much professional activity can threaten the stability of their personalities and lead to their inability to face their ageing and their own identity crisis in a creative and constructive way.

Our first realization of our need to consider whether or not we are being influenced by our own process of ageing may be in the perception of a discrepancy between our ego ideal of how we expect ourselves to function and to be responded to by others and what is actually the case. It may be accompanied by feelings of failure, alienation, and a questioning of the value of what we do, the goals of our work, and even the purpose of life itself. These are the "symptoms" that many psychoanalysts may have experienced at other critical phases in their professional life, and have managed to readjust their expectations of themselves. But there comes a time when it is as though the individual has come to a "T" junction in his life. He can no longer continue in the direction he has been following up to this point in time, and therefore he has to decide to turn either to the left or to the right; that is, he has to make a choice. This choice is between an adaptive reaction (he can accept the changing situation in a creative way) and a maladaptive one (he can try to ignore the problems arising from his ageing). It is when he chooses the latter that he exposes himself to pressures from others and misses the chance to make creative choices about his own future with the accompanying pleasure of feeling that his life is still in his own hands.

In 1974, when I first put forward these ideas, I was fifty-six years old and, of course, getting old seemed set in a distant future for me, although I was aware how it could affect others, who might need help and who should be able to receive it from psychoanalysis. This was the core of my search. I think that some colleagues were beginning to respond to my requests to take seriously the possibilities of taking on older patients in psychoanalysis.

Following these discussions, I was asked to take part in a Symposium that was arranged for the thirty-first IPA Congress in 1979 and the first one to be held in the USA. The papers were concerned with "The life-cycle as indicated by the nature of the transference in the psychoanalysis of children" by Peter B. Neubauer, and Peter Blos dealt with the topic in the psychoanalysis of adolescents. I was asked to speak on "The life-cycle as indicated by the nature of the transference in the psychoanalysis of the middle-aged and elderly". This was the first time that the topic had been allowed on to the programme of an IPA Congress, unless Abraham spoke on that topic years ago!

I was only sixty-one years of age when I gave this paper at the New York Congress in 1979. In 1989, I put together some of my thoughts on this subject for Leo Rangell's Festschrift. My paper was entitled "On being a psychoanalyst: integrity and vulnerability in psychoanalytic organisations" and it was very concerned with the importance of psychoanalysts being able to assess themselves and become responsible for their own mental and physical health as they came to the different phases in their own life-cycle, or felt vulnerable to the pressures of the organization within which they worked.

I then became eighty years old in 1998 and my colleagues in the Independent Group arranged a lovely "Pearl's Day", which was followed later in the year by a Conference arranged by the Society. Much love, care, and appreciation was embodied in those events, concerning what I had been struggling to do for psychoanalysis and my colleagues during my professional life as a psychoanalyst.

The only thing that spoilt my appreciation of these experiences was that I was recovering from an attack of "temporal arthritis" and an unfriendly hip. The former was dealt with by large doses of steroids and the latter by a hip operation. This was the first time for years that I had been ill and I had to face the impermanence of my body . . . that it would not last for ever! Since then I have enjoyed good health.

Hanna Segal and I are almost the same age, and so we shared the same year in which to celebrate with our colleagues our eightieth birthdays and we gave a paper for each other's Festschrifts dealing with our work with older patients, for she was one of the first analysts to publish work on this subject. My paper was entitled "In the end is my beginning". The title was taken from *East Coker* by T. S. Eliot, which is included in his *Four Quartets*. This poem starts with these words and finishes with them. They brought to my mind that my ageing could give me the chance to begin another profession and follow other interests. I could try to publish some of the papers that I had abandoned or had never written. I had never taken seriously the task of publishing my own papers and many colleagues had complained that they had trouble when they wanted to refer to work that we had done together. I was told that it was unfair of me not to take it seriously.

I gradually planned for myself another career doing research and writing. It would mean accepting that I would not see any more patients, which was sad, but on the good side it meant that my days were not fixed to the strict "timetables" that working with patients involves one with. I could plan my time, attend to my garden, arrange to do things with my friends, have time to do research in our archives (which I had helped create) and write about "Helping societies to grow", which was the title of my eightieth birthday Conference arranged by the Independent Group. It felt like being on holiday all the time, even though, with this new regime I have much more work to do!

This title, "Helping societies to grow", brings me back to the beginning of this paper. This was what I was doing when I first met Veikko Tähkä in 1964 when he and Donald Winnicott and I started to help the new Finnish Psychoanalytical Society to come into being in 1967.

I would like to conclude by quoting part of a poem by Longfellow (1940), which he wrote to commemorate the fiftieth anniversary of his class of 1825 in Bowdoin College, USA, which he called "Morituri salutamus":

> It is too late! Ah, nothing is too late
> Till the tired heart shall cease to palpitate.
> Cato learned Greek at eighty; Sophocles
> Wrote his grand Œdipus, and Simonides
> Bore off the prize of verse from his compeers,
> When each had numbered more than four-score years . . .
> Chaucer, at Woodstock with the nightingales,
> At sixty wrote the Canterbury Tales;
> Goethe at Weimar, toiling to the last,
> Completed Faust when eighty years were past.
> These are indeed exceptions; but they show
> How far the gulf-stream of our youth may flow
> Into the arctic regions of our lives . . .
> For age is opportunity no less
> Than youth itself, though in another dress
> And as the evening twilight fades away
> The sky is filled with stars, invisible by day . . .

References

Abraham, K., Bryan, D., & Strachey, A. (1919) [1927]. The applicability of psychoanalytic treatment to patients at an advanced age. In: *Selected Papers on Psychoanalysis*, pp. 312–13. London: Hogarth.

Balint, M. (1957). *Problems of Human Pleasure and Behaviour*. London: Hogarth.

Balint, M. (1968). *The Basic Fault and Therapeutic Aspects of Regression.* London: Tavistock.

Bowlby, J. (1969). *Attachment & Loss* (Volume 1). London: Hogarth.

Erikson, E. H. (1951). *Childhood and Society.* London: Imago.

Erikson, E. H. (1959). *Identity and the Life Cycle* (Psychological issues, monograph No.1). New York: International Universities Press.

Escalona, S. (1953). Emotional development in the first year of life. In: M. J. E. Senn (Ed.), *Problems of Infancy & Childhood,* pp. 136–137. New York: J. Macy Jr Foundation.

Fairbairn, W. R. D. (1952). *Psychoanalytic Studies of the Personality.* London: Tavistock.

Fenichel, O. (1945). *The Psychoanalytic Theory of Neurosis .* London: Routledge & Kegan Paul.

Freud, A. (1966). *Normality and Pathology in Childhood.* London: Hogarth.

Freud, S. (1898a). Sexual aetiology of the neuroses. *S.E., 3*: pp. 282–283. London: Hogarth.

Freud, S. (1905a). On psychotherapy. *S.E., 7*: p. 264. London: Hogarth.

Freud, S. (1912c). Types of onset of neurosis. *S.E., 7*: p. 236. London: Hogarth.

Greenacre, P. (1953). *Trauma, Growth & Personality.* London: Hogarth.

Hartmann, H. (1958). *Ego Psychology & the Problem of Adaptation.* London: Imago.

Hartmann, H. (1964). *Essays on Ego Psychology.* London: Hogarth.

Jacobson, E. (1965). *The Self and the Object World.* London: Hogarth.

Jaques, E. (1965). Death and the mid-life crisis. *International Journal of Psycho-Analysis, 46*: (4), 502–514.

Khan, M. M. R. (1963). The concept of cumulative trauma. In: *Psychoanalytical Study of the Child,* Volume XVIII. London: Routledge.

Khan, M. M. R. (1971). Infantile neurosis as a false-self organisation. *Psychoanalytical Quarterly,* XI: 2.

King, P. (1968). Alienation and the individual. *British Journal of the Society of Clinical Psychologists, 7*: 81–92.

King, P. (1972). Narcissism and sexuality. (Unpublished.)

King, P. (1974). Notes on the psychoanalysis of older patients—reappraisal of the potentialities for change in the second half of life. *Journal of Analytical Psychology, 19*(1): 22–37.

King, P. (1978). Affective response of the analyst to the patient's communications. *International Journal of Psycho-Analysis, 59*: 129–134.

King, P. (1980). The life cycle as indicated by the nature of the transference in the psychoanalysis of the middle aged and elderly. *International Journal of Psycho-Analysis, 61*: 153–160.

King, P. (1983). Identity crises: splits and compromise—adaptive or maladaptive. In: E. D. Joseph & D. Widlocher (Eds.), *The Identity of a Psychoanalyst*, pp. 181–194. IPA Monograph No.2. New York: International Universities Press.

King, P. (1987) [1997]. Talk on September 5th 1987 on the twentieth anniversary of the founding of the Finnish Psychoanalytical Society. In: A. Laine, H. Parland, & E. Roos (Eds.), *The Pioneers of Psychoanalysis in Finland*. Lapin Painotuote.

King, P. (1989). On being a psychoanalyst: integrity and vulnerability in psychoanalytic Organisations. In: E. Weinshel & H. P. Blum (Eds.), *The Psychoanalytic Core: Essays in honour of Leo Rangell, M.D.* (pp. 161–168). New York: International Universities Press.

King, P. (1999). In the end is my beginning. In: D. Bell (Ed.), *Psychoanalysis and Culture: A Kleinian Perspective*, (a celebration of the work of Hanna Segal) (pp. 170–188). London: Duckworth.

King, P. (2002). On becoming an ageing psychoanalyst. *The Bulletin of the British Psychoanalytical Society*, 38(4): 34–37.

Klein, M. (1948). *Contributions to Psychoanalysis*. London: Hogarth.

Klein, M., Heimann, P., Isaacs, S., & Riviere, J. (1952). *Developments in Psychoanalysis*. London: Hogarth.

Klein, M., Heimann, P., & Money-Kyrle, R. A. (1955). *New Directions in Psychoanalysis*. London: Tavistock.

Klein, M. (1957). *Envy and Gratitude*. London: Tavistock.

Laine, A., Parland, H., & Roos, E. (Eds.) (1997). *The Finnish Pioneers of Psychoanalysis*. Finnish Psychoanalytical Society, Lapin Painotuote.

Longfellow, H. W. (1940) [1968]. 'Morturi salutamus'. In: *The Poetical Works of H. W. Longfellow*. London: Oxford University Press.

Main, T. F. (1957). The ailment. *British Journal of Medical Psychology*, 30(3): 129–145.

Milner, M. (1969). *The Hands of the Living God*. London: Hogarth.

Rapaport, D. (1959). A historical survey of psychoanalytic ego psychology. *Psychological Issues*, 1: 5–17.

Rickman, J. (1957). *Selected Contributions to Psychoanalysis*. London: Hogarth.

Segal, H. (1958). Fear of death; notes on the analysis of an old man. *International Journal of Psycho-Analysis*, 39(I): 178–181.

Segal, H. (1973). *Introduction to the Work of Melanie Klein*, p. ix. London: Hogarth.

Spitz, R. A. (1950). Anxiety in infancy: a study of the manifestations in the first year of life. *International Journal of Psycho-Analysis*, 31(1–2), 138–143.

Spitz, R. A. (1956). Transference: the analytical setting and its proto-type. *International Journal of Psycho-Analysis, 37*: (4–5): 380–385.

Strachey, J. (1953). Freud's psychoanalytic procedure. *S.E., 7*: 254. London: Hogarth.

Winnicott, D. W. (1956). Primary maternal pre-occupation. In: *Collected Papers* (pp. 300–306). London: Tavistock.

Winnicott, D. W. (1960). The theory of parent–infant relationship. *International Journal of Psycho-Analysis, 41*(6): 585–595.

Winnicott, D. W. (1965a). Classification: is there a psychoanalytic contribution to psychiatric classification? In: *The Maturational Processes and the Facilitating Environment* (pp. 124–139). London: Hogarth.

Winnicott, D. W. (1965b). Ego distortion in terms of true & false self. In: *The Maturational Processes and the Facilitating Environment* (pp. 140–152). London: Hogarth.

CHAPTER THREE

"Dissidence" in psychoanalysis: a psychoanalytic reflection

Otto F. Kernberg

The present "age of pluralism" in psychoanalytic theorizing justifies a new look at the historical aspects of dissidence and change in the development of psychoanalysis during the past century. A conference on this subject organized around a fundamental contribution to this subject by Martin Bergmann (2001) stimulated this contribution. What follows is a general reflection on dissidence in psychoanalysis.

"Dissidence" is defined (*Concise Oxford Dictionary*) as disagreement, especially with the religious doctrines of an established church. "Dissidence" within psychoanalysis thus implies an ideological or religious quality of psychoanalytic convictions, and implicitly raises questions about the scientific nature of psychoanalysis. Bergmann (2001) quotes Freud as stating that disagreements regarding psychoanalytic theories should be settled with empirical evidence. Yet Freud, Bergmann goes on, also asserted that rejection of some basic psychoanalytic theories reflected psychologically motivated resistance to the truth of psychoanalysis, implying that the perfectly analysed psychoanalyst would not present such opposition. Dissidence, according to this latter view, again has the connotation of opposing ideological or religious belief systems rather than of engaging in scientific discourse.

If one translates the question of dissidence into the question of the nature of scientific evidence in psychoanalysis, the focus shifts to the development of methods for empirical examination of controversial issues. I assume that, even in the current relatively immature stage of methodology of scientific research in psychoanalysis, some issues may be approached empirically. These might include the nature of the analytic relationship, the interaction of technique and process and between process and outcome, the effectiveness of psychoanalytic treatment, for example. But many fundamental questions must remain open, and can only be resolved gradually, by means of the cumulative clinical experience of the profession, and the shared communication and evaluation of this clinical experience over time.

As Bergmann (2001) pointed out in his overview of the main contributions stemming from psychoanalytic dissidents, many of their theories, originally rejected by the psychoanalytic community, were eventually woven into the main fabric of psychoanalytic theory and method. Bergmann raises the fascinating question of what made some of these dissidents "dissidents", and what made some potential dissidents into "modifiers" who enriched psychoanalytic theory with their contributions. His central thesis is that, at least in the early generation of dissidents, the personal relationship with Freud played a major role. It is an open question as to what extent the personal relationship to Freud's thinking continues having such a central role for the dissidents and modifiers who continued to emerge after his death. While I am in essential agreement with the major proposal of Martin Bergmann, in what follows I shall take on the role of a "modifier", building on his rich contributions while focusing on the varying influence that personal, scientific, cultural, and institutional factors have on the emergence of dissidents.

The personal relationship with Freud

Bergmann describes convincingly the importance of the development of personal conflicts, particularly rivalries between Freud and his early disciples, with clear implications of oedipal conflicts and sibling rivalry as major contributors to the development of dissidents. Perhaps the most striking illustration of this dynamic is the gradual sharpening of the disagreements between Freud and Adler, and the eventual departure of Adler from the psychoanalytic group. But it is one among many defections that include Jung, Rank, Ferenczi, Horney, and Wilhelm Reich. All of these dissidents had personal relations with Freud, but at a certain point, when their contributions ran counter to Freud's convictions and the related boundaries of psychoanalytic formulations of the time, they met with sharp criticisms that reinforced their insistence on their particular views, finally leading to a split.

I agree with Bergmann that a personal disappointment either in the dissidents' psychoanalysis or in the relationship with Freud played an important role . Obviously, behind that conflict were issues of the psychopathology of all participants, activated by the regressive effects of the personal psychoanalysis, and the institutional reinforcement of such conflicts as these resonated with the psychoanalytic movement's relationship to its founder and charismatic leader. In fact, one might raise the question whether what appeared on the surface as personal conflicts with Freud might not have been unconsciously stimulated by the "innocent bystanders" of the psychoanalytic movement. I use the term innocent bystanders to refer to the psychology of regressive group processes that enact profound ambivalence toward their leader, expressing the hostility by a selected opponent or sub-group, which permits the silent majority to deny their own aggression by acting as "innocent bystanders." While they admired Freud and followed him without question, their unconscious hostility might have been enacted through fostering the conflict with Freud of a selected "representative"—or scapegoat.

Freud was open to new ideas, and changed his views significantly in the course of time, but was strongly assertive of them at any particular point. His efforts to integrate the thinking of his disciples when it did not correspond entirely to his own at times may have been facilitated by those closest to him. At other times the influence of his close friends may have increased the sharp differences between Freud's views and that of a young challenger. The personalized accentuation of the differences of their theoretical and technical formulations with those of Freud strongly suggest that the young challengers had intense feelings about these differences.

Much of the more subtle dynamics of the early group probably is no longer available for scrutiny, but what we can assess is the influence of cultural factors on the different viewpoints that evolved, and the use of ideology to support and rationalize more personal struggles.

What was the influence of Freud's rigidity in asserting his viewpoints? In all fairness, the enormous scope of Freud's discoveries, the continuous broadening of the world of unconscious conflicts and their consequences that he opened up would make it reasonable to think that it was difficult for the early group to absorb, in addition, the theoretical and clinical breakthroughs stemming from his disciples. When such contributions were presented with an aggressive assertion of revolutionary "uniqueness", like that of Adler and, eventually, Rank, an impatient rejection of their ideas seems understandable. I believe, however, that what haunted the psychoanalytic movement, and continues to haunt organized psychoanalysis to this day, is that the clinical basis of psychoanalytic discoveries, the knowledge learned from psychoanalysis as an investigative tool, is fraught with methodological difficulties. The mutual influences of analysts' theories and patients' regressive deployment render decisions regarding alternative theoretical formulations very difficult to make. The inevitable subjectivity and uncertainty of the clinical process will be resolved (if ever) only after an entire generation of analysts has approached the problem from different viewpoints, and sufficient knowledge has been accumulated for the entire psychoanalytic movement to move on.

For example, Ferenczi's (1949) stress on the importance of the mother–infant relationship, and, with it, the emphasis on pre-oedipal development turned out to be an extremely important advance in psychoanalytic understanding. It was elaborated later on by Melanie Klein, Winnicott, and Mahler, but it would take still another generation to establish a synthetic view that would integrate the pre-oedipal and oedipal stages of development in the concept of the archaic oedipal constellation. Similarly, Adler's stress on the importance of competitiveness and aggression would only later be integrated into the psychoanalytic mainstream, under the influence of newly accumulated information from the psychoanalytic treatment of severe psychopathologies, leading to Freud's discovery of the importance of repetition compulsion and superego pathology.

It might be argued, of course, that psychoanalysis as an institution might have been more open to new ideas had the leadership been more functional and less authoritarian. New ideas might then have been welcomed, studied, elaborated, and integrated, rather than having to undergo periods of dissidence and re-encounter. But the enormous difference between Freud's creativity and the dependent attitude of his disciples probably constituted such a powerful dynamic that a more relaxed search for consensus might have slowed down the pace of Freud's own discoveries and contributions. Here the question of the extent to which it is functional that the psychology of the institution adapts to the personality of the creative leader becomes relevant. In other words, some degree of authoritarianism on the part of an extremely creative leader may represent a reduction in an organization's optimal functioning, but is a price well worth paying for supporting such a leader. In all fairness, one also may grant the dangerous nature of experimenting with a new investigative tool, psychoanalytic exploration, as causative in bringing about the inappropriate aspect of the behaviour of those early disciples.

The impact of ideological cross-currents on the development of dissidence

Bergmann (2001) describes convincingly Jung's deep adherence to religion and mythology, with its linkage to German romanticism, and ultimately to racist nationalism and anti-Semitism, and his irresponsible immersion in the Nazi culture. By the same token, Freud's profound identification with the rationalist and atheist culture of the nineteenth century may have contributed to Jung's rationalization of his departure from the psychoanalytic movement. (McGuire, 1974).

It is only in the last thirty years that various psychoanalytic contributors have reflected on the subtly militant atheism of psychoanalysis's ideological stance towards religion, expressed in the not infrequently heard statements in the 1950s and 1960s that a well-analysed person could no longer be a religious one. The concern over psychoanalysis becoming a "Weltanschauung" was first expressed by Chasseguet-Smirgel (Chasseguet-Smirgel &

Grunberger, 1969), and has led in recent time to a meaningful re-exploration of the relationship between psychoanalysis and religion; for example, in the Mainz seminars in Germany in recent years (Kernberg, 2000b).

Marxism became the ideological cross-current that influenced the dissidence of Wilhelm Reich, was already a factor in Alfred Adler's partisan political stance regarding the social democratic party in Austria, and re-emerged in Erich Fromm's critique of capitalist societies. Perhaps the most extreme representatives of this ideological development were Herbert Marcuse's utilization of psychoanalytic thinking as part of what might be called a Marxist theology of liberation, and Althusser's utilization of the superego concept, bringing together Lacan and Marx in analysing the ideological superstructure of capitalism. The demise of Soviet Communism and the loss of popularity of Marxist ideology in general has brought about a curious disappearance of the psychoanalytic communities' concern with the relationship between psychoanalysis and Marxism, but we must remember how it agitated the entire psychoanalytic generation in the 1960s and 1970s, leading, for example, to the splitting off of Marxist groups from the psychoanalytic societies in Argentina. Those Marxist groups have, in the meantime, disappeared entirely.

The most recent of these cross-cultural currents has been the feminist critique of Freud, expressed along a broad spectrum, from the thoughtful contributions of Melanie Klein and Edith Jacobson, correcting Freud's assumptions about early superego development in women, to the general critique of the primary nature of penis envy in women, and to the dissidence of Karen Horney (Benjamin, 1986; Blum, 1976; Horney, 1967). The marginalizing of Horney is especially to be regretted in the light of the later integration of new understanding of early development in both genders, stemming from both North American and European recent literature. Karen Horney's departure from the New York Psychoanalytic Society was probably determined less by the heretical nature of her ideas than by the internal conflicts of the then monolithic institution to which she belonged.

It is difficult to assess concurrently—rather than with hindsight— to what extent ideological currents infiltrate psychoanalytic thinking and co-determine the differential characteristics of psychoanalytic institutions in different countries today. When a general cultural agreement prevails in a certain region of the world, psychoanalytic institutions may not even be aware of those cultural influences on psychoanalytic development. For example, the strong adaptational stress on the part of American ego psychology, the assumed normal adaptation to an "average expectable environment", the Hartmann era emphasis on the positive functions of the ego in facilitating adaptation, the tendency to reject the concept of a primary aggressive drive (let alone the concept of a death drive) all flourished in the optimistic cultural development of the United States after the end of the Second World War (Bergmann, 2000). Meanwhile, predominance of concern over primitive aggression was strongly developed in Great Britain during and immediately after the war years.

The spread of Lacanian psychoanalysis, with its stress on philosophy and rejection of Anglo-American empiricism, has had a strong impact on Latin American psychoanalytic societies living within a francophone cultural environment, while it has left only the merest traces in the Humanities departments of American universities. It is interesting, furthermore, how the recent stress within the biological sciences on genetics, and the revolution in neurosciences, has prompted psychoanalysts to re-examine the relationship between mind and brain, an interest totally absent from the psychoanalytic culture of only ten or twenty years ago. It is significant, it seems to me, that the idolatrous attitude toward Freud of most of his followers during those years did not include recognition of his great interest in neurology and the relationship of mind and brain.

My point is that during periods of rapid cultural shifts, when new ideological currents clash with traditional influences upon psychoanalytic thinking, that clash may contribute to the development of dissidence, eventually exaggerated as a system of rationalization for opposition that has deeper roots in psychoanalytic institutional dynamics.

*Intrinsic challenges of psychoanalytic theory and technique
to the conventional assumptions of mass culture*

Here I enter a problematic area of argument. One often hears, particularly in conservative psychoanalytic circles, that the hard times psychoanalysis is presently undergoing are related to the ongoing threat of Freud's findings to conventional assumptions of mankind. I believe that this argument tends to underestimate the serious problems that psychoanalysis has created for itself by accepting, indeed enacting, its reputation as isolationist, elitist, and biased against empirical research. However, I believe the argument holds in terms of the persistence, within conventional culture, at least of the Western world, of the myths of the sexual innocence of childhood, the basic goodness of human beings, and the positive consequence of any human encounter in which at least one of the two parties is attempting to help the other. Max Gittelson put it in a simple sentence: "There are many people who believe in psychoanalysis, except sex, aggression, and transference".

These conventional assumptions are often called "resistance" to psychoanalytic concepts, an unfortunate misuse of a term, whose specific meaning in psychoanalysis has to do with the manifestation of defensive operations in the psychoanalytic situation. This definition has particular implications for a contemporary theory of technique: more about this later.

The assumption of infantile sexuality, one of the most revolutionary discoveries of Freud, will probably be accepted in theory by every psychoanalyst. In practice, however, the ignorance or neglect of infantile sexuality shows up again and again, in the theorizing of dissidents as well as in various technical approaches within the psychoanalytic establishment. Thus, Jung's stress on the collective unconscious and archaic archetypes pointedly neglected infantile sexuality, and, as Bergmann pointed out, Jung accused Freud of having elevated sexuality to the equivalent of a religious commitment. Rank's stress on the fundamental importance of the relationship of the infant to mother likewise de-emphasized infantile sexuality, and even Ferenczi, in accentuating the devastating effects of sexual abuse and traumatization of the child, implicitly turned back to that innocent view of childhood.

Melanie Klein's formulations, although they incorporated the concept of the premature oedipalization as a defence against preoedipal aggression, in practice stressed preoedipal conflicts almost to the exclusion of the erotic quality of the relationship between infant and mother. Only in the last ten years, probably under the influence of contacts with French psychoanalysis, has the focus on oedipal conflicts again been accentuated in the work of Kleinian authors. Karen Horney, Kohut's self psychology, the inter-subjective and relational psychoanalytic schools, evince an under-emphasis of unconscious oedipal conflicts. It is as if the vicissitudes of infantile sexuality have to be rediscovered, again and again, against this cultural trend influencing psychoanalytic practice and theorizing.

The rejection of Freud's dual drive theory of libido and aggres-sion, and its replacement by an object relations approach, also reflects the tendency to underestimate both infantile sexuality and aggression (Kernberg, 2001). This shows clearly in the clinical illus-trations of intersubjective, relational, and self psychological case material; for example, in the symposium on "The Good, The Bad, and the Ugly", organized by all the New York based IPA psycho-analytic institutions and the leading psychoanalytic journals, in New York, 1991 (Kernberg, 2004). Perhaps self psychology has been most outspoken in this regard, and Kohut's proposal that aggres-sion derives from the traumatic fragmentation of the self may be the most specific formulation of that view. Erich Fromm's views imply that, in an optimally arranged society, the degree of aggression would decrease significantly (Fromm, 1941). As Bergmann pointed out, Fromm was deeply critical of Freud because of his pessimistic stance in this regard.

The empirical research on attachment, of significant clinical as well as theoretical importance regarding early development, tends to focus primarily on the traumatic effects of mother's lack of normal responsiveness to the baby. Extrapolating from that research, the intersubjective and relational approaches have focused on the analyst's inevitable "failures to understand" as trau-matic, requiring repair via appropriate interpretation before the analytic process can go on. In this regard they follow a path not dissimilar from the techniques of self psychology. As in the theories of Fairbairn, the emphasis on the traumatic origin of neurosis and unconscious conflict implicitly denies the central importance of the disposition to aggression.

In the light of contemporary affect theory, and the probability, as I have suggested, that the drives are supraordinate integrations, respectively, of positive and negative affects, one may question the primary nature of the drives, but not the primary nature of both negative and positive affects, the disposition to rage, anger, hatred, and disgust as well as to joyful contact and erotic pleasure. The primary nature of both intense positive and negative affect states and their influence on structure building supports, I believe, Freud's basic dual drive theory (Kernberg, 1992b). It may be argued that only under pathological circumstances may aggression become so dominant that the effort to destroy all relationships—including the self, may become the dominant motivation, thus crystallizing as a death drive in some severely psychopathological conditions. That is a far cry, however, from the systematic under-emphasis on the importance of the conflict between libido and aggression at all of levels of psychological development implicit in many dissidents' objections to Freud's dual drive theory.

Regarding the transference, the painful reality that unconscious negative dispositions from many sources are an important aspect of the unconscious relationship of the patient with the analyst, of the defensive object relations in the transference that we call "resistance", and an important part of the technical challenges for the analyst, is another culturally supported source of denial. The stress on the "real" relationship between patient and analyst, not as a consequence of transference interpretation but as a precondition for transference analysis, has led to an ever-recurring tendency to induce the patient's cooperation seductively with supportive interventions. The problematic trend in earlier ego psychological approaches to stress the "overcoming" of resistances, and the misinterpretation of their functions only more recently corrected in the work of Paul Gray and Fred Busch, also serve as rationalization for an "anti-authoritarian", implicitly supportive, technical approach (Kernberg, 2001).

Here I cannot resist the temptation to explore somewhat further the issue of resistance, and the culturally influenced questioning of the technical implications of this concept in the service of denial of the importance of the aggressive components of negative transference developments. Resistances should be analysed in terms of the functions of the corresponding object relationship in the transference. Many years ago, Hanna Segal (1964) defined defensive operations, stating that resistances and the impulses against which they had been erected reflect, respectively, object relations activated defensively to deal with object relations activated by impulse. In this connection, I believe that the contemporary stress on a "two person psychology", on the mutual influences of transference and counter-transference, tends to undermine the more subtle aspects of transference analysis represented by a "three person psychology", the analyst being split into one part responding in the counter-transference to the patient's transference, and into another part reflecting on that very development. The analyst's analysis of his counter-transference as a preliminary step to analyse the transference–counter-transference bind tends to be flattened by the premature utilization of counter-transference by either adjusting to the patient's assumed reaction to an assumed stance of the analyst, or by communication of the counter-transference to the patient. Under these conditions, the analytic dialogue shifts excessively into an analysis of the present interpersonal situation, to the detriment of the exploration of the deeper layers of the patient's unconscious conflicts around aggression and eroticism.

My point is that various dissidents, in their global reaction to psychoanalytic theory and technique, have incorporated an identification with conventional cultural assumptions, and that this identification is not necessarily related to any "unanalysed" personal psychopathology. Such cultural adaptation may contribute to the development of dissident theories into a broad replacement of psychoanalytic theory *in toto*.

Perhaps the strangest dissidence in this regard is Lacan's (Benvenuto & Kennedy, 1986; Clement, 1983). Leaving aside the problematic nature of his personality, his mystifying style of communication, and the question of to what extent he distorted some basic Freudian concepts while assuming that he was providing the most faithful clarification and development of Freud's thoughts, Lacan's most significant dissident approach was his complete neglect of transference analysis and of the actual transference–counter-transference relationship. This attitude was reflected in the arbitrary shortening of the analytic session according to the analyst's assessment of whether meaningful communication was coming from the patient. The assumption that "empty talk" warranted ending the session meant brushing aside the analysis of unconscious defence and, in the process, returning to a truly "one person psychology" (or rather, a "one person psychology" being enacted simultaneously by two persons in the same room . . .). To

this day, one of the most problematic aspects of Lacanian psychoanalysis is the lack of presentation of clinical data, which charac-
terizes the entire Lacanian literature. There is no doubt that there
are important theoretical contributions stemming from Lacan,
particularly his proposals regarding archaic oedipal developments,
the transformation of a dyadic relationship marked by the imaginary into a triadic one represented by the symbolic and its relation
to the oedipal situation. So, returning once more to Gittelson's
phrase, I believe it does summarize impressively the nature of the
attitude of major dissenters and "paradissenters" towards basic
psychoanalytic theory and technique.

The influence of institutional dynamics on the development of dissidence

Returning to Bergmann's (2001) comments on the influence of the
personal relationship with Freud on the thinking of the early dissidents, obviously, those who had no direct relationship with Freud
still evinced an intense conflictual attachment to his basic ideas.
I believe that this apparent focus on Freud's thoughts may mask
major institutional dynamics of psychoanalysis, in addition to the
other causal factors of dissidence mentioned so far. Psychoanalytic
institutions developed strongly authoritarian tendencies, perhaps
culminating at the time of maximum cultural prominence and
popularity of psychoanalysis in its major centres in London, the
USA, Buenos Aires, and Paris.

I have referred to this issue in earlier contributions (Kernberg,
1992a, 2000a), and here wish only to summarize briefly my main
proposal, which is that the carrying out of psychoanalytic treatment
within an institutional context led to institutional structures
intended to protect candidates and training analysts from massive
acting out of transference and counter-transference, but these structures in fact had some unfortunate effects. While psychoanalytic
treatment was considered as a combination of a science and an art,
it was taught within an institutional structure that resembled a
combination of a religious seminary and a technical professional
school. The dominant administrative distortion was the development of the training psychoanalysis system, with the concentration

of all authority regarding teaching, supervising, analysing, and administrative leadership in the hands of the training analysts. This created a privileged class and an underclass (the candidates), with chronic institutional aggression acted out in the form of transference splitting, idealization of some subgroups, and paranoid developments regarding other subgroups and outsiders.

An atmosphere of submission and rebelliousness, of monolithic theorizing and indoctrination while professing a flexible analytic understanding, became major characteristics of psychoanalytic institutions, particularly where their social prestige and influence assured the stability and legitimacy of their educational enterprise. Within this atmosphere, I believe, dissidence became an expression of rebelliousness against the status quo, affecting to various degrees both early and particularly later dissidents. The case of Karen Horney illustrates this problem, and so, more dramatically, does the fascinating summary of Rycoff's withdrawal from the psychoanalytic institution that Bergmann (2001) provided in the addendum to his paper. I believe that it is not a coincidence that Kleinian and Kohutian groups developed in the USA within the most conservative ego psychological institutions, and, at times, these same analysts then shifted from a Kleinian commitment to a self psychology or an intersubjective one.

The "controversial discussions" in Great Britain (King & Steiner, 1991) that prevented a split between the groups of Melanie Klein and Anna Freud may have unwittingly permitted the enormous development of psychoanalytic contributions of the British Psychoanalytic Society in the 1940s through to the 1960s, by assuring an institutionalized tolerance of alternative ideas and implicit confrontations of those ideas in the context of evaluation of clinical material over time. Yet, the fact that candidates trained by Kleinian psychoanalysts remained Kleinian, and candidates trained by analysts of the middle group and of Anna Freud's group remained within those respective groups, points to the enormous pressure of institutionalized psychoanalytic ideology in distorting the psychoanalytic process and in determining the position of the student body regarding their respective training analyst's allegiances.

Authoritarian pressures in institutes may brand innovators as dangerous rebels, and force potential "modifiers" into an oppositional stance. Institutional splits or the development of dissidence

can be the result if one of the mutually split groups represents offi-
cialdom and the other is expelled and declared "non-psychoana-
lytic". This is what happened in 1949 with the group of
Schultz-Henke in Germany, expelled from the International
Psychoanalytic Association, not because of what many years later
was assumed to be related to their past contamination by Nazi
influences, but because of the rejection of the concept of the death
drive by Schultz-Henke, and the determination of the International
Psychoanalytic Association at that point that this position was
incompatible with psychoanalytic theory. Little did the psychoanalytic community expect that large segments of it would reject the
concept of a death drive, particularly in the USA, fifty years later.

Institutional dynamics typically show up as conflicts between
groups that appear, on the surface, as conflicts between charismatic
individuals in leadership position of these groups. Charismatic
leadership undoubtedly helps to crystallize groups around the
leader, but the institutional dynamics leading to such mutually
split-off groups, described by Bion as the basic group assumption
of "fight–flight", lie in institutional dynamics. Fortunately, the
psychoanalytic community has painfully learned that the expulsion
of individuals and groups because of differences in theory leads to
dissidence and a potential weakening of the psychoanalytic movement, and that the containment of theoretical differences may have
a beneficial effect on psychoanalysis as a whole. This principle
operated already in the controversial discussions, and later in the
capacity of the American Psychoanalytic Association and the
International Psychoanalytic Association to contain Kohut's self
psychology—in spite of its rejection of basic psychoanalytic theories that earlier would have led to a split. I have recently been able
to observe the surprising development of a strong and articulate
"intersubjectivity" group in the Chilean Psychoanalytic Association
that used to be rigidly Kleinian, a counterpart to the developments
in Argentina, where the traditionally rigidly Kleinian Argentinian
Psychoanalytic Association has experienced the development of a
powerful Lacanian group.

I believe that a variety of controversial issues regarding psychoanalytic technique are influenced by these same institutional
dynamics. The confusion of the concept of resistance as the clinical
manifestation of defensive operations in the transference with

opposition to the psychoanalytic treatment "that has to be over-come" outside as well as inside the consulting room seems to me a typical manifestation of an authoritarian influence of the psycho-analytic institution on psychoanalytic technique. The questioning of the authority of the psychoanalyst on the part of self psychology, the intersubjectivity and relational approaches, seem to me equally an effort to react to institutional authoritarian pressures by injecting a political, democratic ideology into the analytic process. As another example, the transformation of the concept of technical neutrality into the "anonymity" of the psychoanalyst proposed both by ego psychological and Kleinian schools in the 1950s and 1960s seems to me a direct consequence of the efforts to protect the untouchable training analysts from contamination with the candi-dates' social body, rather than the alleged effort to protect the "purity" of the transference.

Implications for the future of the psychoanalytic enterprise

It seems to me that, if the factors I have referred to are indeed fundamental contributors to the development of dissidence within psychoanalytic institutions, and if we are willing to learn from our history in considering the future development of psychoanalysis, we do have some major tasks at this time. First, the development of scientific research in the broadest sense is an urgent task. It will include both the gradual development of psychoanalytic expertise through the analysis of the effects of alternative approaches to the clinical situation over time, and empirical research, in the sense of setting up experimental designs by which alternative theories can be tested and the field developed in this context.

It is obvious that there are enormous difficulties in the objective study of the psychoanalytic process, but we are gradually advanc-ing in our capacity to carry out such studies. There are methods from other sciences that we may appropriate in addition to the use of the psychoanalytic situation *per se* as our major investigation of the unconscious. The dogmatic affirmation that only psychoana-lytic treatment permits us to learn more about the dynamic uncon-scious and to resolve questions about alternative theories and techniques has been used to protect our institutions against the strengthening of psychoanalytic research in the broadest sense, in addition to isolating us from the surrounding world of science.

Second, we must tolerate the development of alternative approaches in our midst, both theories and methods, and see it as our task to evaluate them systematically, not in order to absorb and integrate eclectically everything that comes along, but to develop our understanding in depth of what is essential about the psychoanalytic process and needs to be reaffirmed in the face of new developments. What has been called the "age of pluralism" means only that we have multiple theories and approaches, and not that all of them have to be accepted or integrated. They have to be used as challenges, as tests of our science, and they cannot be avoided, because they confront us with the influence of cross-cultural, ideological, and fundamental scientific discoveries occurring in fields at the boundary of psychoanalysis. The temptation to use neurobiological findings merely to affirm that "Freud was right all along" can be as destructive as the systematic ignorance of such findings. We have to be prepared to modify our theories and techniques in the light of controversies, and not as an effort to politically accept a bland pluralistic eclecticism.

Strengthening our scientific enterprise implies fundamental changes in psychoanalytic education, the development of an authentically scientific atmosphere where faculty and students jointly study our field, openly recognize and articulate areas of uncertainty and ignorance, and discuss how we can proceed to obtain new knowledge. I am aware that every time this challenge is formulated, there is an immediate response of "we are doing all of this anyhow": and it usually takes a long time to show that this may not be so at all.

If the proposed dynamics regarding ideological cross-currents and consistent conventional cultural assumptions are true, there may be some battles that have to be fought again and again: the pendulum switch between genetic and intrapsychic versus environmental and traumatic determinants of unconconscious psychic conflicts also may have to be elaborated again and again. In earlier work (Kernberg, 2001), I pointed to the present development of a mainstream of psychoanalytic technique that combines fundamental contributions from ego psychology, Kleinian psychoanalysis, the British independents, and the French mainstream, while an alternative development has been the consolidation of a relational/intersubjective/self psychological approach. These developments may illustrate the extent to which Freud's basic discoveries regarding aggression, sexuality, and transference have to be worked through, again and again, in the process of the development of psychoanalytic knowledge.

Finally, one of the most astonishing blind spots in the development of psychoanalysis has been the neglect of the development of psychoanalytic psychotherapy for a broad spectrum of patients whose psychopathology does not respond to standard psychoanalytic treatment. The denial of this issue, on the one hand, and the development of significant breakthroughs in psychoanalytic psychotherapies on the other, often outside the context of psychoanalytic institutions, is a major paradox. Veikko Tähkä's book *Mind and Its Treatment* (1993) provides a helpful overview of these new developments. This paradox reflects, I believe, the ongoing insecurity of psychoanalysis regarding the survival of its science, and, therefore, the need to protect the mythical "identity" of psychoanalysis, on the one hand, and a self-destructive avoidance of full integration of some of the most important contributions of psychoanalysis to the field of psychotherapy, on the other. We may be at the beginning of the breakdown of this denial, and of the awareness that a broad spectrum of psychoanalytically derived techniques can be explored, applied, and scientifically evaluated, strengthening the contributions of psychoanalysis to society. The development of independent societies of psychoanalytic psychotherapy functioning in parallel and even in competition with psychoanalytic societies is one form of unrecognized institutional dissidence that has been very damaging to psychoanalysis and needs to be overcome. This is the subject of another paper.

References

Benjamin, J. (1986). The alienation of desire: women's masochism and ideal love. In: J. L. Alpert (Ed.), *Psychoanalysis and Women: Contemporary Reappraisals* (pp. 113–138). Hillsdale, NJ: Lawrence Erlbaum Associates.

Benvenuto, B., & Kennedy, R. (1986). *The Works of Jacques Lacan: An Introduction*. London: Free Association Books.

Bergmann, M. S. (2000). *The Hartmann Era*. New York: Other Press.

Bergmann, M. S. (2001). Rethinking the problem of dissidence and change in the history of psychoanalysis. (Unpublished.)

Blum, H. P. (1976). Masochism, the ego ideal, and the psychology of women. *Journal of the American Psychoanalytic Association, 24*: 157–191.

Chasseguet-Smirgel, J., & Grunberger, B. (1969). *L'Univers Contestation-naire*. Paris: *Petite Bibliothèque Payot*.

Clement, C. (1983). *The Lives and Legends of Jacques Lacan*. New York: Columbia University Press.

Ferenczi, S. (1949). Confusion of tongues between adult and child. *International Journal of Psycho-Analysis, 30*: 225–230.

Fromm, E. (1941). *Escape from Freedom*. New York: Farrar & Rinehart.

Horney, K. (1967). *Feminine Psychology*. London: Routledge & Kegan Paul.

Kernberg, O. F. (1992a). Authoritarianism, culture, and personality in psychoanalytic education. *Journal of the International Association for the History of Psychoanalysis, 5*: 341–354.

Kernberg, O. F. (1992b). *Aggression in Personality Disorders and Perversion*. New Haven: Yale University Press.

Kernberg, O. F. (2000a). A concerned critique of psychoanalytic education. *The International Journal of Psycho-Analysis, 81*: 97–120.

Kernberg, O. F. (2000b). Psychoanalytic perspectives on the religious experience. *American Journal of Psychotherapy, 54*(4): 452–476.

Kernberg, O. F. (2001). Recent developments in the technical approaches of English language psychoanalytic schools. *The Psychoanalytic Quarterly, LXX*(3): 519–547.

Kernberg, O. F. (2004). Editorial comments on the symposium "The Good, the Bad, and the Ugly". Clinical perspectives of the question: How does treatment help? *Journal of the American Psychoanalytic Association* (In press).

King, P., & Steiner, R. (Eds.) (1991). *The Freud–Klein Controversies, 1941–1945*. London: Tavistock/Routledge.

McGuire, W. (Ed.) (1974). *The Freud–Jung Letters: The Correspondence Between Sigmund Freud and C. G. Jung*. (Transl. R. Manheim and R. F. C. Hull.) Bollingen Series XCIV. Princeton: Princeton University Press.

Segal, H. (1964). *Introduction to the work of Melanie Klein*. New York: Basic Books.

Tähkä, V. (1993). *Mind and its Treatment: A Psychoanalytic Approach*. Madison, CT: International Universities Press.

CHAPTER FOUR

Illusion and reality in the psychoanalytic relationship[1]

Riitta Tähkä

T ruthfulness is a foundation pillar of the psychoanalytic treat-ment (Freud, 1915a). It strives towards the true and the real. It is a quest of a person's innermost subjective truth. Finding one's authentic self also opens up the way to another person, seen as more real and less covered up by the veil of illusions. Illusion is usually understood as perceiving and interpreting an aspect of one's experiential world as coloured and distorted by one's needs and wishes, as well as by the expected dangers related to them. Illusion reflects back areas of our inner world that we don't recog-nize as our own, thus distorting or preventing our experience of the objects' self-determined actuality.

Dictionaries define illusion as a mistaken perception that always involves an object, as contrasted to hallucination, in which the object is either lacking or bears little resemblance to the object for which it is mistaken (English & English, 1958). However, both tend to be accompanied by a compelling feeling of reality, even when the subject may simultaneously be intellectually aware of their unreal-istic nature. As contrasted to illusion, a delusion is regularly expe-rienced as representing objective reality.

Illusion, thus, means experiencing something according to an important, persisting wish. Even when there may be some rational knowledge of its unreality, illusion *as an experience* tends to be essentially immune to reality testing. Still, in the formative development of the mind a significant relationship of the self to the reality of the object world seems possible to establish only through the pathway of illusion. Winnicott (1965) described how a mother, fully devoted to the needs of her baby, provides the latter with an illusion of a world that is the very fulfilment of the baby's wish for the moment. The mother has thus created a protective space ("holding") that permits the baby to discover and recognize the awakening impulse arising from his "true self", not as caused by the outer world and therefore amounting to a real and personal experience. This is possible only when the mother is present and ready to receive the baby's "spontaneous gesture" and give it the shape that makes it real and existing. The early illusion includes the possibility of experiencing that there is a reality corresponding with the child's ability to create. Only the early experience that the child's impulse has a receiver that gives it the shape of the child's own desire can act as a foundation for a life felt as real and personally meaningful. Such experiences provide the basis for the self's "continuity of being" on which the personal psychic reality will gradually be built.

This early illusion that includes a sense of omnipotence requires and is dependent on a reliably present and responding other. It lays the foundation for a sense of subjective existence and being a real and meaningful someone in a meaningful relation to an object and to the reality of an object world. This takes place through the mother's gradual helping the child to tolerate more frustration and less illusion in his initial experiencing of the world as a fully possessed and controlled "my world". In this process the world will gradually become experienced as having a self-determined existence to which the child still can relate meaningfully as an authentic self and in which he has a meaningful place of his own.

According to Winnicott (1965), if the mother does not offer the child the original illusion this foundation for being oneself will not be established. It is this illusion that creates the original idea of a world towards which the child can trustingly direct his needs and wishes.

The development of an individual's representational world proceeds through hallucination and illusion towards increasingly non-illusory experiencing that reflects successive levels of structuralization and object relatedness. In this process the necessary illusions change according to the changes in the developing representational world. A little child can only experience his object in an illusory way as long as his world cannot be experienced as shared, but only as possessed by an omnipotent self. The establishment of self and object constancies represents a revolutionary experiential change that thoroughly reorganizes the conception of the world and necessitates renunciation of most of its basic illusory aspects. However, this powerful disillusionment does not rob illusion of its central role in these processes of internalization and structuralization of the representational world that continue to proceed after this particular developmental achievement.

The path towards an increasingly non-illusory way of experiencing reality proceeds through recognizing the reality of one's feelings as a result of finding an inner world of one's own. To be realized, this process requires an interaction with another human being, no matter whether during the original development or in a psychoanalytic relationship later in life. Klauber states ". . . when we know our feelings, we feel more real . . . it is the illusion in psychoanalysis that first brings the patient in touch with the reality of his feelings" (Klauber, 1987, p. 7).

Several authors have described how the individual's experience of himself as meaningful becomes verified in the relationships with his important objects; how another human being is needed to find, confirm, and mirror for him the various aspects of his self-experience. While this is a lifelong process, it is vitally important and necessary when the representational world is still to be developed through processes of proceeding internalization. Winnicott's (1971) well-known description of the mother's face as a mirror in which the child finds an image of himself to be internalized is pertinent in this connection. If this finding of oneself in the mother's eyes fails, the child does not see a mirror but just the mother's face. In such a situation

> . . . perception takes the place of what might have been the beginning of a significant exchange with the world, a two-way process in which self-enrichment alternates with the discovery of meaning in the world of seen things. [Winnicott, 1971, p.113]

Cited by Symington (1987) Klauber maintains that reality cannot be approached directly but only through illusion. In the psychoanalytic relationship he saw transference as a dramatization of the patient's illusions and thus as a potential way to find the reality of his true feelings through illusions.

In my own psychoanalytic work I have become increasingly convinced that illusion, both as a phenomenon and a concept, plays an important role in the understanding that takes place in the psychoanalytic process. Klauber underlines this in his way by stating: ". . . psychoanalysis enables the patient to correct flaws in his or her internal dream or illusion via which reality is perceived" (cited by Symington, 1987, p. 47). For my own part I would want to emphasize the important role of illusions activated in a psychoanalytic relationship in keeping the analyst informed about the nature and level of structuralization of the patient's representational world—in the language of stagnated transference illusions as well as of illusions merely interrupted by lost developmental opportunities.

The relationship between illusion and reality will be impressively dramatized on the stage of transference. Illusion includes the significant vitalizing aims for which the self-experience is striving. Finding and understanding these aims is another way to describe the goals of the psychoanalytic process—just as valid as the goal of truthfulness.

In Freud's thinking, illusion and reality were seen mainly as opposites. It was the task of the analyst to demonstrate, with the help of transference interpretations, that the patient's illusions were repetitions of his unconscious past experience and thus unrealistic and anachronistic from the standpoint of the present reality. It was expected that this would help the analysand to discriminate the present reality from his own meaningful history.

However, while writing about transference love, Freud hesitates to call it entirely unrealistic. The central basis of the psychoanalytic treatment is for Freud the necessity of the transference illusion. He writes:

> He [the analyst] must keep firm hold of the transference-love, but treat it as something unreal, as a situation which has to be gone through in the treatment and traced back to its unconscious origins

and which must assist in bringing all that is most deeply hidden in the patient's erotic life into her consciousness and therefore under her control. [Freud, 1915a, p. 166]

On the stage of transference the conflictual unconscious wishes from the patient's past will be awakened as a vividly experienced present. However, the patient is expected at the same time to be aware of its illusory, make-believe character in the realistic present-day context of the psychoanalytic relationship. In his article Freud emphasizes the unrealistic nature of the transference love as a mere repetition of the past, without any new aspects that would stem from the analysand's present-day relationship to the analyst. In overcoming the transference Freud emphasizes its confrontation with the present reality and its interpretation as a repetition of the patient's past history.

However, to the question of whether transference love should be regarded as altogether unreal and not genuine, Freud elects to answer in the negative. Falling in love always includes repetition of the past, even if its emergence in the psychoanalytic relationship is specifically provoked by the situation and strengthened by the analytic resistance. Transference love in the analysis is also considerably less in need of observing reality than falling in love in more customary circumstances.

The psychoanalytic theory of today tends to regard transference less as a repetition of the past as such, but rather as its new edition that may have been modified by the later life experiences, including the realistic present-day aspects of the analytic relationship. Many authors maintain that the particular form and nature of transference manifestations result from interactions participated in, and influenced by, both parties of the analytic situation. The nature and significance of these elements in the actual analytic relationship have recently become the target of increasing interest among psychoanalytic scholars and clinicians.

While underlining the central role of interpretation in understanding the unconscious determinants of the transference illusion, as well as in opening up new ways to inner reality and truthfulness, Klauber thinks that the analysts tend to shun acknowledging and encountering the intense emotional significance of the illusion by overemphasizing the exclusive importance of interpretation in this process. He states:

The transference illusion is not simply a false perception or a false belief, but the manifestation of the similarity of the subjective experience aroused by an event in the past and in the present. (Klauber, 1987, p. 7]

In the transference illusion, which also includes an illusion of timelessness (i.e., the timelessness of the unconscious and the "timeless" nature of the psychoanalytic setting), will be found the sameness of experience and contact with the authentic feelings that are the bearers of its subjective significance. This contact with one's genuine feelings strengthens the authenticity of the self-experience involved, and is, according to Klauber, an important reason why, after their analyses, patients tend to be reluctant to regard their transference experiences as illusory. Even if Klauber sees the differentiation of illusion and reality with the help of interpretations to be essential in the analytic process, he emphasizes that the transference illusion is not just a medium for solving the underlying conflicts, but also a crucial participant in a new unconscious synthesis of reality and illusion in the analysand's mind. In that synthesis a formerly dissociated aspect of the self will be integrated in the analysand's experience, opening new ways for creative imagination and giving new depth and significance to his present life and object relationships.

While Freud emphasized the importance of the patient's getting rid of his illusory experiencing and the role of analytic abstinence in reaching this goal, there seem to be openings to parallel thoughts when he describes the process as follows:

... [the patient] will then feel safe enough to allow all her preconditions for loving, all the phantasies springing from her sexual desires, all the detailed characteristics of her state of being in love, to come to light; and from these she will herself open the way to the infantile roots of her love (Freud, 1915a, p.166).

Although Klauber (1987) speaks of the analyst's ability to listen, as well as of his spontaneity and honesty as important prerequisites for progress in the analytic process, he does not discuss more closely the elements of the actual interaction between the analyst and his patient in the analytic situation. Loewald (1960, 1975) has developed further this issue in several important writings. He defines transference neurosis (1975) as a new staging and dramatization of the patient's life history, that in its overall development is a unique product of the psychoanalytic process, jointly created by both parties. ". . . [It] is a fantasy creation woven from memories and imaginative elaborations of present actuality" (Loewald, 1975, p. 279), that contains the relationship between the patient and the analyst. Loewald makes it very clear that this brings decisively new elements into the drama of transference.

At first the fantasy character of the transference is not clear to the patient, in whose experience it still represents reality. The analysand and the analyst create together a playful illusion. The patient takes the initiative and brings the material, while the analyst participates in it by understanding, clarifying, and demonstrating its illusory character. The action of this play rests upon the possibility of experiencing it as both real and as a product of fantasy. The analyst takes an active part in its creation and its experiencing, not by adopting roles offered to him by the patient but by responding to him with his organizing and structuring understanding. In this interaction the poignant immediacy of the experience will gradually diminish and its fantasy character become more evident, making the patient increasingly conscious of who is the author of the play. When transference has been revealed as a repetition of the past it becomes a fantasy from the standpoint of present reality, with the resulting differentiation of present and past actualities.

The new experiential elements brought by the analyst into the interaction have a modifying influence on the patient's ability to relive his past in the analytic situation. Loewald (1975, p. 287) states that it is not an abstract realization, nor a response to the analyst's benevolent and warm attitude, but *self-understanding conveyed by the analyst's objectively articulated empathic understanding* that offers the possibility of a higher level representation of the experiential content, with new alternatives for its organization and integration. Both parties regularly experience this transaction in a way that Loewald calls "authentic responsiveness" (*ibid.*, p. 287) and that he regards as an essential aspect of the analytic insight (Loewald, 1960, 1975).

The awareness of the fantasy character of the transference becomes possible for the analysand when he develops the ability to differentiate between those aspects of his experiencing that are purely subjective and those that are responding to the present-day actuality. I will return to this later.

According to Loewald (1975) fantasy (transference) is not an unreal opposite to reality. It is unreal only when its communication with the present-day reality is inhibited or cut off. When this is the case, the present actuality will also become unreal or meaningless. In the analytic process the infantile fantasies become meaningful when they connect with the present actuality of the analytic relationship. Obtaining significance from each other, they will both participate in creating the experiential reality. So-called objective reality is not absolute truth but a human construction created for a particular moment.

According to Loewald, it is essential in the psychoanalytic process to deal with the transference not only as a repetition of the infantile fantasy, but as a dramatic play that is ". . . a re-enactment of life in fantasy, and this fantasy life enters actual life giving it renewed and enriching meaning" (1975, p. 294). Made possible by the analyst's interpretative work, a connection will develop between these different realities. The precondition for this is that the transference neurosis is recognized as a fantasy play that is not rejected, but is permitted to participate in organizing the present reality.

Loewald emphasizes that the development and dissolution of transference neurosis requires the analyst's active presence and "responsive thought interaction" (*ibid.*, p. 297). Resulting from the cooperation between the patient and the analyst, transference neurosis has *a form of reality* that is different from mere thoughts, dreams, day-dreams or remembering. Thus, transference neurosis would not be merely a transitory stage between illness and life, as Freud (1914g) wrote. As is well-known, Freud did not yet see the role and importance of the therapeutic alliance in the analytic relationship. He contents himself with the statement that an "unobjectionable" positive transference (Freud, 1912b) is necessary for the continuation of the analytic work when it becomes threatened by intensifications of transference love.

In discussing and understanding the different levels of experiential reality in the analytic interaction, Winnicott's (1965, 1971) concepts of transitional space and transitional phenomena are pertinent. The "third area" of experiencing to which these concepts refer is the space for play and creative experience as well as for psychotherapy. This "potential space" contains a paradox of experiencing: the object is simultaneously experienced as existing in the external world and as an object created by the subject. The playing child uses the outer reality in the service of his inner reality by pinning the meanings of his subjective dreams on phenomena of the outside reality. It is from these experiences of the intermediary area that abilities to fantasize and think will gradually arise. Winnicott writes:

> Of the transitional object it can be said that it is a matter of agreement between us and the baby that we will never ask the question: "Did you conceive of this or was it presented to you from without?" The important point is that no decision on this point is expected. The question is not to be formulated. [1971, p. 12]

In the psychoanalytic relationship this area of experiencing is different from the usual everyday reality. It is a subject-created variation of the so-called objective reality that is not yet a subjective fantasy but a shared illusion in which both parties to the interaction take part.

The developmental illusion

As discussed above, the neurotic transference illusion reflecting dissociated infantile fantasies has, in the beginning, to be experienced by the analysand as emotionally meaningful present-day reality. However, it is essential that its fantasy character will be revealed, and that past and present realities become differentiated in the analytic interaction. It seems that connection with reality is necessary for illusion to be changed to self-understanding and its content integrated into the self.

So, what kind of reality is being referred to here? Transference illusion is, by definition, impossible to fulfil. The neurotic transference tells a story of an illusion *and* its inevitable failure. That story cannot have any other outcome. In the analytic process the patient has to abandon seeking actualization of this illusion, an experiential change to which the analyst's interpretations open the way and build the bridge between illusion and reality. However, merely confronting the analysand with the present-day reality is not enough to make him responsive to interpretation, as Freud seemed to think. It seems necessary that the analysand should have experiences in his analytic relationship in which different levels of reality are simultaneously present. The patient can recognize his transference as an illusion only when there exists alongside it another significant reality in the analytic relationship, that includes joint striving of its parties to understand the patient's world of experience—i.e., the area of therapeutic alliance. That the patient and her illusions become understood in a never before experienced way through the analyst's empathically conveyed interpretations is itself the very experience that makes possible the integration of illusion and reality. In that shared understanding the dead-end of transference will be opened, an occurrence that Tähkä (1993) has described as the birth of a new developmental object on the side of the transference object. To that I would want to add that at this moment the illusions that bring forward reactivated processes of internalization also become possible and, therefore, I call them *developmental illusions*.

In my analytic work I have repeatedly encountered the emergence of illusions that are different from transference illusions from the point of view of both interacting parties. The emotional responses they give rise to in the analyst are different, and so are their significance and utilization in the analytic process. I call them developmental illusions for two reasons: first, because they seem to be analogous to the developmentally necessary illusions in the mother–child relationship as well as to the transitional phenomena as described by Winnicott, and second, because they emerge in that area of the analytic relationship that Tähkä (1993) has described as the relationship between the emergent "developing child" in the patient and the analyst as its new developmental object.

The authors who have approached phenomena similar or related to those described above tend to ascribe them to the transferential area of the analytic relationship (e.g. Modell, 1990). According to my experience, however, this is not conducive to a full understanding of this particular kind of illusion, nor to its adequate encountering in the analytic situation.

A developmental illusion brings an experience into the analytic situation in which some important aspect from the developmental interaction between the child and the parent becomes actualized, not as a concrete reality, nor as an elaborated fantasy, but only on the symbolic level of illusion. Although its experiential content refers to a wish of a child, it is not a repetition of the past but reflects a developmental interaction that never had the opportunity to materialize. The analytic relationship makes it possible for the patient to approach the analyst as a new object for wishes never responded to and to experience them being met by the analyst on the level of illusion. It is not enough that the analysand becomes conscious of his buried interactional wish and understands it as a present-day adult. What is essential is the experience that another human being responds to it. This responding does not refer to any concrete interaction or role-playing but simply to *the analyst understanding the meaning and nature of the patient's wish* and sharing this understanding with the patient in a way that the latter can experience as a deeply significant connection with the object. This is the virtually needed experience of meaningful sharing, becoming mirrored, found, acknowledged, and confirmed that makes it possible for the patient to experience and represent the content of his mind as a meaningfully existing part of his self. Structuralization of a meaningful self-experience, subjective finding of a "good" self, is dependent on another sharing and participating human being. A developmental illusion is always related to a "good" libidinal object while the transference object is always ambivalently experienced. Correspondingly, the analyst's complementary and empathic responses to the patient in the area of developmental illusion are libidinal and generative in nature (Tähkä, 1993).

Although the wish inherent in the developmental illusion is a wish that has not been responded to adequately during the patient's early development, its interpretation as belonging to the past does not offer any solution to it. Describing to the patient the nature of the wish and what would have been needed from the object does not lead to any similar change in the patient's world of experience, than in the case of a transference wish, where a correct interpretation can be expected to be followed by a new, significant insight in the patient's mind. Instead, in the area of developmental illusion, the analysand needs the experience of a receiving and responding object that would let him feel found and understood on a symbolic level.

Although the developmental illusion is a creation of the analysand, the analyst must participate in it with his understanding in order to make it a shared process. However, it will not be interpreted as a subjective creation of the patient, nor as a repetition of his past. That would not be adequate because the developmental illusion is simultaneously true and not-true, belonging to the "third area" of experiencing (Winnicott, 1965, 1971) where such questions do not count. Still, there is no conflict between the developmental illusion and the present reality, which it does not strive to deny or dissociate. This holds true even with the real contemporaneity of the analytic relationship, although it has little relevance for the moment.

The situation is very different when a transference illusion becomes activated. A transference fantasy is always ambivalent, involving unconscious conflicts and inevitable frustrations of the transferential wishes. Thus, transference always represents a dead-end aspect from the patient's arrested past (cf. Tähkä, 1993). It cannot be actualized as an illusion experienced on the symbolic level. When a transference illusion becomes intensified in the analytic relationship no different levels of reality will exist; it only strives for its concrete actualization here and now. It tries to destroy the analytic working alliance that can be restored only by a transference interpretation. It is *the understanding* inherent in the interpretation that makes possible the return of a shared reality and of a cooperative relationship between the parties.

Transference illusion strives to create a single-level reality, that would deny the present-day reality and the impossibility of concrete actualization of the transference wishes. It is the destiny of the transference wishes to become frustrated, the transference illusion being an arrested play with ready representations of something once experienced without possibilities of change. The role of the object is defined in advance as a part of a manuscript in which there is no room for new creative elements (cf. Tähkä, 1993), unless an interpretative understanding will restore the cooperative relationship and make a change possible in the patient's way of experiencing and understanding himself. A transference illusion strives for forcing the reality to correspond with one's own wishes. An extreme example of this is represented by a psychotic delusion, in which a marginal experience of an own existence is possible only by grossly distorting the present-day reality.

As contrasted to the transference illusion, the wish activated in a developmental illusion means taking a new and risky step towards the object, a step that had not been possible hitherto. It is here that the analyst is specifically needed as a new developmental object. As a rule, it is a point at which some of the analysand's once interrupted, important developmental strivings and wishes become activated in the analytic relationship (Tähkä, 1993). Like transference illusion, the developmental illusion emerges from the soil of trauma and frustration but, unlike the transference wish, it does not represent in itself a repetition of a past conflict and its management. Instead, it represents a new opening up towards the object, the subject's venturing to let an important aspect of his or her self-experience once again be dependent upon the object's response.

Still, the emphasis is on *the analysand's wish*; how she or he will be able to approach the object from this particular starting point. This expectation of the object's response is not predestined and closed as it is in a transference illusion. The developmental illusion is open, and what matters is whether the analyst responds to it by understanding its inherent message, thus confirming the significance of the patient's expectation, or whether the message will remain unresponded to and banished back to insignificance. Although the object's understanding thus is necessary for giving significance to the analysand's expectation, the question in the developmental illusion is entirely about the analysand's experiential reality and not of that of the analyst. The developmental illusion calls back to life an area of the analysand's inner life from its previous state of muteness.

For such a step towards the object to become possible, a trusting enough analytic relationship should have been established. Generally, this is possible only when important aspects of the patient's transference have already been understood and worked through. Since transference always represents the best possible solution for the "transference child" in the analysand, sticking to it is the most tenacious obstacle to the new developmental strivings of the "developing child" in him. The wishes of the latter are therefore concealed by, and intermingled with, the destinies of the "transference child" and can be detected only by simultaneous understanding of the transference repetitions (Tähkä, 1993). At the moment when the developmental illusion becomes actualized in the analytic relationship, the analysand has given up the shelter offered by the transference to his self-image and gives himself into the hands of the object as far as an important developmental wish is concerned.

In this situation, a lack of, or failure in, understanding from the object's side can be a crushing experience for the patient. An example of such a traumatizing failure of the analyst's understanding is provided by the latter erroneously interpreting the wish inherent in the patient's activated developmental illusion as a transference wish belonging to his past history. The result tends to be self damage of a different degree.

The obstacles experienced by the analysand to the emergence of his developmental illusion directed to the analyst are related to negative feelings and contents stemming from his past traumatic interactions with the original developmental objects. According to my experience *shame* regularly represents the crucial obstacle for this experiencing, as it tends to be the case in general when an interactional wish for a mirroring and self-confirming response from the object becomes frustrated (Ikonen & Rechardt, 1993). The analysands often feel crushingly ashamed to experience and express some of their central developmental wishes and dreams from their childhood in their here-and-now-relationship to the analyst. In my experience, it is exceedingly important that the analyst responds to the patient's messages in a way that allows these wishes to develop further and become integrated to his self under the shelter provided by the developmental illusions activated in the analytic situation. It is my impression that a majority of the analysands harbour an intensive reluctance to admit and express these very wishes, which they tend to experience as exceedingly shameful, childish, and stupid.

In the area of developmental illusion there is a real dependence on the object. Venturing to enter a developmental illusion undoubtedly presupposes previously internalized experiences of a "good object". Therefore, and since in the phenomena that I have called developmental illusion the question is about the needs of a developmentally inhibited "child" in the analysand, it might seem reasonable to see it as a part of transference, as, for instance, Modell (1990) seems to do.

Modell discriminates between two different transferences that are always present in the analytic interaction: "iconic/projective" and "dependent/containing" (1990, pp. 46–49). The former corresponds with the transference neurosis proper, while the latter is based on the psychoanalytic setting itself, which, besides its concrete features, includes the analytic atmosphere with strivings and attitudes conveyed by the analyst as its essentially influential elements. In the analysand's mind this setting will acquire symbolic meanings that transfer his experience of the relationship to a level of reality that is different from ordinary life and on which the analysand's early mother–child relationship will be re-experienced. This "dependent/containing" transference Modell sees as an impersonal and universal area in the psychoanalytic process. He writes: "This form of the transference differs fundamentally from what has been traditionally described as the transference neurosis" (*ibid.*, p. 48).

According to Modell there is "widespread agreement on this distinction" (*ibid.*) although it has been given numerous different names. He thinks that the most usual description of this state of affairs is the term "holding environment".

> The experience of the analytic setting as a holding environment is not uncommonly elaborated further into the illusion that this setting functions as a protective alternative environment that stands between the patient and a dangerous world. This is truly a transformation into another level of reality that is not the "real" world, nor is it the world of imagination and pure fantasy. [Modell, 1990, p. 47]

To my mind, the limitations in Modell's description of this form of transference lie in its sole emphasis of non-specific dependence conflicts and symbolic actualization of the earliest interactions. I find Tähkä's (1993) conceptualization of the analysand's relationship to the analyst as "new developmental object" more pertinent and useful. According to Tähkä, this relationship represents an essential element in the analytic relationship throughout the analytic process. His description covers and demonstrates the crucial significance of such a relationship on all levels of relatedness and structuralization taking place during the analytic interaction with its different individual contents and goals.

Similarly, the developmental illusions in the analytic situation do not limit themselves to universal symbolic meanings of the psychoanalytic setting. They refer to and include interactional wishes and fantasies from all levels of development and are of utmost importance in the processes of structuralization and integration that take place in the psychoanalytic treatment. Thus, for instance, in the oedipal terrain there are, as a rule, important developmental illusions to be encountered alongside the central transference illusions. Although the question is about developmental, and therefore universal interactional needs and their "symbolic actualization" (Modell, 1984), the illusion created together by the parties of the interaction is always unique, and the more so the more individuated is the analysand in whose inner world the wish actualized in the illusion originates. Holding alone is not a sufficient concept to define and cover this multi-layered group of phenomena.

I am in disagreement with Modell's and many other authors' way of placing these heterogenous areas and processes under the general heading of transference. However, I agree with Modell that the difference between these two forms of relatedness is visible in their different ways of responding to interpretation. In the area of developmental illusion and relatedness, the understanding offered by the analyst gives strength, shape, and significance to the analysand's wish, whereas interpretation of transferential wishes and illusions is apt to lessen their strength, thus prompting their gradual extinction.

At the most intense moments of the transference illusion the wishes involved represent the whole reality for the analysand. The only acceptable response and outcome is felt to be the concrete actualization of those wishes here and now. Other realities and goals have lost their meaningfulness, notably the cooperative relationship with the analyst, aimed at a joint understanding of the analysand's way of experiencing. At this point the analysand ignores and denies the existence of other levels of reality, including the dimension of "play" in the analytic interaction. Only when this is restored by the patient—with or without the analyst's interpretations—does understanding become possible again as the element that is indispensable for continuing progress in the patient's analysis.

In the area of developmental illusion, the patient's being confronted with the reality of the analytic working relationship is not needed. A developmental illusion does not deny the present reality, nor does it strive for concrete actualization in the analytic relationship. The response needed by the developmental wish is simply to be understood (Tähkä, 1993). Words that convey the right understanding are enough. Being confronted with the realistic nature of the analytic relationship when a developmental illusion is active in the analysand's mind tends to break down the illusion and make it feel like a ridiculous fantasy, the actualization of which as a meaningfully shared common experience could only occur in one's stupid and childish day-dreams. In contrast to the transference illusions that are stubborn and unwilling to give up their goals, the developmental illusions are typically exceedingly vulnerable and fragile.

As Winnicott (1971) points out, it is important that in the area of this type of illusion no questions about its experiential reality should be presented. Developmental illusions do not represent resistance to the aims of the analytic process; on the contrary, their adequate encountering leads to emergence and discovery of crucially important dimensions of the patient's self- and object-images and to their integration into an improved sense of psychic reality.

As stated above, the existence of the real analytic relationship is not denied in a developmental illusion, although its significance for the moment is brushed aside in order to maintain the quality of truth that is necessary for the maintenance of the illusion. Many patients suffering from more severe disturbances, in which the need for a developmental object is most fundamental, tend to experience this "truth" in their developmental illusions in an especially intensive way, although even then it remains in the context of the analytic relationship and in the service of developmental aims.

As is well-known, a transference wish has to be experienced here and now for its strength and living significance to be recognized by the patient and for it to make him receptive to interpretations about its repetitive origins. The developmental illusion, for its part, will become actualized in the transitional present of the analytic relationship and will be internalized as part of the patient's significant self-representation. Having completed its task it will disappear as a necessary intermediate step in the analysand's finding and completing his autonomous self-image.

While transference illusions are ubiquitously present in the analytic situation as defensive dead-end solutions to developmental arrests and unconscious conflicts, the developmental illusions usually become activated and visible later in analysis as gateways to resumed developmental interaction in the analytic relationship. Still, the vicissitudes of both groups of illusion are always intimately intervowen in the analytic process. Only when it has been possible to understand the "transference child" in the patient, with its stubborn wishes and defences, can ways be opened to wishes— often unarticulated and hesitating—that belong to the emerging "developing child" in the analysand (cf. Tähkä, 1993).

The goals of the analytic process can only be reached through the analysand's venturing to experience his illusions. As Freud states, the symptoms and conflicts behind them "can only be resolved and washed away by a fresh high tide of the same passions" (Freud, 1907a, p. 90). However, letting oneself experience according to one's illusions is not easy even in regard to transference illusions, despite their compulsive pressure to repetition and actualization, together with the features of the analytic setting that facilitate their emergence. A common way to try to keep the transference illusions hidden is the analysand's attempt to stick to such interactions with the analyst that underline rationality and here-and-now-reality of the relationship, in which an emergence of transferential passions and conflicts would represent a frightening and humiliating danger. This would protect and keep in force the central transferential solutions as the best ways he knows to retain a tolerable self-experience.

Sticking to the "reality" of the analytic relationship is no less usual a hindrance to the analysand's allowing himself to experience and express the developmental illusions necessary for his proceeding from the cul-de-sac solutions of the transference. Typically, this will be expressed by statements like: ". . . this is only analysis, nothing real, I don't even know you, . . . you are not really interested, . . . this does not mean anything to you, . . . you are just doing your work", etc.

A developmental trauma means losing trust in the object's reciprocity in the area of a wish, important for definition and confirmation of the subject's self-image. How deep and decisive will be the ensuing distrust of the object's responsiveness depends on the vital importance of the wish to the subject's self-experience. Such wishes are the more desperate the more the object's response is needed for retaining the subject's self-experience. The more difficult or impossible will then be venturing to approach again such interaction with the object that would actualize the once traumatically rejected or ignored emergence of a developmental illusion. At this point there will remain the original, traumatically interrupted need that would require response from a human object here and now. This need is buried in a self-image that protects itself against a repetition of the frustration by sheltering fantasies about itself and the object in ways observed as the analysand's transference to his analyst.

When enough understanding of the significance, dynamics and history of this repetition has been reached, it is the turn of the interrupted developmental wishes to become experienced in the relationship to an object here and now in their full vivacity and meaningfulness. At this point many analysands tend to stick to the "real reality", trying to prove to themselves that the wish has to be buried and abandoned as impossible to be actualized ever more, and thus to leave its frustration and disillusionment to be kept in force. Venturing to try again to expose the wish to the object's response is felt to be a foolhardy step, and the more so the earlier and the more fundamental are the analysand's developmental traumas.

This was the case with Sara, who, in her early childhood, had suffered a traumatic separation from her mother due to the mother's illness. For her, sticking to an omnipotent, self-sufficient self-image was vitally important. When the early traumatized—and therefore dangerous—need for a good and close reciprocity became activated in her analytic relationship with me, it mobilized hateful transferential images of an all-bad object, as well as a self-image that was totally outside any loving relation to an object that could provide her with the possibility of re-experiencing that she was worth loving and thus able to love herself again.

This possibility she attacked vehemently with negative transferential images and fantasies, as well as by sticking to the concrete "reality", disdainfully devaluing and denying any real reciprocity in her analytic relationship. Her endlessly repeated message to me was that this was just an analysis and could therefore never give her what she would need. Therefore, she had to wipe out and deny all her unrepresented needs and potentials for an object-directed developmental illusion. Although knowing intellectually that encountering and understanding one's feelings and wishes was essential in psychoanalysis, she refused to accept that this would be useful or even possible in her case. She did not belong to those who could be enticed into experiencing and expressing feelings and wishes in an artificial interaction created by the analyst for purely professional purposes. It was just an humiliating play in which she could not be persuaded to participate. The analyst merely did her work and would not really care for her.

In Sara's case, the early nature of her developmental trauma had obviously made a transference solution inevitable, in which retaining self-experience had remained dependent on the maintenance of an omnipotently self-sufficient self-image, as well as on an image of the object from which nothing good was ever expected. This prevented her effectively from even contemplating approaching developmental illusions in her analytic relationship, thus allowing them to be included in the interaction only as dormant and unarticulated potentials.

While the fundamental nature of Sara's early trauma made even the cautious approach of a developmental illusion impossible for her for a long time in her analysis, this was not the case with Nina, who was capable of visiting her developmental illusions from time to time in her analytic relationship. However, especially in the beginning these visits were invariably followed by a headlong retreat from the illusion with intolerable feelings of shame.

Nina had intense wishes, both transferential and developmental, for getting my interest and attention. When feeling these wishes as true in her analytic interaction she experienced intense love feelings toward me—an ardent love of the little girl in her. However, after weekends and other separations she usually returned to me either filled with cold rage, or as completely hopeless and with tears flooding from her eyes. A disillusionment of both her transferential and developmental illusions had taken place, making her images of me and herself totally worthless for the moment. She told me how, during the separation, she had "faced reality" and understood how ridiculous were the feelings she had directed toward me, how miserably childish and stupid had been her fantasies about her importance to me, and how intolerably shameful and humiliating it felt to think and speak of all this today.

This same succession was repeated even between sessions. Her experiences and expressions of her love for me were invariably followed by a violent disillusionment and crushing feelings of shame.

The following vignette from this period of Nina's analysis demonstrates the differences between her transference illusion and her emerging developmental illusion:

> Nina comes to her hour feeling that everything has once again become disgusting, lifeless, and of no importance. She is convinced that I would feel similarly sick and tired of her, without any motivation to cathect her analysis with interest. Everything I say is only felt to strengthen these transferential images of me and herself. Yesterday she felt different, though, she says. She had felt glad and happy about my way of listening to her with real interest, sensitively sharing her inner experience. Now all that feels ridiculous and stupid. Tortured by all-pervasive shame, she devalues all good interactional experiences with me on the day before, thus completely wiping out the wishes inherent in her activated developmental illusion.

> However, this time she is better able than before to respond to my comments by accepting a joint investigation of what had taken place in her mind since the session on the previous day. Despite her crushingly humiliating feelings of shame she is now able to tell me about the fantasies of contact and close togetherness that were stirred up by my way of relating to her the day before, making her feel so happy. After her analytic hour she had felt that she should buy a bottle of wine and drink it alone while trying to relive what she had experienced with me during the session. She followed this plan with results visible in her way of experiencing me and herself today.

This was her repeating defensive pattern, in which she managed to destroy the activated developmental illusion by retiring into the simultaneously activated transference illusion. Her positive experiences with me had provided her with both transferential and developmental satisfaction. When left alone she was not able to preserve my representation in her mind as a new object (as a preliminary step towards internalization). Instead, she arranged a session with a wine bottle, in which she tried first to extract all possible transference satisfaction from the experiences in her analytic hour. However, in accordance with the manuscript of her central transferential solution, this was inevitably followed by increasing feelings of lonely omnipotence, with a simultaneous devaluation of any images of a good object. In this process the wishes inherent in the developmental illusion activated in her analytic relationship were totally wiped out, making recalling and thinking of any good experiences with me extremely shameful and humiliating. This efficiently closed all doors to any meaningful reciprocity with me as a new developmental object.

When I verbalized my understanding of her inner necessity to resort to her defensive transference illusions in order to combat the wishes inherent in her developmental illusion that was activated in her relationship to me, Nina replied: "I agree, it's as simple as that, the issue is simply whether you like me or not—a stupid, childish wish." The oscillation from activated developmental wishes to her customary transferential illusions continued in Nina's analysis but the ice was broken and she started to become more and more able to experience her developmental illusions as her own and to make use of me as a new developmental object. The feelings of shame associated with her developmental wishes gradually diminished, and utterances like the following became possible: "Why could I not just let myself enjoy your understanding me and maybe at times liking me—what's there to be ashamed of?"

There are situations in which it is not easy for the analyst to find words to help and protect the analysand's developmental illusion. Such are the moments when the analysand's mind becomes filled with disturbing feelings of the "real nature" of the relationship. When the patient keeps repeating: "This is not true, it is only fantasy", the analyst cannot take a stand on this dilemma because the questions of "real" and "unreal" do not belong to this area of experiencing (cf. Winnicott, 1965, 1971). The question here is about what has been called "unevenness" of the analytic relationship. It is true from the standpoint of the present reality and a necessary prerequisite for the analytic process. However, inside the developmental illusion, where the experience is shared, this "unevenness" loses its significance and does not exist for the moment. Basically the analyst's problems of proper responding to the analysand's developmental illusion are the same as in his encountering the latter's transference illusions, i.e., how to use his own emotional responses to the patient and her messages for understanding her inner experience and not for assuming roles and functions that would correspond with the analysand's transference expectations or for trying to offer concrete parent–child interactions for an adult patient's developmental needs (Tähkä, 1993).

The following vignette is aimed to exemplify how different levels of reality manifest themselves in the psychoanalytic relationship.

Nora, who had suffered several traumatic losses , both in her early and adult life, is in the process of finishing her long analytic relationship with me. Her analytic material during these hours has been both deeply felt and rich in content. She ponders over her life, past as well as future, and on the different ways she has changed during her analysis. She mourns for the ending of the analysis and returns repeatedly to the question: what will end when the analysis ends? When this question had arisen earlier in her analysis, it had always caused in her a twinge of pain and fear of losing the only one who understands her.

While speaking of this, Nora is well aware of both the significant reality of her analytic working relationship and of the meaning of her central transference fantasies that one last time are activated by the approaching end of her analysis. In her hour today she says: "This room means harmony for me, maybe belief in goodness." [I find myself thinking that Nora speaks of her former ideals that now have been internalized and integrated in the self-ideal of an autonomous self.] We then discuss at great length Nora's experiences of loss and mourning— past and present. She speaks in tears, "I am not really so afraid of ending the analysis, but I will miss the goodness here; like I would have found a home and allowed to grow up there as an adopted child . . . It is too great to express . . . gratitude . . . one should make a speech . . . fine words . . .".

I: "These were fine words."
Nora: "I have not had a mother to help me with my children. You have been like a grandma for my children. It is so important for a woman to speak to another woman."

[I am surprised. Nora has always had especially good relationships with her children who, during her analysis, had reached adulthood.] Nora reflects upon the end of an important human relationship and that her own death would be almost easier to think of, for then everything else, too, would cease to exist. She goes on, "Someone comes close, gradually one knows everything about the other . . . (pause) . . . although I cannot say that I really know you . . . yes, I do know you as my analyst."

I: "As your analyst you know me very well."
Nora: "The other knows everything about oneself, becomes like part of oneself, one's life—even when at home . . . Everything one has created, learned to trust—and all of the sudden—while everything else goes on, *it* is not there any more . . .".

Nora cries, deeply and silently.

The question in an illusion is about finding and maintaining significant meanings; even when the illusion is in conflict with reality or downright delusional, it amounts to preserving and protecting of an important self-image, and may therefore be exceedingly difficult to give up.

In the area of developmental illusion its illusory aspects will normally be withdrawn from the developmental interaction as such, and become internalized as aspects of the subject's personal reality. However, even there the illusions continue to remain in use to varying degree. It can be asked for good reasons whether illusions are needed by a human being throughout life. Loewald (1975) speaks of disillusioned adults who have lost contact between the dreams of their youth and the routine everyday life of today. Loewald thinks that reality testing is much more than a merely intellectual and cognitive function.

> It may be understood more comprehensively as the experiential testing of fantasy—its potential and suitability for actualization—and the testing of actuality—its potential for encompassing it in, and penetrating it with one's fantasy life. [Loewald, 1975, p. 296]

Such sayings of the patient as "you don't really love", or "I don't really mean anything to you", have to be encountered and worked through repeatedly during the analytic process. It amounts to the analysand's gradual accepting that past realities cannot be relived, whereas the meaningfully existing levels of reality are included in the analytic interaction aiming at finding the reality and genuineness of the analysand's inner world. As was seen in Nora's case, meaningful reality of the analytic relationship will, as a rule, clear up towards the end of a successful analysis. In Nora's mind there were no longer doubts about the reciprocal meaningfulness of the relationship for its both parties.

The need for a shared experience, held up by the illusion, will be present throughout life as a striving for discovery and maintenance of meaningfulness and authenticity of self-experience. In different phases of life this meaningfulness has repeatedly to be found and defined anew (cf. Erikson, 1950).

Without the activation of developmental illusions the analyst cannot secure the position of a new developmental object in the analysand's mind. This new relationship will emerge and develop further only as the result of meaningfully shared emotional experiences in the analytic interaction. In the area of developmental illusion there will emerge a proceeding common story of the interrupted and, therefore, essentially unrepresented developmental needs and wishes of the analysand. The story is created together by the activated developing child in the analysand and the analyst as his new developmental object. It is not reconstructing a story of the analysand's past history, as is the case in working through the analysand's transference illusions, but a living interaction that creates a new and so far unwritten story about the unused and neglected potentials of the patient's inner world. Its nature is deeply personal and idiosyncratic and may therefore appear incomprehensible to anyone else but the analyst participating in the illusion. From the analyst, this requires that he dares, and is able, to use the totality of his responsiveness in a creative and continuously renewable way, while at the same time firmly observing analytic abstinence as the necessary frame for developmental illusions.

The usual everyday reality provides the basis for the analytic interaction. Transference illusions represent a world that is repetitive, closed, and unchanging. Although the transference illusion does not originate in the present day, its mere confrontation with the reality of today does not lead to self-understanding and new integration. This will be possible only when a living connection and interpretative understanding has been established in the analytic relationship with the wish inherent in the transference illusion. In a developmental illusion, the question is about unfulfilled wishes and dreams, which may be consciously and intellectually represented but lack such fantasy contents of self and object that can be discovered and internalized to a meaningful inner reality only in emotionally meaningful new interactions.

The developmental illusion represents a gateway from the repetition compulsion by opening up possibilities to a new kind of experiencing. Sheltered by the analytic setting and by the limitations set by the analytic abstinence, the developmental illusion can be experienced truly enough to allow symbolic actualization of even the most primitive layers of the mind. Analysands suffering from very early and severe problems often strive to protect those features of the analytic situation that support this other level of reality, even when they are still structurally unable to develop a therapeutic alliance proper with their analyst.

The analysand's change in the analysis does not take place in the present reality, nor in her fantasy. It takes place in the context of the analytic relationship, where its core is *understanding*; the striving of both parties towards understanding experienced as shared and real, the giving and receiving of understanding in a way that motivates and prompts a resumed growth in the analysand's way of experiencing himself and the object world. If understanding ceases, so does the analytic process.

Note

1. This paper appeared in *The Scandinavian Psychoanalytic Review* (2000), 23: 25–88. Reprinted by permission. Copyright (c) Munksgaard International Publishers. Copenhagen.

References

English, H. B., & English, A. C. (1958). *A Comprehensive Dictionary of Psychological and Psychoanalytical Terms*. New York: Longmans, Green.

Erikson, E. H. (1950). *Childhood and Society*. New York: W. W. Norton.

Freud, S. (1907a). Delusions and dreams in Jensen's *Gradiva*. *S. E., 9*: 7–93. London: Hogarth.

Freud, S. (1912b). The dynamics of transference. *S.E., 12*: 99–108. London: Hogarth.

Freud, S. (1914g). Remembering, repeating and working through. *S.E.*, 12: 147–156. London: Hogarth.

Freud, S. (1915a). Observations on transference-love. *S.E., 12I*: 159–171. London: Hogarth.

Ikonen, P., & Rechard, E. (1993). The origin of shame and of its vicissitudes. *Scandinavian Psychoanalytic Review, 16*: 100–124.

Klauber, J. (1987). The role of illusion in the psychoanalytic cure. In: John Klauber and others, *Illusion and Spontaneity in Psychoanalysis*. London: Free Association Books.

Loewald, H. W. (1960). On the therapeutic action of psychoanalysis. *International Journal of Psycho-Analysis, 41*: 16–33.

Loewald, H. W. (1975). Psychoanalysis as an art and the fantasy character of the psychoanalytic situation. *Journal of the American Psychoanalytical Association, 23*: 277–299.

Modell, A. H. (1984). *Psychoanalysis in a New Context*. New York: International Universities Press.

Modell, A. H. (1990). *Other Times, Other Realities. Toward a Theory of Psychoanalytic Treatment*. Cambridge, MA: Harvard University Press.

Symington, N. (1987). John Klauber—independent clinician. In: John Klauber and others, *Illusion and Spontaneity in Psychoanalysis*. London: Free Association Books.

Tähkä, V. (1993). *Mind and its Treatment. A Psychoanalytic Approach*. Madison, CT: International Universities Press, Inc.

Winnicott, D. W. (1965). *The Maturational Processes and the Facilitating Environment*. London: The Hogarth Press and the Institute of Psychoanalysis.

Winnicott, D. W. (1971). *Playing and Reality*. London: Tavistock Publications.

CHAPTER FIVE

Transference: an historical and present-day perspective[1]

Eero Rechardt

The birth of psychoanalysis

I t is little known that Freud's thinking was not far away from the scientific thinking of his day and was close to Helmholtz's conception of perceptual psychology (Makari, 1994; Rechardt, 2000).

Freud belonged to a scientific tradition started by Immanuel Kant, with the great German physiologist Helmholtz being one of the most famous representatives. Freud admired Helmholtz, and apparently considered him his scientific ideal. Helmholtz had a magnificent scientific career, and can be considered the "super scientist" of his era. His many scientific achievements include the founding of perceptual psychology and, in physics, the law of the conservation of energy. Freud's students did not see the connection between Freud and Helmholtz, as they were chiefly interested in the clinical applications of psychoanalysis. Only a few of them had the inclination to follow Freud's thinking as he was laying the foundation for psychoanalysis, a foundation which is very close to Helmholtz's ideas on perceptual psychology. These parallels, which were overlooked at the time, have been revealed only by much later research on the history of psychoanalytic thought (Makari, 1994).

The origins of psychology, or scientific research into the events and functioning of the human mind, are strongly tied to perceptual psychology and sensory physiology. The traditional view of the functioning of the human mind was the idea originating with Aristotle that an observation was an exact representation of reality. Tentative attempts to question this theory of "immaculate perception" (Makari, 1994) had been made before by Kant (1724–1804), but his chief work *The Critique of Pure Reason* (1781), caused a final, permanent Copernican shift, i.e., a revolution in our world view, in our ideas about the human mind and the nature of our sense perceptions. The concept of "active observer" who creates for him the contents of what he observes now permanently entered the epistemology of European philosophy. Kant's intention was not to subjectify reality, but rather to illustrate that we cannot make observations about reality, "the thing itself" (*Das Ding an Sich*), but only about reflections of reality. These reflections are born from universal *a priori* ways of seeing the world.

Even more significant than the thoughts of the philosophers was a new area of research called perceptual psychology, which was built on the foundation of Kant's thought. Posterity has erroneously viewed Helmholtz (1821–1894) as a representative of biological research—antagonistic to philosophy, hostile to psychology, mechanistic in his views, and purely physiological in his orientation. People have forgotten that Kant's philosophy is a basis for Helmholtz's thought.

Another widespread misunderstanding concerns Freud's place in the scientific field of his day. He has been depicted as a controversial, solitary genius, detached from contemporary scientific thought. In fact, Freud admired Helmholtz, and in his own psychology he expanded Helmholtz's perceptual psychology in the direction of *inner perceptions* in a very original way (Makari, 1994). Helmholtz's famous model about psychological illusions, or hallucinations, was based on a staggeringly simply observation. If we press hard on our right eyeball, we see a light phenomenon with the left eye. The optical nerves crossing on their way to the brain cause the switching of sides. Helmholtz explained the light phenomenon as a memory of previous intense light stimuli, and he called this illusion, i.e. hallucination, an "unconscious inference" where the familiar past mingles with the unfamiliar present (Helmholtz, 1868, quoted in Makari, 1994). The memory of the light phenomenon is familiar from the past; the unfamiliar present is the eye being pressed instead of receiving a light stimulus. The experience of a sense perception thus does not provide one with knowledge of the nature of the stimulus, but only of its existence. Helmholtz considered himself a disciple of Kant, and thought he had elaborated on Kant's view of *a priori*, which was now replaced by a memory.

Thinking of that time could be called dual-aspect monism. It included the principle already laid out by Kant that scientific knowledge concerning reality is quantitative, but also believed that psychological, meaning-related knowledge about experiences is qualitative. Neither quantitative nor qualitative knowledge was given precedence, but together they allowed scientists to be both biological materialists and psychological idealists without contradiction (Makari, 1994). Helmholtz and his disciples, however, did deride the romantic post-Kantian philosophy, which considered experience merely to be dream-like, but did not underestimate the crucial importance of personal meanings in the formation of sensory experiences. However, qualitative differences were not universal transcendental categories but experience-based memories. Perceptual psychology, the new area of research opened up by Helmholtz, and the rest of his scientific endeavours were much more significant to the scientific world of their time than was the tinkering of the philosophers, which did not interest Freud much. It is possible that Freud's belittling attitude towards philosophy was based on the fact that he considered Helmholtz's research as his ideal.

The psychology of misunderstanding

According to Helmholtz, a sense perception does not provide us with a reliable account of the external world. He presented the idea that characteristics we associate with an object are not characteristics of the object itself, but represent the effects that the object has on our sense organs. A perception is not immediate knowledge about the object, but rather a psychological process where the object is clad in inner meanings, i.e. the qualities of observer.

During the first stage of his psychoanalytic research, Freud attempted to create a common model for psychology (Freud, 1895), which he called "Project", or "Psychology for neurologists". The French psychological philosopher Hippolyte Taine (1828–1893) and the German psychologist Theodore Lipps (1851–1914) were both trying to build a model for the psychology of normal humans following Helmholtz's dual-aspect monism, which considers qualifiable subjective perception and quantifiable material truth as parallel to one another. They took Holmholz's illusion model as the starting point. According to them, perceptions are at first illusions largely formed as a result of flawed unconscious reasoning, with experience gradually forcing the person to correct them.

The influence of Kant, Miller, Schopenhauer, and Helmholtz has led to the emergence of the tradition of critical psychology in Europe, the starting point of which has been to question the idea of immaculate perception and to focus on how our picture of the world is formed through illusion or misunderstanding. Understanding is born out of misunderstanding.

In his own individual way, Sigmund Freud also belonged to this tradition, his interest being focused primarily on psychopathology. According to Kant, the "actual reality", the external world, the *Das Ding an Sich*, is unknown. Freud expanded this view to apply also to the perception of the internal world. The inner world is likewise unknown at first, but through trial and error, guided by our failures, we gradually find functional meanings that are based on memories. The development of a human being is a process of slowly expanding one's worldview towards an awareness of one's own limits. It is a development that is constantly at risk of stalling at apparent truths.

Wishes and inner perceptions

In his "The interpretation of dreams" (1900a), Freud discussed the theory of dreams from the viewpoint of Helmholtz's illusory perception. Helmholtz's research assistant, Wilhelm Wundt (1832–1920), claimed that dreams interpret external stimuli just as when we are awake we experience visual illusions. Freud summarizes Wundt's thoughts as follows:

> The mind receives stimuli that reach it during sleep. . . . A sense-impression is recognized by us and correctly interpreted—that is, it is placed in the group of memories to which, in accordance with all our previous experiences, it belongs. . . . If these conditions are not fulfilled, we mistake the object, which is the source of the impression: we form an illusion about it. [Freud, 1900a, p. 29]

Freud accepted Wundt's Helmholtzian theory, which stated that "dreams interpret objective sensory stimuli just as illusions do", but he adds that "we have found a motive which provides the reason for that interpretation, a reason which has been left unspecified by other writers".

What Freud means is that the motivating force in his model of illusions and dreams is an inner cause, a *wish*. In "The interpretation of dreams", Freud added a new essential dimension to the post-Kantian model of perception. Not only was the "actual" reality of exogenous stimuli unknowable, as Kant had shown, but so too were endogenous unconscious stimuli. As Freud notes:

> In its innermost nature it [the unconscious] is as much unknown to us as the reality of the external world, and it is as incompletely presented by the data of consciousness as is the external world by the communications of our sense organs. [Freud, 1900a, p. 613]

Helmholtz and his successors used Kantian ideas in order to understand our perception of the external world. Freud turned this inward to encompass the perception of our inner world and attempted to conceptualize through analogies how unconscious inner events became conscious.

According to Freud, awareness of the unconscious was "subjectively distorted in the same manner that sensory perception of the external world was flawed," as Makari (1994, p. 568) explains. Makari adds that Freud thought that "unconscious quantities . . . were only allowed into consciousness and perceived as qualities of pleasure or unpleasure" (Makari, 1994, p. 570).

Freud drew a parallel between the perceptual system and consciousness. According to Freud, consciousness is a part of the perceptual system; it is the sense organ for psychological qualities. As Makari explains, Freud relied on dual-aspect monism,

> declaring that the unconscious presented its unknowable quantities to consciousness which was [in Freud's words] a "sense organ for the perception of Psychical qualities" [Makari, 1994, p. 569]

By drawing parallels between consciousness and a sense organ Freud utilized an existing model made familiar by Helmholtz's theory of perception. This helped him to describe unconscious events in a language which was understandable to his colleagues.

Transference

When discussing the manifestation of a wish, Freud also assumed the existence of another form through which unconscious quantities can be in contact with the conscious. The same underlying principle of Helmholtz's theory of perception helped Freud to articulate and explain a phenomenon he called transference. In Helmholtz's model, the experience of an illusion emerged when an unusual and unidentified stimulus was incorrectly identified as some familiar memory. Freud emphasized that his model differed from Helmholtz's in that it expressed the motive behind an illusion. An unconscious memory does not randomly and "accidentally" attach itself to the wrong stimulus: the false identification is motivated. *The motivating force is an unconscious wish looking for an opportunity to become fulfilled.* An unconscious quantity finds a conscious form and an indirect expression by emptying itself into a preconscious mental content.

In "The interpretation of dreams" Freud called this phenomenon transference. Freud explained that

> ... an unconscious idea is as such quite incapable of entering the preconscious and it can only exercise any effect there by establishing a connection with an idea which already belongs to the preconscious, by transferring its intensity on to and by getting itself "covered" by it. Here we have the fact of "transference", which provides an explanation of so many striking phenomena in the mental life of neurotics [Freud, 1900a, pp. 562–563]

By cloaking itself in already existing psychic contents, transference does not penetrate into the conscious like an hallucination, but rather distorts previously formed observations and presents impressions and thoughts which, as such, are neutral and indifferent, thus lending them its own intensity and content.

Transference had an important place in Freud's model of the mind, as, in Makari's words "it was a metapsychologic concept that formalized the way unconscious processes invaded and distorted preconscious psychic contents and hence both consciousness and perception" (Makari, 1994, p. 573). For Freud, transference was as central a concept as illusion was to Helmholtz. It was one of those unusual phenomena that enabled identifying unconscious phenomena in awake and non-psychotic people.

The concept of transference is important to the formation of our entire view of the human being. It describes how unconscious mental processes distort and subjectify awake experiences, impressions, and thoughts. It shows not only that people misinterpret and misunderstand external objects, but also the limitations of their ability to observe and to know. The unknowable repressed inner expresses itself only by its ability to distort the preconscious. It penetrates thought and the perception of the external world, and fills them with pleasant and unpleasant emotions that have originated in other contexts and other interrelationships (Makari, 1994; Rechardt, 1998).

The clinical aim of psychoanalysis

Psychoanalysis started from clinical need, the attempt of Breuer and Freud (1895d) to find a treatment method for hysterical symptoms. It was about the flesh and blood of acute reality. The primary target of the psychoanalytical method is the suffering of the self, helplessness, disturbances of bodily existence, the feeling of being threatened, and lack of control of life. In this situation the study of unconscious meanings finds a concrete target. The focus of study was shifted from the mind in general to its disturbances. The task of psychoanalysis is to detect the existence of isolated parts of the mind, and to help in integrating them with ego in the expectation that the ego strengthens and is able to exist in a less threatened state. This resulted in research, characteristic of psychoanalysis, which has self-understanding as its goal and seeks contact with those experiences that have shaped the meanings of perceptions of self and the outside world, and the origins of which are not in the region of conscious self-understanding. Thus, the aim is to find connections to personal, perhaps quite early, experiences, and memories of them. During individual development, those memories have gone through many phases and have generated many derivatives, which Freud calls "subsequent". The German expression used by Freud is *Nachträglich*. French psychoanalysis uses the term *aprés coup*, which has a distinctive role in the theory of French psychoanalysis. "Each word that we use includes its earlier meanings. The task of a psychoanalyst is to find out about these meanings." (Green, 1998). Strachey's English translation "deferred action" is different in the respect that it implies action despite the fact that the issue is about meaning, which emerges later and after some delay.

Interpretation of transference

The concept "transference" was a part of the theory of dreams. According to this concept all our perceptions, whether concerning the outside world or originating from inner perception, are memories. They are originally unknown, i.e., unconscious, as Helmholtz (1868) put it. To Helmholtz's perceptions of the outside world, Freud added inner perceptions, *wishes*. The term *wish* comprises yearnings for pleasure, satisfaction, and relief. In their archaic form they seek fulfilment without regard to the consequences and at any cost. Expressed in the more familiar clinical words, wishes can be destructive, libido-oriented, or a mixture of both.

In order to discover transference it is not enough to be conscious of the possibility of its existence. Although Freud had already written about transference and explained the theory of it, he had later to acknowledge, in the case of Dora, that he had not discovered her transference in relation to him, her analyst (Freud, 1905e). Freud states often that discovering and processing transference is crucial as far as the results of the analysis are concerned. This is a problem that each analyst continually has to face.

Memory and transference

Helmholtz reached the conclusion, essential to perceptual psychology, that the meanings our minds give to our perceptions are the results of *memories* of our experiences. Freud added inner perceptions to Helmholtz's outside world perceptions. All our perceptions are originally unknown, i.e. unconscious, as Helmholtz expressed it. They get their meaning, emotional content, verbal expression, and their name through memories of experiences, in the context of which they have entered our mind. Perhaps the forgotten bond between Freud and Helmholtz is the reason why the role of memory in the formation of transference was disregarded for so long. If we begin our reflections with the process of remembering, we have to change our traditional ideas about transference.

During recent years, psychoanalysis has adopted from cognitive psychology a theory that there are two kinds of remembering: procedural memory, i.e., programmed memory, and personal, i.e., situational memory. These varieties of memory are stored differently, although a slow conversion from one type to the other is possible. Procedural memory cannot be expressed verbally, and instead it manifests in action. It is stored separate from personal situational memory, which is expressed verbally and is more easily reached by psychoanalytical work. The actual act of remembering involves parts from both, such as programmed motor memories with fixed motor content and situation-bound, specifiable, analysable, and verbally expressed memories. Therefore, the act of remembering is usually more or less unreliable. It involves components that are felt to have an indisputable verity, however delusional this belief may be. Personal situational memory may lack components because, although perceptions and experiences of them must exist, the mind is unable to retrieve them. Paradoxically, amnesia, too, is a form of remembering. It may be that experiences that have not been recorded in situational memory, but are stored instead in procedural memory, surge to the mind as delusional experiences. I am inclined to think that traumatic experiences especially predispose the procedural memory to become unreasonably dominant. Then action displaces thinking and imagining abilities, so that images requiring action disturb our interrelations, or memories of positive experiences are consigned to the background of our experienced world. Procedural memory should not, however, be labelled simply as "bad memory". A satisfactory, sufficiently protective caring experienced by a small child forms a good basis in our procedural memory for later life. It may be that those persons whom we now call "narcissistically damaged" may, in future, be described as persons dominated by traumatized procedural memory.

Experiencing self

According to traditional psychoanalytical ideas, experiencing the self as separate from objects is possible only after the border between the other and separateness from the other has been formed. Lacan argues that the child finds his or her ego in the mirror. From that point on, self is also the other, in an internal relationship with it. Kohut thinks differently: the first mirror of a child is the mother's approving look (Kohut, 1971). This starting point is emphasized in Stern's work *The Interpersonal World of the Infant* (1985), in which the author features contemporary studies on development in early childhood. He has an interesting point of view on the development of the experiencing self. He assumes that a baby's self originates from reciprocity with its environment, and that from the beginning of life experiencing self is a central organizing principle in the development of a child. A particularly interesting feature of this book is that Stern has introduced a new psychoanalytical paradigm: the central meaning of *reciprocal communication*.

Stern has tried to understand the world of an infant from the first moments of existence. A new-born may react to the external world by sucking, turning his head, or looking. By monitoring the sucking movements it has been found that a baby becomes more excited by the sound of a human voice than by other, similar sounds. By recording the turns of babies' heads, it has been discovered that an infant recognizes the smell of his own mother's milk, differentiating between it and the milk of other mothers. Observing where a baby looks has revealed that he is more interested in pictures of faces than in other pictures. All these things reflect the abilities of a baby to form early object relations. Many other research results have proved that the ability to seek for a contact is

fully operable in a baby right from birth. Importantly, these perceptions have changed ideas about the early developmental stage of
autism. Stern claims that the effort to find reciprocity and the ongoing expanding experience of the self are present in a baby's life
from the very beginning. Earlier, it was thought impossible to have
experience of the self in this phase, because the differentiated self,
a unit that is independent of its environment, does not exist at this
stage. Stern argues that self is experiences of cohesive and differen-
tiative psychic functions. The capabilities that a baby demonstrates
in the securing presence of its mother (such as the ability to form
perceptions or to understand their inner relations) are, in fact, the
same as experiencing the birth of the self. A well-cared-for baby
may also be in a state of peaceful, passive activity that recurs regularly. At these times the baby observes its environment by looking,
and seeks new things. The baby processes his perceptions through
inborn inclinations. The self includes both the forming and perma-
nence of the new organization. It is, first and foremost, an experience of achievement and functioning, an experience of being alive
(Rechardt, 1988).

The new dimension of psychoanalysis

The idea of the role of transference is common to different psychoanalytical schools. However, different schools view transference
differently: some emphasize its—often difficult—verbalized
features linked to procedural memory, others focus on personal
situational memory reflected by transference. From the point of
view of reciprocity, transference reflects whatever forms of
reciprocity early wishes, needs, and desires have confronted, and
what kind of reciprocity has been missing. The idea of an ever-
present need for reciprocity existing since earliest childhood has
given a new dimension to psychoanalytical knowledge. This
resulted in a turning point, signs of which have been present
in many directions during recent years. The importance of being
understood, and experiences in reciprocal understanding, are
gaining new significance. Stern, with his colleagues (Stern *et al.*,
1998), has talked about "moments of meeting" between the
psychotherapist and the person receiving therapy, an event that is

characterized by a moment of mutual understanding. This moment expands the consciousness of the person receiving psychotherapy and forms new angles for understanding. Stern aims to locate in his clients such regions of the mind in which verbally transferable understanding can be found. Fonagy (1999a) crystallized his thoughts on the subject in an editorial article, saying that we ought to forget the archaeological metaphor and that understanding of the past does not necessarily guarantee achieving results in the treatment. Goldberg replied by suggesting that Fonagy's article was unworthy of publication, arguing that reconstruction of the past remains as one of the cornerstones of psychoanalytical work (Goldberg, 1999). Fonagy then responded (1999b), underlining that an understanding of the mind's present state comes first, and this is why it is necessary to process that part of the transference that is connected with the non-verbal process memory. Tähkä's (1993) approach is simpler, and closer to practice. He emphasizes that a borderline patient does not benefit from having the transference pointed out, but from the analyst's ability to express the patient's moods and feelings, something the patient himself is incapable of doing. He calls it *emphatic description* (*ibid.*, pp. 349–360).

The differences between the theory and the practice of psychoanalysis, described above, become so tense because they do not—except for Tähkä's thoughts—fully take into account what kind of disturbance it is that is being treated. Böhm (1999) has said that an experienced analyst will find the problematic areas of the analysand best by just listening to the uncontrolled thoughts that the patient's speech evokes in him. In Böhm's opinion, different types of programme—for example, those offered by the Kleinian tradition—merely serve to distract this process. He emphasizes that even the transference should not be made the key to the solution. The analyst should listen without preconceptions to whatever comes into his mind as the patient speaks. The method Böhm has described probably suits best those patients whose transference is mainly located in the area of the personal situational memory. In order to reach a mutual understanding, even for just a moment, the analyst needs, as Tähkä wrote, to recognize and name the moods and feelings the patient (who is narrowed down by the non-verbal motor process memory) is going through.

The analyst as a new object

The aim of discovering transference is, thus, to find connections to personal, perhaps quite early, memories and their derivatives. Often it is a time-consuming process that demands much working through and reprocessing of memories again and again in different contexts. However, experience has shown that even dealing painstakingly with transference does not always bring results. Recent views on remembering make this understandable. It has been found essential to seek new viewpoints in order to reach ever more disturbed analysands. It has become common to say that an analysand needs a new object in the analyst. It means that the person receiving analysis gains an experience of communicating with someone who can understand him or her in another way than have important people in his or her past (Fonagy, 1999; Loewald, 1960; Tähkä, 1993). The focus shifts from the past and history into the present, to the fact that the analyst finds verbal expressions for the moods and states of mind of the analysand, which he or she has not previously possessed, but which are acceptable for him or her. It expands the analysand's ability to achieve self-understanding.

The stupor of shame as a disturbance of the process memory

The research on early development is crucial to the psychoanalysis of today. In terms of biology, also, it has proved how important it is to find accepting reciprocity in human relationships and how difficult and lasting may be the effects of the lack of it on a child. An extreme example of this importance is a child who has been raised by monkeys, and who will never develop human ways of thinking and social skills. From early infancy onwards, reactions to babies' mutuality needs affect their relations with other people in ways that influence their whole life. The reactions we get to our search for reciprocal interaction form our social language. It is possible—although difficult—to learn a new language later. Good enough mutuality in relationships forms the basis of a baby's feelings of security, self-experience, self-esteem, and ability to cooperate.

Experimental research has been done on the reactions of a baby to his mother's lack of mutuality. Mothers were instructed to stay expressionless and not to look or smile back at the babies looking for their mother's gaze. The babies were confused for a while, but pulled themselves together quickly and were ready to try again to reach for mother's gaze. If the mother's reply was still flat, almost all the babies reacted the same way: their self broke down, their motor activity became uncontrollable, and they regressed to painful crying. We can guess that if this happens often a baby would soon learn not to look for contact and not to expect anyone to understand him when his self has broken down in pieces. In this state "you are avoided like someone with the plague and you have to avoid others as well", as the Swedish psychoanalyst Kjellqvist (1993) says in her book on shame. The language of shame is our natural-born language of morality, something that has begun to be understood better in recent years. Earlier, shame was regarded as typical phenomena of the personal situational memory, a passing, uncomfortable feeling. However, an accentuated tendency to feel shame is an important disturbance in the process memory. It leads to both a higher risk of becoming paralysed by shame and many forms of anti-sociality in order to protect oneself from the stupor. What has been missed is the archaic nature of shame, which makes us believe that every effort of mutuality is unreasonable and leads to complete inner stupor and fading of the lust for life.

Summary

The intention of this paper has been to emphasize that transference is remembering past experiences, albeit this remembering has many features that do not fit into our everyday thinking. As Freud assumed in accordance with Helmholtz, our perceptions—even those about our inner world—do not have a "typical" meaning. We interpret our perceptions based on our memories. Our memories programme the meanings for our perceptions, but this process is very much an unconscious one. Also, memories change as time goes by. It may well be that how, in an early stage of life, a perception was formed, or how traumatic it was, affects how well it is processed. Freud investigated the remembering event from the point of view of making it more conscious and less dissociative. One of the present theories is that there is no single "memory", but different forms of memory that are saved in different ways. The first of these is non-verbal and action related, and another is situational memory, which can be put into words and processed psychologically. This form of remembering also demands contact with the unconscious, but it is easier to access in psychoanalytical work. Those patients who are difficult to treat (borderline, narcissistically traumatized, and psychotic persons) are controlled by the former, and they need their own strategy to experience mutuality. This has been written about by Fonagy, Loewald, Tähkä, and Stern's group.

The additions that have been made to the psychoanalytical theory and practice during the last one or two decades represent a step forward and an increased integration of psychoanalysis. According to Pine (1998) psychoanalytical knowledge develops by growing, not by shutting out. In our everyday work we do not "get by" with just one god, as Fonagy has said; we need many gods whom we will use when we need them and be unfaithful to them according to present need, situation, and client. It is necessary to do as Böhm recommended (and what Freud knew as well) to listen to the patient through the analyst's own impressions, and to generalize this also to the area of knowledge. Theoretical knowledge should always be, in practice, something that one can move around freely, although it is impossible to avoid the fact that some of the hypotheses may steal all our interests and narrow our horizons.

Note

1. Published by permission. The first version was published in Finnish in E. Roos, V. Manninen & J. Välimäki (Eds.), 2001, *Rakkaus, Toive, Todellisuus* (*Love, Wish, Reality*). Helsinki: Yliopistopaino.

References

Böhm, T. (1999). The difficult freedom from a plan. *International Journal of Psycho-Analysis, 80*: 493–506.

Fonagy, P. (1999a) Memory and therapeutic action. *International Journal of Psycho-Analysis, 80*: 215–224.

Fonagy, P. (1999b). Response. *International Journal of Psycho-Analysis, 80*: 1011–1012.

Freud, S. (1895) Project for a scientific psychology. *S.E.*, *1*: 281–392. London: Hogarth.

Freud, S. (1895d) Studies on hysteria. *S.E.*, *2*: 3–305. London: Hogarth.

Freud, S. (1900a). The interpretation of dreams. *S.E.*, *5*: 509–627. London: Hogarth.

Freud, S. (1905e) Fragment of an analysis of a case of hysteria. *S.E.*, *7*: 3–122. London: Hogarth.

Green, A. (1998). Personal comment. IPA Symposium, Paris.

Helmholtz, H. von (1971) [1868]. Recent progress in the theory of vision. In: R. Kahl (Ed.), *Selected Writings of Hermann von Helmholtz* (pp. 144–222). Middletown, CT: Wesleyan University Press.

Kant, I. (1965) [1781]. *The Critique of Pure Reason*. New York: St Martin's Press.

Kohut, H. (1971). *The Analysis of the Self*. New York: International Universities Press.

Lacan, J. (1988).*The Seminars of Jacques Lacan. Books I and II*. J.-A. Miller (Ed.). Cambridge: Cambridge University Press.

Lipps, T. (1905) [1926]. *Psychological Studies*. Baltimore: Williams and Wilkins.

Loewald, H. (1960). On the therapeutic action of psychoanalysis. *International Journal of Psycho-Analysis*, *41*: 16–33.

Makari, G. J. (1994). In the eye of the beholder: Helmholtzian perception and the origin of Freud's 1900 theory of transference. *Journal of the American Psychoanalytical Association*, *42*: 549–580.

Pine, F. (1998). *Diversity and Direction in Psychoanalytic Technique*. New Haven: Yale University Press.

Rechardt, E. (2000). Transferensseista (On transferences). Paper read at the symposium of the Finnish Psychoanalytical Society, January 2000.

Schwaber, E. (1998). Travelling affectively alone. *Journal of the American Psychoanalytic Association*, *46*: 1044–1065.

Stern, D. (1985) *The Interpersonal World of the Infant*. New York: Basic Books.

Stern, D., Sander, L., Nahum, J., Harrison, A., Lyons-Ruth, K., Morgan, A., Bruschweiter-Stern, N., & Tonick, E. (1998). Non-interpretive mechanisms in psychoanalytic therapy. *International Journal of Psycho-Analysis*, *79*: 741–756.

Taine, H. (1872). *On Intelligence*. New York: Holt and Williams.

Tähkä, V. (1993). *Mind and Its Treatment. A Psychoanalytic Approach*. Madison, CT: International Universities Press.

Wundt, W. (1900) Grundzilge der physiologischen psychologies Leipzig 1874. Ref: Freud, S., "The interpretation of dreams" (1900a). *S.E.*, 5. London: Hogarth.

CHAPTER SIX

Actualized unconscious fantasies and "therapeutic play" in adults' analyses: further study of these concepts

Vamik D. Volkan

One of the major contributions of Veikko Tähkä to psycho-analysis is his illustration of how some hallmarks of psychoanalytic technique, canonized by Freud's classical papers, have become blurred and require re-examination (1984, 1993). For example, he reexamined the concept of "interpretation", defined as bringing to the patient's awareness mental conflicts and their contents that were previously unconscious. Tähkä states that the classical definition of interpretation links it with the phenomena of repression and dynamic unconscious. Therefore, interpretation as a therapeutic tool can be utilized only for those patients with neurotic pathology whose main defence mechanism is repression. Since we as psychoanalysts have extended our practice to include patients who are more severely disturbed than neurotic patients, we need to seek new technical concepts. For example, interpretation in the classical sense cannot correspond to a borderline patient's subjective experience; even a borderline may grasp an interpreta-tion intellectually. Therefore, Tähkä tells us, a borderline patient will not respond to interpretation. However, the borderline patient will respond to the analyst's catching and describing the patient's way of experiencing in a method that is analogous to a primary developmental object's (i.e., mother's) understanding of her offspring and conveying that understanding to the patient, who then can identify with the analyst's description as a step towards further internal structuralization. For example, when an analyst understands how a borderline patient felt during a weekend break, the analyst

> should simply try to describe it to the patient as fully as possible. It is not sufficient that he tells the patient that he understands how the patient must have felt, but rather he should try to convey that understanding in detail, to do it with respect and empathy. [Tähkä, 1993, pp. 355–356]

Tähkä calls his technique "empathic description" (*ibid.*, p. 349). When it is repeated often enough—let us say in relation to a patient's many weekend breaks—it becomes the patient's own attitude towards him or herself during any breaks in treatment in the future and leads to selective identification with the analyst. Thus, empathic description essentially addresses a primary lack of structure, while interpretation deals with a secondary loss of available structure.

It is beyond the scope of this chapter to give further details of Tähkä's differentiation between interpretation and empathic description. His point is well taken and can be summarized with a simple statement: interpretation, in the classic sense, is not an appropriate tool in the treatment of patients who are functioning at borderline or psychotic levels because they do not possess a cohesive sense of self and cannot fully utilize repression as their central defence mechanism.

The focus of this chapter parallels Tähkä's ideas about patients for whom the analyst's essential therapeutic consideration should not be—or at least should go beyond—interpretation in the classic sense. The patients I will refer to in this chapter need empathic descriptions *as well as* involvement in certain actions that Ast and I called "therapeutic play" (Volkan & Ast, 2001). As the patient carries out these actions, he or she develops certain nurturing, repairing, and integrating transference images of the analyst and eventually identifies with such images.

Once more, we need to re-examine some hallmarks of psychoanalysis and, like Tähkä, without removing ourselves from the mainstream of psychoanalytic practice, consider new tools for psychoanalytic technique that are designed for the specific psychological conditions of some of our patients: in this case, the conditions are related to the patients' early severe actual trauma or substantial accumulation of trauma. Interpretations, not actions, were considered to be the main therapeutic tool of psychoanalysis. Otto Fenichel (1945) summarizes the classical view of action as something that "impede(s) the ego from being confronted with unconscious material" (p. 570). He argues that action "relates to the present and does not make the patient conscious of being dominated by his past to be effective in the present" (p. 571). Fenichel is referring to "acting out" of neurotic conflict. Since "acting out" was considered an undesirable concept (Freud, 1914g)—and in its classical sense, this is still true—it was not frequently mentioned or studied in the psychoanalytic literature. In recent decades, "action" or "re-enactment" has become popular in certain circles. A close look at writings about these terms suggests various conceptualizations; some can be thought of as belonging to mainstream psychoanalysis, and others cannot be considered truly psychoanalytic. I will not review such conceptualizations here. But it is imperative that I describe clearly what I mean by therapeutic play in order to avoid confusing it with these other conceptualizations.

Patients involved in therapeutic play in order to fully recover from their mental problems are those who experienced *actual* traumatic experiences in their developmental years. Furthermore, these patients may "encapsulate" (D. Rosenfeld, 1992; H. Rosenfeld, 1965; Volkan, 1976, 1995) their traumatized self-images with their corresponding object images and affects. Some unconscious fantasies that link the real trauma in the external world with its perceived and/or experienced mental representation become *actualized*, as I will soon illustrate. Actualized unconscious fantasies do not respond to interpretation in the classical sense; they do not initiate new internal structuralization, even when the patient can understand intellectually the interpretations of the content of such fantasies. The patient needs to be involved in an action, a therapeutic play, in order to tame, modify, and master the influence of his or her concretized beliefs, even when they are no longer unconscious due to therapeutic work. The personality organizations of patients with actualized unconscious fantasies may be on psychotic,

borderline, narcissistic, or even neurotic levels. Even if these individuals are on a neurotic level, because of the encapsulation of their
traumatized self-images with their associated object images and
affects, we should consider such individuals as not having fully
cohesive selves. Before giving clinical examples, I will examine the
two principal concepts I already mentioned: actualized unconscious fantasies and therapeutic play.

Actualized unconscious fantasies

In 1908, Freud described two types of unconscious fantasies:

> Unconscious phantasies have been unconscious all along and have
> been formed in the unconscious; or—as is more often the case—
> they were once conscious phantasies, day-dreams, and have been
> purposely forgotten and have become unconscious through
> "repression". [Freud, 1908a, p. 161]

In this chapter, my focus is on the second type of unconscious
fantasy: a child making an "interpretation" of an event that tries to
satisfy both wishes and defences against those wishes according to
the phase-specific ego functions available to him or her and also
contaminating this "interpretation" with primary process thinking.
For example, a child who witnesses a primal scene may develop an
unconscious fantasy that, when naked and holding each other, a
man eats or chokes a woman. Obviously, unconscious fantasies do
not have a formed thought process, but they refer to a mental
content that is initiated by an external event; that is a collection of
the child's available cognition, affect, wish, defence; that is influenced by whichever psychological developmental tasks he or she is
dealing with at the time; and that is contaminated with primary
process thinking. In treatment, when the influence of this mental
content on the patient becomes observable, then the patient and the
analyst develop a "storyline", a content that transfers the unconscious fantasy into a formed thought process, however illogical it
sounds, due to its absorption of primary process thinking. Once the
storyline of an unconscious fantasy is found, the unconscious
fantasy then resembles an ordinary conscious fantasy or daydream.

Most unconscious fantasies concern themselves with body functions, birth, death, sex, aggression, early object relations, separation–individuation, oedipal issues, family romance, mother's pregnancy, father's penis, and siblings. Classical psychoanalysis states that the original mental content is repressed and, as a repressed "mental content", the unconscious fantasy exerts an interminable psychodynamic effect on subsequent perceptions, affects, behaviour, thinking, responses to reality, and adaptive or maladaptive compromise formations (see also: Arlow, 1969; Beres, 1962; Inderbitzin & Levy, 1990). Some unconscious fantasies are common: for example, Ast and I illustrated the commonality of various types of sibling-related womb fantasies (Volkan & Ast, 1977). A storyline of such a womb fantasy could be: "I want to be my mother's only child in her womb. I will enter there and kill my sibling, but my sibling in turn may kill me." An adult under the influence of such an unconscious fantasy, obviously without knowing why, will have anxiety about entering a cave that symbolically represents his or her mother's womb.

There are unconscious fantasies that are very specific and belong *only* to the individual who has it. This occurs especially if the initiation of the unconscious fantasy is due to a trauma specific to the child or a collection of specific traumas. For example, Ast and I described the case of Gitta, a woman who had gone through multiple surgeries and extended hospitalizations as a child (Volkan & Ast, 2001). Her unconscious fantasy was that she had a leaking body and that as long as her body leaked, she was alive. For example, as an adult, at times she "believed" that her menstrual flow was constant.

Actualization of an unconscious fantasy occurs when the actual trauma is severe or a series of actual traumas are accumulated, and when they interfere with "the usual restriction of fantasy only or mostly to the psychological realm" (Volkan & Ast, 2001, p. 569). A girl's unconscious oedipal fantasy, in a routine developmental process, remains in the psychological realm and it will psychologically influence the individual as an adult according to its *content* (which only becomes fully available during analytic work). If the influence of the girl's unconscious fantasy that is related to her wish to possess her father is very strong, she, as an adult, may have a tendency to marry an older man (a father figure). But as long as her unconscious fantasy stays within the psychological realm, as she grows up she may use her unconscious fantasy to satisfy her infantile sexual desires mentally, to enhance self-esteem, to create competitor-mother images, and so on. In routine development, she will be able to further repress and modify the unconscious fantasy. But if, while developing unconscious oedipal fantasies, the little girl is most severely traumatized, such as through being sexually assaulted by her father or a father substitute, such as an uncle, her unconscious oedipal fantasy becomes "actualized". Because there is a strong link between the unconscious fantasy and reality, the little girl's unconscious fantasy will exist in *both* the psychological and experiential realms. During her adult sexual relations, the actualized unconscious fantasy, as the heir of her severe traumatic childhood event, will be experienced as "real", or at least "partly real", and existing in the present time. For example, if a man makes sexual advances to her, at times she will experience this man as the original traumatizing and victimizing father or uncle, even though in reality the man's advances remain within socially acceptable patterns. The man is not someone behaving *like* the original assaulting person; in the patient's mind, he *is* the assaulting person.

Besides incest or repeated sexual stimulation by parents or siblings, severe bodily injuries, surgeries, near-death experiences, drastic object losses, and exposure to massive destruction like earthquakes or war during childhood make an individual prone to developing actualized unconscious fantasies. Actualized unconscious fantasies link real events that traumatize a child with their mental representations. They also link patients' developmental defects with their early object-relations conflicts. Early severe actual traumas or accumulation of such traumas may lead to developmental defects in mental structuring. Whenever there are defects, there are also object-relations conflicts. I do not separate such patients into those having only defects or only early object-relations conflicts. They have both: actualized unconscious fantasies deal with defects and early object-relations conflicts and link them.

If the individual encapsulates his or her childhood traumatized self with associated object images and affects, the actualized unconscious fantasy not only plays a role in recalling the original trauma and its mental representation, but also plays a role in safeguarding encapsulation. If encapsulation breaks down, the rest of the individual's self-system will be assaulted by the previously encap-sulated part and the individual will experience anxiety. Effective repression of unconscious fantasies (the mental content) will take place among neurotic patients, but for practical purposes, I believe that actualized unconscious fantasies are not fully repressed. Usually the individual is aware of a version of it, now more symbol-ized, distorted, and often disassociated from the individual's other mental phenomena. If a person with an actualized unconscious fantasy enters into psychoanalysis as an adult, through therapeutic work he or she may become further aware of the storyline of his or her unconscious fantasy that was previously repressed and/or disassociated. But when this person's actualized unconscious fantasy is reactivated either in his or her daily life or in the trans-ference relationship to the analyst, the individual will have diffi-culty differentiating where his or her (now conscious) fantasy ends and where reality begins. Such patients then experience symbols or objects of displacement representing various aspects of the actual-ized fantasies as "protosymbols" (Werner & Kaplan, 1963). That is to say, to the patient, they *are* what in actuality they *represent*. When the *content* of such fantasies is understood and interpreted by the analyst, this does not lead to therapeutic progress. To extend Tähkä's term, the analyst can make an "empathic description" of both the content and the *functions* of such fantasy. This may lead to progressive therapeutic movements, especially if there are oppor-tunities to repeat such emphatic description and if the patient iden-tifies with the analyst's insights. In certain cases, however, empathic descriptions are not enough. In such a circumstance, the patient needs to get involved in therapeutic play—which will be described in the next section—in order to get well. The following case illus-trates actualized unconscious fantasies.

Anna: detached penises made of clay

During the time that she was negotiating oedipal issues as a child, Anna was in reality sexually assaulted by her father on many occa-sions when he was drunk. Once in treatment, in her thirties, she and I could put a storyline to her unconscious fantasy: men have detachable penises that are made of clay and men, by playing with the clay, can make their detached penises huge, hard, and dangerous. The *content* of this unconscious fantasy was understood: little Anna loved her oedipal father when he was not drunk, at which times he was indeed kind. By giving him a detachable penis, little Anna split her kind father image from her rapist father image by detaching or attaching a "good" or "bad" penis. Anna's mother was a potter, and, as a child, Anna had played often with clay. By having her father's detachable penis made of clay, she wanted to control the size of his penis or destroy it: when erect, it was monstrous, but she could make the penis smaller by squeezing off part of the clay or crumbling it like a dried piece of clay. Anna "understood" the meaning of her now-conscious fantasy. But, since her fantasy was actualized, she also *believed* that her analyst's penis was made of clay, that it was detachable, and that it, as a "bad" penis, could enter her unexpectedly when she was not on guard. Even though Anna had been married twice, and thus, in reality, knew what a penis looked like and was made of, she still believed in the analyst's detachable penis made of clay. In order to get well—that is, integrate "good" and "bad" fathers and her corresponding self-images and know the "truth" for sure—Anna demanded that the analyst show her his penis. The treatment for practical purposes came to a standstill in spite of the analyst's interpretations and empathic descriptions. Some months later, Anna became involved in an action: she fell "in love" with a professor who was the same age as her analyst and who was teaching at the same university. Their sexual union was centred primarily on her "playing" with his penis for hours. Through such activity, she began putting together what she knew a penis looked like in reality with what she "knew" a penis looked like in another reality, her actualized unconscious fantasy. After such activities, she began to put her kind and rapist father images together, stopped asking her analyst to show her his penis, gave up her lover, and developed a "routine" oedipal transference, which had good therapeutic consequences.

Therapeutic play

Human beings are constantly involved in actions and our patients routinely speak about their past, current, and planned actions.

Consider a patient beginning his session with a description of an action that he was involved in the day before. The patient says that he had a toothache the day before and had to visit the dentist. Then the patient describes what happened between himself and the aggressive dentist and how the dentist hurt him. There will be several factors if the patient's reported action, his unexpected visit to the dentist, will be examined in the session. Imagine that the patient is in the middle of a transference neurosis in that he expects castration in the hands of the analyst/father and that, during his free associations, he links the analyst's image with the dentist's image. The analyst then makes a clinical decision to explain or not to explain this connection to his patient. For example, the analyst may decide to say nothing to the patient if the analyst feels that his silence will induce necessary anxiety in his patient so that the patient can therapeutically regress further and make his transference neurosis "hotter". If the analyst and the patient, with a close working alliance, are in the middle of collecting evidence of the existence of the patient's castration anxiety, the analyst may say something about how the patient's perception of the dentist was another piece of evidence of his castration anxiety. Or the analyst finds no connection between the patient's report on his visit to the dentist and what the patient is currently negotiating in his analysis, and what is "hot". Then, the analyst treats the patient's reported action as one of the routine events that does not merit special attention at the time.

When I speak of the concept of an adult patient's therapeutic play, I am referring to a specific type of action that continues for days, weeks, or months. The patient is preoccupied with it and reporting it becomes the central focus of his verbal communication from session to session. The action reflects a storyline and as the patient's action continues, it becomes clear that this storyline is related to the patient's actualized unconscious fantasy. The analyst's various images, especially his or her repairing and integrating images, appear prominently in this storyline. The action comes to an end days, weeks, or months later when the storyline, which first expressed itself in actions, also can be verbalized. At which time, the story is fully in the awareness of the patient and he or she comprehends its various meanings. Such actions are not "acting out" in the classical sense; while they include elements of

remembering in action and resistance to verbalization of the transference, their *ultimate aim* is to crystallize insights about one's
conflicts and/or to repair structural defects. To differentiate therapeutic play from acting out, let me first further describe the latter.

Acting out: The aim of "acting out" is the opposite of the aim of
therapeutic play: "acting out" is part of resistance to verbalizing the
current derivatives of wishes and defences against them and they
are in the service of preventing the repairing of defects or working
through conflicts. Some "acting out" is short-lived: when I went on
vacation, a patient of mine, Harry, who had severe separation anxiety, left the town where we both lived, and went to a nearby place
called "Peaks of Otter", three mountaintops forming a triangle and
surrounding a lake. He rented a room at a nearby lodge and sat in
the window, from which he could gaze up at two of the three mountains. When both of us resumed our work together, the patient
exhibited no anxiety or other feelings about my leaving him. When
Harry told me of his trip and of his gazing at the two mountains,
and when I realized that the two mountaintops side by side represented my "breasts", I interpreted how his action "cancelled" his
anxiety pertaining to the separation between us. Then, the patient
brought his separation anxiety to the surface once more so that we
could examine what it signalled within his sessions.

Another type of "acting out" on the surface resembles therapeutic play in that it goes on for days, weeks, or months. But close
observation shows its dominant meaning: to resist working
through a specific transference issues. This is exemplified in the
case of a young woman, Linda, whose mother was her father's
second wife. Her father's first marriage had ended with the death
of his young child, but he never forgot his beautiful first wife or
their dead son, and when my patient was born into this second
marriage, he treated her as a representation of both of them. As an
adult, my patient had a series of love affairs with married men,
becoming their "other wife" in each case. Her analysis showed that
in this way, she was responding to her father's needs and experiencing oedipal triumph until the guilt of "incestuous" closeness
made her break off each relationship, only to launch herself into
another.

When, in the middle of her analysis, Linda worked on these
issues, she began to experience erotic feelings for me and proposed

a liaison, changing her mind when she fell "in love" with another married man, a university professor like myself, and began to fill her hours with accounts of the many, sometimes frantic, activities in which the lovers engaged. Unlike Anna, who had become involved with a university professor as a part of separating the reality of a penis from the reality of a clay penis, Linda used her involvement with a professor as a means to resist working through her erotic transference feelings for the analyst. Linda and her lover's activities took their own course and became one continuous event in what was a good example of "acting out" in the classical negative sense. She would not undergo structural change until this "acting out" was interpreted systematically and she abandoned the affair. It was only then that she could experience her erotic transference fully and work through it. But her "acting out" (in a negative sense) persisted over months and provided stubborn dominant resistance to the analytic process. It seemed at times even to threaten the process itself.

Three types of therapeutic play

Now, let me return to therapeutic play. I first reported such actions in 1984 and named them "therapeutic *stories*", or special aspects of a developing and resolving neurosis. Later, Ast and I differentiated "therapeutic stories", which are exhibited by neurotic individuals or narcissistic and borderline patients after their evolving more integrated self-representations, from "therapeutic *play*", which is usually exhibited by individuals in treatment who do not have integrated self-representations and who, when interpretations in the classical sense are provided to them, do not utilize them therapeutically (Volkan & Ast, 2001). On a descriptive level, it is difficult to differentiate a "therapeutic story" from a "therapeutic play". Both have the same characteristics that I described above. Thus, now, I prefer to call all such actions that continue for days, weeks, or months and that provide a storyline in relation to an actualized unconscious fantasy, as adult patients' "therapeutic plays". But, when I go beyond description of them and look at their *functions*, I divide them, for practical purposes, into three categories. The first two types of therapeutic play occur during the treatment of neurotic-level individuals. They use repression effectively—even their actualized fantasies reflect an encapsulated area in their personalities. The third occurs in individuals below neurotic type, those with psychotic, borderline, or narcissistic personality organizations and structural defects.

The first type

The first type of therapeutic play takes place *after* the resolution of transference neurosis has begun—largely, in fact, *after* it has taken place. It is in the service of recapturing or summarizing the already properly interpreted transference neurosis. It is in the service of crystallizing mastery over the influence of (previously) actualized unconscious fantasy before the termination of the analysis.

William started his analysis when he was in his mid-thirties. His father had died when the boy was in the middle of his oedipal struggle. He had childhood memories of lying next to his father, who was in an alcoholic stupor and had saliva dripping from his mouth. The child wished for his father to be dead, and his father actually died after one of his drinking binges. For a year after his father's death, William slept with his mother. His oedipal fantasies were actualized: he had killed his father and possessed his mother. When his mother married suddenly a year after her first husband's death, William had to move to his stepfather's house. Literally overnight, he was separated from his mother, who now slept on the first floor with her new husband. The children of William's new stepfather slept on the second floor of the house, and William was "exiled" into a dark and scary attic. William went from feeling like a prince to feeling like a slave; he was consumed with rage, but had to develop surface masochistic tendencies in order to survive in the new environment. The new home was on a farm. As an adolescent, William shot and killed some puppies and chickens representing his step-siblings. These actions further crystallized his unconscious fantasy that he was his father's "killer" and that one can actually kill other competitors for a mother's love. William became an adult with extreme inhibitions. His analysis was successful. As the termination phase neared, he developed a dramatic "story" in action about dangers to the analyst's life. The patient checked the tyres of the analyst's car parked in front of his office, declared that the tyres were worn, and warned the analyst that he may have a fatal accident. Since "killing" the analyst had become a very familiar story by this point, and since the analyst and the patient both knew what it meant, the analyst remained silent. By the next session, the patient had checked the electrical wires in the analyst's building with the same idea: that the analyst may meet his death in an accident, this time in a fire. The patient's telling a story through his actions of how the analyst will die went on for several weeks. Finally, one session, the analysand suddenly began to laugh with relief: "You know," he said, "I have been trying to kill you. I knew all along what I have been doing. But you are still alive! I now surely know that I did not kill my father. Now I feel free of guilt." There was nothing for the analyst to interpret; he offered only his affirmative "Hm! Hm!" and soon the patient entered the termination phase of his analysis.

The second type

This type of therapeutic play appears in a neurotic individual as he or she is in the middle of assimilating interpretations of an actualized unconscious fantasy. The action is necessary for the assimilation of the interpretation.

Like William, Roger—who was also in his thirties when he started analysis—had many inhibitions and suffered from an obsessional neurosis. He was obsessed with conscious fantasies (daydreams) of inventing something that would bring sunlight to the earth's dark side during the night. His fantasies included thoughts of a spaceship with a vast mirror that would reflect to the dark side of the world the sunlight from its bright side. As his analysis progressed, the meaning of Roger's day-dreams were understood. As an only child born to parents in their early forties, Roger lived in an apartment so small that all the family slept in the same room. Roger was exposed to multiple primal scene activities. One night when Roger was twelve years old and lying in his bed, which was alongside his parents' bed, his father unexpectedly turned on the light and Roger caught a glimpse of his mother preparing for intercourse by putting Vaseline in her vagina. The light was quickly extinguished. But this event became a symbol of his previously actualized unconscious fantasy in that witnessing a primal scene would blind him, as the light turned on quickly (temporarily) would blind him. The unconscious fantasy also included his "belief" that his mother had a vagina with teeth, *vagina dentata*. He wanted to see it so that he could master his fear of it, but the light necessary for seeing his mother's vagina also would blind him (castrate him). His conscious day-dreams about bringing light to the darker side of the earth reflected the globalization of his actualized unconscious fantasy.

As a neurotic individual, Roger was able to develop a workable transference neurosis. He understood interpretations, including the interpretation of his actualized unconscious fantasy when they were reflected in his transference neurosis. He had many dreams concerning his actualized unconscious fantasy and they were also interpreted. Yet, Roger could not fully work through the influence of his previously unconscious actual fantasy. At this point, he became involved in a "therapeutic play". He began speaking of his preoccupation with an inanimate object, an adult toy. He had answered an advertisement in a magazine offering material for a Viking ship model. He was like a child whose eye had been caught by a toy in a shop window. Should he buy a kit, or shouldn't he? He kept asking me, but I gave no answer. At times, I felt as though he were asking me to buy it for him. After a month or so, he came to a decision, and sent for the kit, which was expensive. When it arrived, he was like a child playing with building blocks. He filled his hours with me with accounts of his work on the model. I felt like a spectator as he planned aloud each successive step of its construction, pondering over it without letting me become at all involved in his "play". I did observe that he was launching forth into some original "creativity" beyond what was indicated in the instructions; he wanted to add a lantern that would blink and quickly alternate light with darkness. The original model called for one unisex head (lavatory), but he wanted to add a head suitable for a woman to use.

I then came to understand what his "toy" and his activities and "creativity" pertaining to it meant to him. In his analysis, he had gone over the ramifications of the event that had taken place when he was twelve. He had repeated it "out there" in action, in transference, in dreams, in order to authenticate the existence of his incestuous desires, his fear of castration (going blind) at the hand of his father, his fear of female genitalia, and the reasons for his symptoms and behaviour patterns. My interpretations now provided the authenticity he sought—and the capacity for related affect. Old desires and old fears had lost their ferocity; the old dreams about vaginas that bite and about Oedipus had lost their frightening force. I came to see his new play with the Viking ship as something like seeing a frightening film for the second time and no longer being terrified by the monsters in it, instead, being amused by the monsters' actions and being able to enjoy the film light-heartedly. The making of the symbolic toy was an activity in the service of gaining comfortable immunity from being sucked into neurotic seductions. The play with the ship had positive qualities because of the following: the ship had a feminine shape, and his measuring and remeasuring its narrow length led me to understand that it represented his mother's vagina. The dragon's head he used for the figurehead on the prow was the oedipal father getting ready to possess the mother and lead her away from her boy child. The blinking lantern (which he had added) recalled the bedroom disclosure when he was twelve, as did the head designed for a woman. He was concerned over where to put this convenience on a ship so narrow; the manufacturer's plans made allowance for only one common toilet. By trying to add a head for women only, he was trying to gratify his wish to separate the father's penis from the mother's vagina. He was concerned that it be so situated in the ship that no one would see a woman urinating in it; his desire and dread about seeing the mother's vagina was being repeated in this. Also, his serious attention to the details of the ship's interior reflected his old fear of *vagina dentata*.

I must emphasize that his "play" with the ship model came after he had worked through in transference the repetition of the bedroom episode—or, at least, was in the process of doing so. When I made some efforts to show him that his work on the ship model also reflected similar phenomena, he seemed simply a child absorbed in serious play, unaware of his surroundings. I gave up trying to interpret, and contented myself with being a "spectator". But when his ship model was completed, after some months, he was able to listen to my interpretations and to join me in describing what he had accomplished psychologically by taking the action he had. He felt different, and turned to a new chapter in his analysis once his "play" was over. The Viking ship was no longer important; he had worked through the influence of his previously actualized conscious fantasies and had crystallized the working-through of his oedipal conflict with his "good" actions.

During the next phase of his analysis, there was exaggerated identification with my analytic attitude, like a child's identification with the father in order to consolidate superego development and to rearrange the internal psychic organization in general.

The third type

The third type of therapeutic play, while descriptively similar, is very *different* from the first two types as far as its function is concerned, and refers directly to this chapter's theme: patients who possess psychotic, borderline, or narcissistic personality organizations or have structural defects do not hear interpretations in the classical sense. Some other therapeutic manoeuvre, such as Tähkä's "emphatic descriptions", needs to take place before they move toward a neurotic level.

Among these therapeutic manoeuvres, there is one that is initiated by the patient him or herself: initiating a therapeutic play. As stated earlier, the analyst does not offer them such activity. Obviously, this play occurs as part of a patient telling his or her internal story and object-relations conflicts, defects, wishes, and defences through action. In such cases, the therapeutic play *precedes* utilization of interpretations and empathic descriptions and appears almost necessary in order for therapeutic progress to take place. None of these patients have cohesive self-representations; they cannot use repression effectively. In fact, their unconscious fantasies are not fully repressed and symbolized as much as a neurotic person's are. They are constantly under the influence of this actualized unconscious fantasy in a rather obvious way. While they can do routine things like going to the shops, buying bread, or keeping a job, the other part of them that is under the influence of the actual unconscious fantasy is constantly expressed.

Sepp underwent circumcision at age five and again at age eleven. Both were surgeries to correct his phimosis and both were extremely traumatic. In his unconscious fantasy, he "believed" that he was a castrated individual.

Sepp grew up on a farm and had a rather bad mothering. His early recollections of his mother was her coming after him and forcing him to eat, and in his adult mind, he had symbolized this interaction of his mother's offerings of food to Chinese water torture, where one drop of water is followed by another, and then another, until the person is driven crazy. Everybody told him that in his early childhood, he was a cry-baby, most probably representing disturbances of the infant–mother interactions. In turn, Sepp idealized his father and tried to be close to him, but this came to an abrupt end when he went for his first surgery. The day after the surgery, his father came to visit to him and said to him in front of everybody, "What a pity; you no longer have anything to play with." Sepp believed that his father thought that he no longer was "a man" and that his penis was damaged. He regressed a great deal and began going to sleep by putting his arms around his body and rocking himself, sometimes for hours.

For the first circumcision, medical procedures themselves supported the actualization of his unconscious fantasy that he had lost his penis. For example, one procedure involved fitting a plastic ring around the glans penis and then pulling up the skin covering the glans penis and tying a string around it. Part of the skin was then tightly squeezed between the string and the ring, stopping the blood flow to the top part of the skin. Within three or four days, the skin above the squeezed area turned blue and was destroyed. Eventually, the dead skin was pulled off. Apparently, the surgeons who took care of him preferred this method of curing phimosis to the actual cutting off of the skin; they considered this type of procedure to be less susceptible to infection. It was, in actuality, a painful procedure, and mentally created a psychic reality that his penis was being constantly cut off, so that the fantasy of being castrated and actuality merged.

There are many stories to indicate how the oedipal issues were kept alive with young Sepp's interaction with his father. For example, six months after his first surgery, Sepp was playing with a female cousin in a silo. Both had taken their clothes off and were exploring each other's bodies. They were discovered by Sepp's father, who became angry when he observed the children's sex play. In an attempt to quickly dress and come out of the silo, Sepp lost one of his socks. Since the silo had an unpleasant odour that infused

Sepp's body and clothes, he was not allowed to enter the farmhouse. He stayed out of the house for hours, feeling humiliated, before the odour dissipated and he was allowed to enter the house. From that day on, his father would aggressively joke with him and continue humiliating him by asking "Sepp, have you found your sock yet?" and then laughing. The loss of the sock also represented the loss of his penis. One solution concerning his oedipal issues was to crystallize his unconscious fantasy about being castrated so that he, in turn, would not have "power" to "kill" his father.

When Sepp was ten years old, his phimosis reappeared. One day, while in a bathtub, he pulled the skin covering his glans penis back. This resulted in the skin squeezing his penis. In pain, Sepp showed his penis to his mother. Thinking that there was a possibility of acute necrosis, she took Sepp to the hospital, where, without anaesthesia, four hospital attendants pinned him down on the operating table while a physician pulled up his penis in order to make the penis "thinner". This manoeuvre enabled the physician to pull up the skin that was squeezing Sepp's penis. During this humiliating and very painful experience, Sepp had a thought that the doctor pulling his penis might tear it off. After the danger of necrosis had passed, Sepp, this time under anaesthesia, went through a second circumcision. The second circumcision further crystallized his fantasy that he was castrated.

It is beyond the scope of this chapter to give details of Sepp's analytic work. His analyst, Dr Gabriele Ast, who began to see Sepp when he was in his mid-thirties and who consulted with me about Sepp's treatment, had a feeling that her patient was "untouchable". He was behaving as if he was maintaining his posture in order to avoid damage, or recastration, by her. Sepp was not ready to develop a therapeutic alliance that would allow him to hear interpretations, clarification, explanations, and so on. But deep down, he was so dependent that he kept coming to his analytic hours.

During the first three years of analysis, obviously the analyst learned a great deal about Sepp's internal world. Sepp had conscious day-dreams about his first surgery. For example, in one of them, his penis was being peeled like the skin of a banana is peeled. Sometimes, he would day-dream about the "skin" of a carrot being shaved. Carrots and bananas were symbols, but they were so common that he knew what they meant. At other times, he daydreamed about a symbolized penis, such as a mountaintop set ablaze. The fire would burn the brush and the trees and destroy the land.

Not only had he had conscious fantasies rather directly reflecting his unconscious fantasies, but most of his night dreams also centred on his childhood trauma. For example, he would dream about holding a large water hose and watering a green area, and then fearing that he would be found and punished as if he had done something wrong. Then he would go into hiding. Since he did not have much repression, he could easily translate his dream and talk about an event before his first circumcision. After he was put on the operating table, he had to urinate, and was allowed to go to the bathroom to do so. But unfortunately, he had to come back to the operating table and undergo the operation. In the dream, there was a wish that he could hide and not return to the operating table. Other dreams included operating room lights, catheters, plastic tubes used to dilate his urethra (he had oedema after the second circumcision), and a mountaintop (glans penis) that would be bruised and damaged.

The analyst, joining the patient in exploring the "meanings" of these verbal productions in the sessions and sometimes their hit-and-run type transference reflections, would go nowhere. In real life, too, Sepp was living "in hiding". In spite of his intelligence, he worked in a psychiatric hospital where the patients represented himself, and he could not leave his job.

In the third year of his treatment, Sepp acquired a "uniform" that included a helmet with a dark visor. The helmet had a red picture of a biker. He also bought shoes with high heels to make him appear taller and began coming to his sessions wearing them. He reported that he had bought a motorbike that was absolutely in ruins, and that he would repair it. The analyst sensed that the broken-down motorbike represented Sepp's castrated penis and that Sepp was entering into a therapeutic play. For six months, mainly what Sepp reported was repairing this almost-unrepairable motorbike.

After six months, Sepp called his father and asked the older man's help in transporting the motorbike, now not working at all, to a dealer's store. Sepp's father arrived with a truck from the farm. The father and the son put the non-functioning motorbike in the truck and took it to the dealer, where Sepp exchanged the vehicle for a brand-new, powerful, and big motorbike. Interestingly, he had asked his father to buy a big, strong motorbike too. The father did not buy one, and Sepp felt very disappointed. (I think that the wish that the father also had a strong motorbike (penis) would make his image as a strong oedipal father with whom Sepp could identify.) Nevertheless, Sepp drove the new motorbike back to his apartment and became involved with a woman whose first name is identical to that of Sepp's analyst and had intercourse with this woman (Sepp's previous sexual relations were full of object-relations conflicts and unsatisfactory, and fear of castrations, the details of which I need not report here). Since his father would not buy a strong motorcycle, and Sepp was disappointed with him, in a sense, he was trying to receive approval from his mother/analyst for having a penis.

At times, Dr Ast would try to give interpretations and/or empathic descriptions of what Sepp was going through, but she had the impression that such verbal communications to Sepp about what he was doing would go in one ear and out the other. It soon became clear that what Sepp had done by buying this "superbike" was to go from having a non-functional penis to a "superpenis." And obviously, the opposites are the same. He received an anti-anxiety drug from another physician who did not know Sepp's psychology, and began taking these drugs and driving his motorbike recklessly. Despite the fact that Dr Ast knew that Sepp could not hear interpretation, she still "interpreted" Sepp's searching for and creation of a penis, searching for a strong father to model himself on, his disappointment at not finding such a father, trying to receive approval from a mother. By doing so, Dr Ast tried to convey to Sepp that she was understanding his dilemma and that she could put his frantic activities into a storyline. When Sepp's reckless driving became very dangerous, the analyst told Sepp that she had a responsibility to stop him from driving recklessly. She explained that the activity with the superpenis could be done at a slower pace. She told him that if he were injured badly or killed, she would not be able to continue his analysis and that she was a protector of the analytic process. Thus, the analyst acted as a strong parent figure, putting realistic boundaries for Sepp's expensive and dangerous "celebration" of finding a superpenis; to have a superpenis was not an adaptive solution for Sepp's internal problems.

Soon after this, a drastic change in Sepp's real life situation was initiated. Identifying with Dr Ast, he wanted the motorbike to be "safe". Thus, he left his work at the psychiatric hospital, where the motorbike could be stolen or damaged, and moved into a new apartment where there was a safe parking lot. Eventually, he began "sublimating" his activity. He found a job transporting small packages or mail using his bike. His new boss, in fact, had many motorbikes and was a man with good humour, and he hired Sepp to be a courier. For Sepp, this meant the systematic study of a map of the city and memorizing streets. In a sense, he had to learn new ego functions to move out from his restricted external and internal world. When Sepp accepted the job, he made sure he could keep his psychoanalytic appointments and he made arrangements accordingly. One day, Sepp came to his appointments wearing the uniform of the courier company and reported that the superbike was now gone because it was not practical to use. He felt sad giving up his superbike, but he now knew that it was not an item that he wanted to keep. He said that he appreciated his analyst's interest in him in that she was trying to stop him from damaging his body. Instead, he bought a smaller, more realistic motorbike that could go through the city streets safely. Now in his sessions, he reflected the idea that "a bike is a bike" and not a penis. The symbolic representation of the bike was enhanced and Sepp's further ability for repression began to take place.

Concluding remarks

Working through structural conflicts and even remnants of some object relations conflicts to a great extent *precedes* the appearance of a therapeutic play among neurotic individuals in treatment, whereas gaining insights into and beginning to work through object relations conflicts and ego deficiencies typically *follows* the completion of therapeutic play with people who are not on the neurotic level. I consider a therapeutic play of a person who does not yet possess a cohesive self-representation and effective repressive ability to serve the following aims.

(1) Differentiating actual experience from the mental images of

traumatic events associated with an actualized unconscious fantasy.

(2) Evolving protosymbols into symbols.

(3) Increasing capacity for mourning (for "losing" previous self and object representations).

(4) Developing the ability to tame and tolerate aggressive drive derivatives.

(5) Learning to experience and master painful reality.

(6) Building ego identifications with the analyst as a "new object".

(7) Achieving cohesiveness of self-representation.

(8) Becoming capable of the creative living associated with societal and cultural adaptations.

To accomplish these objectives, the working through the meaning and the function of the "play", should take place in the therapeutic space between the analyst and the patient—a space into which the analyst must not intrude on counter-transference impulses.

References

Arlow, J. (1969). Unconscious fantasy and disturbances of conscious experience. *Psychoanalytic Quarterly, 38*: 1–27.

Beres, D. (1962). The unconscious fantasy. *The Psychoanalytic Quarterly, 31*: 309–328.

Fenichel, O. (1945). *The Psychoanalytic Theory of Neurosis.* New York: W. W. Norton.

Freud, S. (1908a). On hysterical phantasies and their relation to bisexuality. *S.E., 9*: 155–166. London: Hogarth Press.

Freud, S. (1914g). Remembering, repeating and working through. *S.E., 12*: 147–156. London: Hogarth Press.

Inderbitzin, L. B., & Levy, S. T. (1990). Unconscious fantasy: A reconsideration of the concept. *Journal of the American Psychoanalytic Association, 38*: 113–130.

Rosenfeld, D. (1992). *The Psychotic: Aspects of the Personality.* London: Karmac.

Rosenfeld, H. A. (1965). *Psychotic States: A Psychoanalytic Approach.* London: Hogarth Press.

Tähkä, V. (1984). Psychoanalytic treatment as a developmental continuum: considerations on disturbed structuralization and its phase-specific encounter. *Scandinavian Psychoanalytic Review, 7*: 133–159

Tähkä, V. (1993). *Mind and Its Treatment: A Psychoanalytic Approach*. Madison, CT: International Universities Press.

Volkan, V. D. (1976). *Primitive Internalized Object Relations*. New York: International Universities Press.

Volkan, V. D. (1995). *The Infantile Psychotic Self: Understanding and Treating Schizophrenics and Other Difficult Patients*. Northvale, NJ: Jason Aronson.

Volkan, V. D., & Ast, G. (1977). *Siblings in the Unconscious and Psychopathology*. Madison, CT: International Universities Press.

Volkan, V. D. & Ast, G. (2001). Curing Gitta's "leaking body": actualized unconscious fantasies and therapeutic play. *Journal of Clinical Psychoanalysis, 10*: 567–606.

Werner, H. & Kaplan, B. (1963). *Symbol Formation*. New York: Wiley.

CHAPTER SEVEN

The past in the present: a case vignette

Anne-Marie Sandler

In his book *Mind and Its Treatment*, Veikko Tähkä described in illuminating detail the various roles of the analyst in the course of a psychoanalytic encounter. He based his view on a careful account of the complex developmental steps taken by the growing child in creating a representational world of self and objects. This approach reminded me of my husband's and my own struggles in our effort to try to conceptualize better the role of the analyst in the psychoanalytic work. Our own formulation of the concept of the past and present unconscious was an attempt to locate and clarify at what levels of psychic development analysts operate.

With the arrival in the consulting room of Miss R, new thoughts about development were forced upon me. I was especially struck how for this patient the past was so constantly and so vividly alive in the present, as if time had stood still for her. I hoped that working with Miss R would elicit some deeper understanding of this process and how the concept of the past and the present unconscious could help in this.

Miss R

When Miss R came to see me, she told me that she desperately wanted to have a baby, but having reached her middle thirties she had no boyfriend. She felt clearly heterosexual but had never had a lasting sexual relationship. Her sister, sixteen months her junior, had announced that she was engaged to be married, and Miss R feared that her sister would soon become pregnant.

I learned that Miss R felt that the birth of her sister had blighted her whole life. She was at pains to assure me that as a child, instead of resenting her sister, she had looked after her like a mother, helping her along and sharing her own friends with her. She now feels very bitter that her sister never reciprocated her generosity and dedication and that her parents, especially her mother, never showed any gratitude for such devotion.

Miss R seemed to be an intelligent and gifted person, a professional artist and teacher. She appeared to have been academically successful at school and at university, but the shadow of her sister's achievements followed her throughout life. She always felt ignored or outwitted, so that her own successes never gave her much pleasure. She never had a best friend, always secretly worrying that her sister's friends were more desirable than her own. Her interest in boys started in her early teens. She always attempted to win the most popular and self-assured boys and tried to make herself irresistible by pretending to be very mature and sophisticated.

She told me that at University she never managed to get a steady boyfriend. Her only passionate love affair had occurred about five years previously, when she fell in love with a waiter, Jose, whom she met in a restaurant on the occasion of a birthday party. She decided to visit the restaurant regularly, waiting for Jose's shift to end and inviting him to her flat. She knew very little about him, only that he had a girlfriend with whom he often quarrelled. Finally they made love and after a few days of intense sexual activity he returned to his previous girlfriend. Miss R had been indignant, feeling terribly betrayed and rejected. She could not let go and a pattern of violent quarrels and reconciliations, followed by new betrayals, became established. This lasted for over a year and was only interrupted because Jose left London. The sadomasochistic nature of the relation seemed evident.

Miss R described her parents as quite a happy couple, although she complained that her mother, like her sister, was rather cold and withholding. She was much more like her father, passionate, moody, and generous, but she could not bear his terrible intrusiveness, his sexualizing behaviour and his frequent panics. She recalled vividly the knots in her stomach when her father raged and ranted and everyone in the house ran to try to find what he had misplaced. Her description had such immediacy that I had to remind myself that the patient had not lived at home for more than fifteen years.

Even though Miss R appeared to speak very easily, openly, and fluently as she was giving me this information, I realized how her narrative corresponded to a pre-set and rigid story to which she clung, fearful that I would disturb it or intrude into it. The discrepancy between her apparently articulate and open presentation and her reluctance to engage in a true dialogue betrayed, I thought, her anxiety and distrust of any kind of close relationships. She considered me with deep anxiety and suspicion, trying to persuade me that she was in full control of her life but that fate had treated her very badly.

The treatment, I thought, would be challenging. Miss R showed a number of borderline traits. She presented with strong intellectual defences, important sadistic and envious wishes, considerable paranoid elements in her relationships and the very special pressure on her, caused by her awareness that her child-bearing time would not last forever. Centrally, I thought that the patient was terrified of close relationships as well as of sexuality, which she felt undermined dangerously her view of herself as being in charge and self-contained. The deep anxieties, which prevented her from opening up, were linked in my mind to her private and primitive view of herself as dangerous and wicked, a view that she had to keep secret from the enquiring eyes of the objects. I was also intrigued by the specific challenge paused by the way Miss R seemed to have psychically organized most of the inner and outer events of her life as a direct consequence of her sister's birth. In some ways her private, personal, internal time had ceased to unfold. The birth of her sister was clearly a highly traumatic event for the patient and had become an organizer of all her future experiences.

The past unconscious and the present unconscious

Before attempting to explore how the past so dominated the present in the case of Miss R, I would like to describe briefly the concepts of the past unconscious and the present unconscious, concepts that my late husband and I used as a helpful technical frame of reference.

Freud's introduction in "The ego and the id" (1923b) of the structural model was never fully integrated with the topographical one. This preoccupied a number of analysts, among them Eissler who wrote that

> ... ego, id and superego do not suffice to outline the whole area of psychoanalytic topography and that on clinical and theoretical grounds it is necessary to assume the existence of something that comes close to, without being identical with, what Freud meant by the system Conscious, the system Preconscious and the system Unconscious. [Eissler, 1962, p. 13]

By introducing the concept of the past and present unconscious (Sandler & Sandler, 1984, 1994), my husband and I felt the need to reabsorb quite explicitly the topographical dimension, the dimension of depth to surface, into our technical frame of reference. We also adopted an essentially developmental point of view, developmental referring not only to temporal development from infancy onward but also to the developmental process in regard to the movement from depths to surface that is consistently going on in the present.

We saw the *past unconscious* as the developmental product of the first few years of life. It evolves in the young child

- who has made important developmental steps, achieved with varying amount of success;
- who may or may not have had a deviant development;
- whose drives, unconscious wishes, and phantasies have undergone many vicissitudes;
- who has experienced successive phases of cognitive development, resulting in significant changes in the type of thought processes;
- who has taken major steps forward with regard to separation–individuation;
- who has narcissistic assets and vulnerabilities;
- who has specific fears and anxieties;

- who may have achieved useful sublimations;
- who has devised a number of solutions to conflict and adaptations to his specific environment.

The past unconscious evolving in the young child is, above all, a developmental product of an object-related child, one who has made significant interactions and identifications with significant others that have become internalized, a child with a phantasy life profoundly affected by such structured internal object relationships, including those that have been viewed as interactions with the superego. It is a child with specific strengths and weaknesses, who will have a greater or lesser tendency to regress in the face of conflict or any other source of unpleasant affect. We saw the past unconscious as acting as a dynamic template, as structuring organisations that form the underpinning for the immediate here-and-now unconscious strivings and responses of the older individual.

The *present unconscious*, on the other hand, resembles Freud's Preconscious system in some ways. It can be regarded as the area of the mind containing the current preoccupations and the unconscious wishful phantasies, which represent the present-day counterparts of, developments from, and derivatives of, those infantile reactions, which we attribute to, and locate in, the past unconscious. The present unconscious is much more accessible to us, although not entirely so, and is the central domain of the analytic investigation and the direct source of transference manifestations.

It is important to clarify that we refer to "unconscious phantasies" as a designation for internal processes, as they exist in the present unconscious. They have to be distinguished from the so-called "deep" unconscious phantasies, attributed to the earliest period of life. In our model, unconscious phantasies do not arise in the depths of the past unconscious, but in the depths of the present unconscious. These unconscious phantasies have then to be dealt with by the person of the present. They will tend to arouse conflict and disturb the inner equilibrium and are mostly dealt with outside consciousness. They are, therefore, modified, disguised, or repressed. The defence mechanisms used by the individual to regulate the content of the present unconscious serve to disguise these unconscious phantasies by means of manipulations of the self and objects representations involved in the phantasy. Parts of the self-representation may be split off and displaced to the object representation, and vice versa.

All this is a consequence of the "stabilizing function" of the present unconscious. It is, indeed, a major part of the work of the present unconscious to maintain inner equilibrium, to maintain feelings of safety and the integrity of the self, by reorganizing the unconscious representations of the threatening content through the use of a variety of defensive measures, essentially measures by which the unconscious content of the present unconscious is transformed.

In our model, we conceive of this unconscious content, however motivated, as arising in the individual *as if* he or she were a particular young child. This unconscious content is not conceived of as arising in the past unconscious, which is viewed as acting as *dynamic templates*. The dynamic templates of the past unconscious are sets of procedures or schemas reflecting the modes of mental functioning of the specific young child within each adult. The impulse, wish, or memory that arises in the depths of the present unconscious is not, in this model, one that has passed in disguised form through a repression barrier between the Unconscious and the Preconscious. The censoring takes place *within and throughout* the present unconscious, with a final defensive transformation occurring before admission to conscious awareness. An unconscious wish arising in the depths of the present unconscious can be regarded as modelled on the template of the inner child's wishes, but the objects involved are objects of the present.

To summarize: as the analyst becomes aware of the ever-repeating themes—through observing and reacting to the patient's phantasies, anxieties, defences, behaviour, actualizations, and so on—he is forced to think of the strength of the repetition compulsion and of a kind of blueprint or template that organizes the specificity of these repetitions. The past unconscious gives structure and form to all the experiential content in each specific individual child, with its individual personality reflecting its individual development. The present Unconscious is based on this past unconscious and is moulded by it.

Let us return to Miss R and ask ourselves how the model of the past and present unconscious can guide us in finding our way through her material.

Miss R again (some remarks about the analytic process)

From the very first encounter with this patient, it was possible to notice with unusual clarity how her version of the past was dominating her internal world and influencing her every thought. Having created for herself a scenario where she felt that she had been rejected and deeply wronged, she was caught in the need for revenge and was thus unable to overcome her past in order to begin to envisage the present and the future.

Miss R refused to lie down. For months she filled the sessions with an endless stream of complaints; for instance, her disappointment with her mother and her sister, whom she experienced as uninterested and cold, and her bitterness towards her father, whom she had so loved as a young child but who had increasingly let her down. In puberty he had become for her a source of shame and embarrassment. Her incessant pouring out of material made it very difficult for me to think and whenever I tried to make contact with her by naming her apparent emotional state or by trying to sympathize with how stuck and lonely she must feel, she tended immediately to refute what I had said. She complained that I was not helpful, that I was only criticizing her, making her feel insecure.

She attempted to persuade me that the only thing which would really help her to feel better would be for me to agree that she has been deeply wronged by the birth of her sister. If I did this, she would feel understood for the first time in her life. As I attempted to make sense of her early experience and her need to recruit me as a witness and supporter in what she had experienced as her early victimization, it became possible to address her feeling of mistrust and isolation. We were able to start and explore how her inner world was constantly fighting accusatory objects against whom she had to justify herself. She plaintively attempted to persuade me that she is a good person, but that her sister and her parents did not seem to appreciate this. I could point out to her that in her repeated efforts to force them to change, she faced a hopeless task, which tied her to them and put her at their mercy. I could add that she also had to control me in the sessions because of her secret terror that I would unearth another aspect of her, less generous and caring.

I understood the nature of her inner struggles better when I witnessed the strength of her magical thinking and her extreme vulnerability and internal violence. On the occasion of a visit from her father to help her with some odd jobs in her flat, he enquired whether she had yet met a man. She described how she had felt abused and intruded upon. She seemed to have become quite hysterical, accusing him of being a voyeur, a pervert. She insisted that he leave at once. A day later, her father had a bad fall and broke his arm. He had a slight concussion and he was kept in hospital overnight. Miss R felt convinced that she had been the cause of the accident. Her reaction was to avoid all contact with her father, feeling then the more despicable for it. When I suggested that she acted as if she felt that she had personally damaged him, she confessed that she was never sure how dangerous she could be. I thought that I could witness here how she had felt suddenly terrifyingly intruded upon by her father's enquiry and how, in a very concrete way, she felt that her uncontrolled, violent, and destructive attack on her father had been the cause of his fall.

In his paper entitled "On the early formation of the mind: from differentiation to self and object constancy", Veikko Tähkä writes:

> It seems likely that the early self experiences the gratifying object as its self-evident possession. The object and its services are felt to exist only for the child's sake and . . . these functions cannot yet be experienced as belonging to a self-determined somebody beyond the immediate control and possession of the self. It is not until the object can be experienced as having an inner world of its own as a result of the establishment of self and object constancy, that the object world ceases to belong experientially exclusively to the self. [Tähkä, 1988, p. 119]

The early arrival of a sister, when Miss R was sixteen months old, may have presented her with a formidable threat to her as yet precarious sense of self. It is possible to wonder if the major upheaval in the mother's availability led in Miss R to the "fading of the all-good" introject with a corresponding strengthening of the image of the "all-bad" object." As a consequence "the only way for the self to preserve differentiation in an experiential world, saturated by frustration and aggression, seems to be to identify with that part of the object" (*ibid.*, p. 116).

Miss R appears to have felt early in life that she had always to be grown up, in control, and independent. She seemed to have made immense efforts to mother her sister. Partly it helped her to feel that she was special, admired by the grown-ups, and irreplaceable, but it also allowed the grandiose illusion that she was the mother, the favourite of the father, and the bearer of babies. In the transference she often dreaded my understanding and my interpretations because it punctured her precarious sense of omnipotence. In the course of the analysis, Miss R divulged an internal representation of herself, which contained a feeling that there is something terribly wrong about her, something totally unacceptable, monstrous, destructive, and hateful that she has to hide at all cost. She had revealed with intense anxiety and embarrassment that, after the birth of her sister, she would frequently have temper tantrums that would totally overwhelm her. Apparently, they continued for several years, well into latency. It seemed to underline the great strain that existed between her need for control and the danger that she perceived unconsciously of being completely overwhelmed by her impulses.

As the analytic work proceeded, I could feel that Miss R was becoming increasingly attached to me. Some of her defences were getting slowly lowered and she could start to acknowledge the existence in her of some important anxieties and conflicts. She often told me that she could only continue her analysis because I appeared to her to be cheerful and really engaged in the work. It would be impossible for her to have to face someone depressed and self-preoccupied. I felt that she probably had some awareness of her terror of her own depressive tendencies. Despite these developments in her ability to confide in me, I kept being aware that she struggled with a kind of bedrock of extreme vulnerability in which she lost all sense of safety. I became persuaded that this vulnerability had its origin in her very early childhood, and probably belonged to a pre-verbal period of her life. This can be illustrated with an example taken from a session of that period of her analysis.

A detailed session

A week before the first two-week Christmas holiday, I fell ill and had to cancel a Friday session. When Miss R came for her next appointment on Monday, there was something unpleasantly penetrating and suspicious in her look. At first I thought that she wanted to make sure that

I was better, but then she said in an angry tone of voice that she had thought of cancelling the session, as it is really no use meeting just for a week and then have a long break. In any case this treatment did not help her at all. She still has no boyfriend and was thus no nearer to having a child.

She then added, with what I felt was an unmistakeable excitement, that she had gone to dinner with her parents on Friday night. As the conversation drifted to her sister and her new-born baby, she had exploded, reproaching all of them for being besotted with the new grandchild and her sister and for ignoring her needs and her problems. She accused her father of having made it impossible for her to have relationships with men and told her mother that she had always been cold and distant. She managed to get herself so worked up that she cried hysterically and also threatened that she would kill herself if things were not going to improve. Her mother started to cry and her father tried to quiet her down, but she was having none of this. Miss R also told me that her mother had commented that she did not think that Miss R should continue her analysis. It clearly did not help her and even made her worse.

I felt helpless and irritated. We had explored her jealousy towards her sister repeatedly and I had thought that she had gained some insight into her rage and resentment towards her parents for having produced this rival. She had appeared also to begin to see how much she had felt ignored in what she called her baby needs, and how bitter she was about this. The way she was describing the scene with her family seemed clearly aimed at making me feel accused for having let her down. I wondered aloud whether she had possibly felt cross that I had cancelled the Friday session. She denied this vehemently and said that she has felt for sometime now that treatment was not helping her. She was still thinking most days about Jose who had left her. He had seemed so eager. They had made love for hours on the first night and then he simply went back to his former girlfriend. How could somebody behave like that? She feels so betrayed, she can't let it be.

I had heard Miss R tell me the same story many times before, but in this session I felt the special intensity of her grudge and the impossibility for her to let go. I also felt that she could not allow herself to be influenced by what I might have to say. Every time that she thought that I was going to speak, she would rush to add another detail to her description, forcing me into silence.

As we were nearing the end of the session, Miss R stopped suddenly. I was not sure whether she had exhausted the virulence of her anger or whether she had become anxious, as she may have realized that most of the session had been taken up. After a very brief silence, she asked in an angry, challenging voice: "So what do you have to say?" I replied that I wasn't sure that I had anything useful to say at the moment, but that I was concerned about how upset she was and that we were getting to the end of the session. She ignored my remark and turned on me about my having been silent and useless to her. I felt greatly provoked and put under pressure to say something, even though I feared that she was in no state to listen. I finally said that I thought she was in a great conflict about the row on Friday night and about the relationship with Jose and that she felt quite awful about me and about herself. She became indignant. Of course, she felt awful. Indeed, what she needed were friends who would make her feel strong by supporting her, not this weird analytic approach that made her feel dreadful.

Time was up, but Miss R just refused to go. She complained that I was just dumping her now, as if I could not bear her any longer, just like her mother who had no patience with her. I got up, reminded her that we could go on thinking about all this tomorrow. I was getting anxious, as I expected a new patient, and increasingly furious towards Miss R. I opened the door and repeated that the time was up for today. She said that that might be so, but reminded me that I had said some weeks previously that she felt sometimes compelled to behave like a sixteen-month-old and that was how she was feeling just now. She added that she didn't give a "fuck" about my concern about time. She would go when she was ready. I responded by saying in a rather threatening voice that I wished her to leave this instant. At that point, with a smile of triumph, she left saying: "This time, I really managed to make you angry!"

When I had recovered and able to reflect on this session, I realized more fully how often Miss R seemed inaccessible or intensely provocative. I started to wonder if I had encountered in Miss R a fundamental vulnerability, from which she had to save herself through an explosion of rage, reproach, and rejection. I certainly felt that she had shown me a very primitive aspect of her personality, one that she could not reflect or elaborate upon, but one that needed immediate enactment.

The model of the present and the past unconscious is mainly aimed at clarifying the psychoanalytic premises that guide technique. Faced with the neurotic elements of the patients, the role of the past in the present is being reconstructed, on the basis of verbal material and transference manifestations. However, when working with aspects of ego disintegration or distortions, which are both the reason and the the cause of severe development imbalance, the analyst has to postulate the presence of pathological templates. These have, in part, been created on the basis of procedural modes of behaviour, not on declarative ones; thus, they are not based on recoverable memories of the past.

As the vignette from Miss R has illustrated, this kind of primitive behaviour by the patient evokes powerful counter-transference reactions, which are not easy to handle. Veikko Tähkä writes in *Mind and Its Treatment* that

> Empathic description of the borderline patient's inner experiencing presupposes that the analyst is capable of being aware and tolerating the feelings and fantasies that are aroused in him as responses to the patient's intense and ambivalently fluctuating, verbal and non-verbal communications and messages. Making use of these responses, the analyst is supposed to identify temporarily with the patient's way of experiencing, and finally, the analyst is expected to put that shared experience into words as accurately and empathically as possible. [Tähkä, 1993, p. 358]

On many occasions, as the analyst feels attacked by the patient, he or she may be tempted to interpret the patient's behaviour as aiming to provoke, but to my mind, this would carry the danger of imputing designs to the patient that he or she might not have. Often no more can be done than to contain the onslaught from the patient, but, as soon as possible, the analyst may be able to describe and to name the underlying emotions, the feeling states which have been experienced in the here and now of the session. This requires from the analyst a capacity to contain the primitive mental state stirred in him or her by the patient's behaviour. If this work is allowed to occur, the patient realizes that the analyst continues to be present and to reflect on the material or behaviour. Tähkä comments that

> ... conveying empathic understanding to the patient at the time of his frustration with the analyst is the most effective way of promoting structure-building identifications in a borderline patient. When repeated frequently enough, it will be seen ... that the analyst's

empathic and respectful way of sharing the patient's experiencing will gradually become the patient's own attitude toward himself. [*ibid.*, p. 356]

Miss R felt overwhelmed and very threatened by her outbursts, which she felt were both shameful and unexpected. She often gave the impression that she felt compelled to get rid of intolerable tensions. It seemed useful to help her to recognize the existence of these tensions, and she gradually became able to acknowledge them and to become aware of their paranoid flavour. Gradually, Miss R became able to identify with the analyst's own reflecting and empathic enquiring. It seems, to quote Tähkä again, that the patient

gradually built up important aspects of his self structure, and gain a progressively expanding store of informative representations of himself and the object. The patient may gradually start to differentiate between feelings other than just anxiety, rage, and elation, as well as to give names to various, so far only vaguely perceived impressions. [*ibid.*, p. 356]

Conclusion

The model of the past and present unconscious helped me to differentiate between the past unconscious with its dynamic templates and the present unconscious, the locus of the analytic work. Borderline patients like Miss R have taken important developmental steps early in childhood, but also show signs of severe early dysfunction. The blueprint of their early years discloses poorly structured dynamic templates, containing specific vulnerabilities or often showing some basic faults. As a consequence of their specific disturbance, these patients require another kind of interpretations from those given to the neurotic ones.

Miss R could feel good about herself only very intermittently, being frequently afraid of her severe destructiveness. She experienced the presence in herself of unremitting internal attacks and she felt driven to get rid of her aggressive experiences into others. She had become suspicious and most easily persecuted. Her love for her father, whom she had felt was much warmer than her mother, had supported her during early latency. With her entry into pre-puberty, however, the father began to be experienced as seductive and she withdrew, terrified by her sexual wishes, which she sensed were mixed with strong sadistic urges.

I thought that I had witnessed in the session where Miss R refused to leave the direct enactment of a sense of panic, created by a fear of inner disintegration. This alternated with times when she could bring material of a higher level, bring dreams or verbal associations, which yielded to ordinary interpretations and brought new insights. However, the important clinical point that I am trying to bring across in this chapter is that, in my view, her inner experience of being attacked which led her to becoming the attacker had to be understood as resulting from faulty primitive structures of her self-representation. The work of Veikko Tähkä has been an inspiring influence in my clinical journey.

References

Eissler, K. R. (1962). On the metapsychology of the preconscious: a tentative contribution to psycho-analytic morphology. *Psychoanalytic Study of the Child*, 17: 9–41.

Freud, S. (1923b). The ego and the id. *S.E.*, 19: London: Hogarth.

Sandler, J. (1974). Psychogical conflict and the structural model: some clinical and theoretical implications. *International Journal of Psycho-Analysis*. 55: 53–62.

Sandler, J., & Sandler, A. M. (1984). The past unconscious, the present unconscious and interpretation of the transference. *Psychoanalytic Inquiry*, 4: 367–399.

Sandler, J. & Sandler, A. M. (1994). The past unconscious and the present unconscious: a contribution to a technical frame of reference. *Psychoanalytic Study of the Child*, 44: 278–291.

Tähkä, V. (1988). On the early formation of the mind: from differentiation to self and object constancy. *Psychoanalytic Study of the Child*, 43: 101–134.

Tähkä, V. (1993). *Mind and Its Treatment: A Psychoanalytic Approach*. Madison, CT: International Universities Press.

CHAPTER EIGHT

Sexualities and neosexualities

Joyce McDougall

Sexual creations and deviations

Ever since Freud, the belief that there is such an entity as "normal sexuality" has been profoundly shaken. Freud states in his famous "Three essays" (1905e) that the sexual drive has no pre-formed, natural object and illustrated this hypothesis in his study of what he called sexual perversions. He deduced that there was no qualitative difference between the so-called "normal" and the "pathological" regarding sexual aim and object; furthermore, he held that there was no specific relationship between sexual orientation and one's biological sex—and that the notion of something called "normality" was fictitious.

From my own perspective, all psychological symptoms are in a sense "creations" constructed by a child who once desperately sought a solution to the problems of being human; that is to say that *all symptoms are attempts at self-cure*—and this includes what might be called symptomatic sexuality. So, in addition to what we deem "sublimations", which, as we know, are socially esteemed activities, many other psychic "creations" do not carry this social value—such as neurosis and psychosis, sexual deviations, and psychosomatic illness. However, although these phenomena do not qualify as sublimations, nevertheless they are *creations of the self*— and as such have been *constructed in the service of psychic survival*. It is my contention that psychological symptoms, as well as sublime creations, all spring from the same source: the attempt to deal with early psychic conflict and primitive forms of mental pain. Some of these archaic psychic dramas are part and parcel of the universal traumata of human life: such as the existence of otherness, the discovery of the difference between the sexes and the inevitability of death; then to these must be added the biparental unconscious which may hold traumatic potential, as well as atypical traumata: for example, the untimely death of a parent, psychosis in a family member, being brought into the world to replace a dead child, or living through a socially traumatic period.

Regarding sexual deviations as a solution to early psychic trauma, most analysts would agree that the analysands themselves, whatever their sexual pattern may be, rarely wish to lose their erotic solutions. This is understandable in that, in many cases, these intricate erotic scenarios serve not only to safeguard a feeling of sexual identity but frequently reveal themselves to be techniques of psychic survival and are required, therefore, to preserve one's feeling of *subjective* identity.

In both heterosexual and homosexual deviations—that is erotic scenarios that differ from what we might call the homosexual "norm" or the heterosexual "norm"—there is an apparent need to "reinvent" the sexual relationship, in other words, requiring something over and beyond a sexual relationship between two consenting adults. In these cases the relationship demands complicated manoeuvres, such as sado-masochistic conditions, the erotic use of urinary or faecal matter or the requirement of "accoutrements" which may resemble stage settings for the production of a play. This need to reinvent the sexual relationship can usually be traced to disturbing childhood events or misleading parental communications regarding sexual identity, sexual roles and the concepts of "femininity" and "masculinity " (if these terms are able to be accurately defined).

One characteristic that has struck me over the years, with those of my analysands who have created complicated sexual deviations, was that frequently they were terrified to imagine the slightest change in their ritualized scenarios. Many of them appeared to be unable even to day-dream freely around their erotic fantasy.

Now, in humankind's psychic economy, one of the leading functions of day-dreaming is to be able to accomplish in imagination that which is believed to be forbidden or impossible to enact in reality. Thus a restricted capacity to use phantasy, as manifested in many deviant sexualities, points to some breakdown in the important introjections that take place in what Winnicott named "transitional phenomena"; in consequence there has been a failure in childhood to create freely an illusion in the space that separates one being from another; or to use a variety of illusions to support absence, frustration, and delay. In all other respects these sexual creators differ little from so called "normal" homosexual and heterosexual individuals, who invest with equally vital significance their sexual drives and relationships, as well as the sublimation of these in their professional work.

What is meant by "sexual choice"?

Nobody freely *chooses* to engage in the highly restricted and exigent conditions imposed by such compulsive sexual inventions, nor the loneliness of a sexual life that is sometimes largely confined to auto-erotic sexual creations. As regards the "choice" of sexual acts and erotic objects, the same reasoning applies to heterosexual and homosexual orientations. Few people have the impression of "choosing", for example, to be homosexual in a predominantly heterosexual society, or for that matter, of "choosing" heterosexuality in order to conform to the social majority. With regard to deviant heterosexual, homosexual, and autoerotic inventions, these creations represent the best possible *solutions* that the child of the past was able to find in the face of contradictory parental communications concerning core gender identity, masculinity, femininity, and sexual role.

The early mother–child relationship may be a decisive factor in laying the foundations for deviant sexual patterns. A "good-enough" mother (in the Winnicottian sense) experiences a feeling of merging with her baby in the earliest weeks of its life. However, as Winnicott points out, if this fusional attitude persists beyond the first weeks of life, the interaction runs the risk of becoming persecutory and pathological for the infant. In their state of total dependency on their mothers, infants tend to conform to what whatever is projected upon them. A baby's motility, emotional liveliness, intelligence, sensuality, and bodily erogenicity can only develop to the extent that the mother herself invests these dimensions positively. But she may just as readily *inhibit* the narcissistic enhancement of these aspects in her infant's somatopsychic structure, particularly if her baby is serving to palliate an unfulfilled need in her own internal world.

This mother–baby pattern then affects the development of transitional phenomena and tends to create a fear in the infant of developing its own psychic resources for dealing with tension. The growth of what Winnicott terms "the capacity to be alone" may be endangered, so that the infant constantly seeks the mother's presence in order to deal with any affective experience, thus instilling in her nursling what may be conceptualized as an *addictive relationship to her presence* and her caretaking functions. This addictive dependency may readily be carried over to the sexual and love relations of the future adult.

Consequently, there is a potential risk that the small child will fail to establish an inner representation of a caretaking maternal (and later paternal) figure, performing functions that include the capacity for containing and dealing with psychological pain or states of over-excitement. Unable to identify with such an inner representation, the child remains incapable of self-soothing and self-care in times of either inner or outer tension. An attempted solution to this lack of self-caring introjects is then inevitably sought in the external world as it was in early infancy. In this way drugs, food, alcohol, tobacco, or compulsive sexual pursuits are discovered as objects that may be used to alleviate painful states of mind—fulfilling a maternal function that the individual is unable to provide for him or herself. These addictive pursuits take the place of the transitional objects of childhood, which embodied the maternal environment and at the same time liberated the child from total dependence on the mother's presence. Unlike transitional objects, however, addictive objects and pursuits necessarily fail in that they are *somatic rather than psychological attempts to deal with absence* and therefore provide only temporary relief. For this reason in earlier writings (McDougall, 1986, pp. 66–78) I referred to addictive objects as "transitory" rather than as "transitional" objects.

In the same vein, therefore, *addictive sexualities*, whether in a heterosexual, homosexual or autoerotic context, may also be conceptualized as a breakdown in the internalization of parental functions—in particular of the environmental mother who is experienced by the helpless infant as unable to modify its physical or psychological suffering. In this eventuality, sexual relations may come to represent a dramatic and compulsive way of preventing one's narcissistic self-image from disintegrating. The sexual act itself is then needed not only to dispel affective overcharge or to repair a damaged narcissistic image of one's gender identity, but also to deflect the forces of infantile rage from being turned back upon the self or against the internalized parental representations. In consequence, a drug-like utilization of sexuality becomes necessary to suspend feelings of violence as well as to anaesthetize, if only temporarily, a castrated image of the self, a threatened loss of ego boundaries, or feelings of inner deadness. Partners and sexual scenarios become containers for the addicted individual's dangerous and damaged parts, which are then over-ridden in illusory fashion through a game of mastery within the parameters of a sexual scenario. At the same time, the partners become substitutes for the missing or damaged parental introjects, and as such are used to repair the fragile sexual image constructed by the child of the past from negative biparental communications.

Thus, the experience of pain, anxiety, and even the threat of death may become an essential accompaniment to sexual activity.

Sexual theory and psychoanalysis

I would now like to reflect briefly upon the place of human sexuality in the psychoanalytic theories of today. For certain schools of thought sexuality is presented as a theory of inter-subjective and intra-subjective relationships with the significant objects of the external world; for some, it is the concept of an internal psychic world populated by relationships between internal objects; other theorists conceive sexuality as being comprised of the concepts of core gender and sexual role identity and of the relations between the two; for others again sexuality even appears to be a clinical conception of analytic practice itself within the transference–counter-transference relationship.

Whatever value one may give to these different perspectives, these concepts, they all tend to occlude the place of sexuality as a *somato-psychic universe: the libidinal basis of all sublimations as well as of the life and death impulses*—whether such views are manifested in the handling of the psychoanalytic process or in the Freudian metapsychology.

In a recent book, *The Many Faces of Eros* (1995, pp. 3–30) I was not seeking to add a new theoretical approach to the above perspectives, but simply to emphasize the *universality* of libidinal impulses—and to explore the thousand and one disguises through which our psychosexuality may be expressed. Following this line of thought I proposed, in the opening lines of this book, that human *sexuality is inherently traumatic and forces humankind to an eternal quest for solutions*. I shall briefly resume some of the leading notions in that work.

In taking as my starting point the dawn of psychic life, I emphasized that the first sensual encounter of the baby with the mother's body already gives rise to a multitude of psychic conflicts which originate from the inevitable clash between the infant's internal impulses and the constraints of external reality. At this phase of the baby's psychic existence erotic impulses are indistinguishable from sadistic ones; we might in fact call this phase the era of cannibalistic love. Along with this confusion we find one further indistinction—that between the baby's body and self and the body and self of the Other. The notion of "Another", as an Object or Place distinct from oneself and one's own psychic space, only comes into existence as a result of the inevitable frustrations that the new human being is bound to encounter and which are destined to arouse feelings of rage followed by a primitive form of depression that every nursling experiences.

Thus, we are not surprised to find, in the course of a psychoanalytic voyage, many traces of what we might term "archaic sexualities" in which feelings of love are scarcely distinguishable from those of hate. At the same time the tension that emanates from this early dichotomy is destined to form a vital substratum to all expressions of sexuality, erotism, and love in the adult to be.

Since the drives only become significant within the mother–nursling dyad which brings them into being, any attempt to disallow the space and the separate existence of the Other gives rise, in the future adult, to an incessant search for the lost illusory fusion.

To this eternal quest are added phantasies of vampirization, implosion and later, anguish in face of the danger of losing the feeling of one's subjective identity or one's bodily limits—all of which form an integral part of the psychic world of the infant. However, when adult sexuality is permeated with such archaic phantasies, sexual and love relations run the risk of being experienced as a threat of castration, of narcissistic annihilation or the menace of death itself. It is evident that should such terrors predominate, they will inevitably require "deviant" solutions in order to permit the individual to have access to sexual and love relationships.

Then, following the catastrophic discovery of otherness comes the equally traumatic revelation of the difference between the sexes. Incidentally, in this respect it is interesting to note that recent psychoanalytic research clearly demonstrates that, long before the oedipal crisis, the little child's discovery of anatomical sexual differences (usually around fifteen months of age) arouses considerable anxiety in children of both sexes (as reported by Roiphe & Galenson (1981) in their pioneering work into the genesis of the feeling of sexual identity). Thus, we learn that "that which does not resemble me", far from being a source of attraction or envy, arouses aversion and revulsion in the little girl as well as the little boy. (It would seem that human children are fundamentally racist!)

Coming now to the "primal scene" and the various troubling phantasies that the parents' sexuality is liable to evoke in their children, clinical observation and children's play both confirm that, prior to the phallic–oedipal psychic phase, this scene is imagined in every form of *pregenital* excitement such as phantasies of mutual devouring, or of urinary, faecal and anal-erotic or anal-sadistic exchanges. When these fundamental elements have failed to be integrated into adult genital eroticism, they in turn will require deviant solutions in order that the individual may have access to sexual and love relations in adulthood.

Then, at the oedipal phase, in both its homosexual and heterosexual dimensions, children are faced with multiple frustrations and impossible dreams—in particular the wish to belong to both sexes and to possess the genital organs of both mother and father (since these are usually taken to symbolize the parents and their magical gifts). Grafted on to these envious wishes there is also the desire to possess both parents sexually. This psychosexual phase of development is further complicated by the fact that the homosexual oedipal constellation always has a double aim: first there is the wish *to sexually possess the same-sex parent* and second the equally strong wish *to be the opposite-sex parent*; this double longing implies, therefore, the desire to possess all the prerogatives and magical powers attributed in phantasy to each parent. These two homosexual aims, both complementary and contradictory, coexist in the psychosexual domain of every child, and moreover, persist in the unconscious of every adult as clinical observation constantly confirms (provided the psychoanalytic voyage continues sufficiently to allow such fantasies of desire to come to the surface and thereby find verbal expression).

The obligation to relinquish these instinctual bisexual aims requires a mourning process that is not accomplished with ease. Perhaps one of humankind's most scandalous narcissistic wounds for its megalomaniac childhood desires is inflicted by the necessity to accept our inescapable *monosexuality*.

Then in parallel with the oedipal crisis, every child must manage to identify itself as either "masculine" or "feminine". In order to be in conformity with his or her sense of core gender identity, he or she must now acquire a sexual identity, which, like one's anatomical identity, is not attained without a struggle. (Here I would like to underline that Freud, who was constantly preoccupied with the difficulties facing the girl-child on the path to attaining adult femininity, leaves us to suppose, by his silence in this respect, that the attainment of adult masculinity is an effortless achievement—which is far from being the case, as every analyst knows!)

To sum up, we can assuredly propose that the attainment of these two fundamental identities, our sense of gender identity as well as our sense of sexual identity, are in no way transmitted by biological inheritance; these psychic constructions are transmitted, first of all, by the discourse of our parents along with the important transmissions stemming from the biparental unconscious. To this, of course, is added the input of the socio-cultural discourse of which the parents are themselves an emanation, concerning the sense of core gender and sexual identity.

Primary bisexuality

The above considerations lead us to further consideration of the universal bisexual wishes of infancy. The primary homosexuality of the little girl includes her wish to possess her mother sexually, to penetrate her vagina, enter her body, perhaps devour her, as a means to total possession of the mother and her magic powers, in a world from which all men are excluded. But her phantasies also include the wish to be a man like her father, to have his genital organs and thus come into possession of all the power and qualities she attributes to him and thereby play, in the life of her mother, the role of the father.

As for the little boy, he imagines himself as his father's sexual partner, phantasizing that he incorporates orally or anally his father's penis and thus, by possessing his genital organs and his privileges, he will himself "become a man". But this same little boy will also be invaded by the wish to take his mother's place in sexual relations—and psychotherapeutic work with children frequently reveals the desire on the part of the little boy that the father would place a baby in his own inner space. Thus, he dreams not only of being penetrated by his father as he imagines his mother to be and of receiving a baby in his own inner space, but he also has phantasies of penetrating his father as well.

It is evident that these processes of identificatory incorporation imply, for both sexes, a measure of destruction of the other, with the concomitant risk of provoking feelings of guilt and depression. It is therefore quasi inevitable that a constellation of complex emotions will be grafted onto these universal bisexual wishes, and that the desires mobilized by the primary homosexualities of both sexes will bear the imprint of narcissistic injury and will run the risk of being infiltrated by feelings of envy and aggressivity towards both parents. Thus, it is understandable that the homosexual components of human sexuality run the risk of being marked by powerful and conflictual affects, both positive and negative.

Of course these same reflections may be applied to the hetero-sexual components of psychosexuality since it is evident that these are in no way lacking in negative feelings of hate, envy, and destructivity, but they encounter less obstacles than those derived from the homosexual strata because of the predominantly hetero-sexual social discourse—a factor of psychic stress that is empha-sized by many gay and lesbian analysands.

This brings to mind a memory recounted by a gay analysand in a recent session. A man in his mid-thirties, a successful artist who assumes his sexual orientation without difficulty, had come into analysis because of multiple phobias, including a constant preoccu-pation with his appearance. He recalled recently his first experience of smoking marijuana when he was sixteen. Invited by some class-mates to enjoy this new experience, after smoking his joint he was suddenly invaded by a sensation that his whole body and being had become "monstrous"; his terror was such that he left his friends precipitately and ran from one bar to another, seeking his image in a mirror to see if he had changed into a monster. He vividly remem-bered the horror of gazing into one mirror after another to see whether he could still recognize himself. He asked in one session if this was the indication of a psychotic core; when I asked what he thought might be crazy within himself he said that he had no sexual interest in girls from as far back as he could remember, whereas his adolescent comrades talked about nothing else. I then asked him whether he thought the "monstrous image" might have been associated with a fear of being revealed as homosexual. This led him to recount, for the first time, how deeply troubled he had been throughout his adolescence by his constant preoccu-pation with homosexual fantasies and desires and the conviction that if his family or friends discovered this he would have to commit suicide. His associations then allowed me to link these terrors with a recent nightmare in which he "had touched a sick person and had contracted leprosy". We were able from then on to better understand his persistent terror concerning his appearance, his constant fear of discovering skin cancers, eczema, and similar allergies that would affect his appearance. Such a moving session conveys in an exemplary way the anguish that a certain number of homosexual analysands have experienced in childhood and adolescence.

The primary homosexual wishes of all children, in their dual version—the wish to possess the same-sex parent and the wish to be the opposite-sex parent—also demand solutions in the sexuality of the adult-to-be. There are, of course, innumerable potential paths through which this universal libidinal current may find expression and consequently be integrated into the psychosexual organization. Although these drives may give rise to neurotic suffering or psychotic anxiety they may just as readily become a factor of psychic enrichment. The bisexual substratum of human beings serves not only to enrich and stabilize love and social relationships, it also furnishes one of the elements apt to stimulate creative activity (although it must be admitted that this same dimension may be the source of creative blockage if unconscious bisexual wishes are a source of conflict or interdiction!).

Before leaving this brief survey of the evolution of human sexuality I would like to open a parenthesis regarding those children destined to seek transsexualization in adulthood. Recent psychoanalytic research leads us to understand that in the majority of cases this desire is not the expression of a psychotic wish, as some colleagues have suggested. The transsexual's desire (like that of all children) is the determination to be in conformity with the mother's wish; in consequence, such individuals will seek, throughout childhood and adolescence, the means by which sexual reassignment may be attained in order to render their anatomical sex in conformity with the persistent conviction of belonging psychically to the opposite sex. This determination is basically the expression of the profound wish to exist as a sexual being in the eyes of the mother (and frequently in the father's eyes also). A question of *psychic survival!* Psychically we are not born "male" or "female" but we become so according to what is authorized by the fears and wishes transmitted by the biparental unconscious, as well as the family and social discourse that continues throughout infancy and adolescence.

In short, in order to attain a satisfactory sexual and love life many individuals, faced with biparental fears and wishes, as well as frightening archaic, pregenital, and bisexual phantasies, find themselves obliged to invent the means by which anguished feelings of castration, annihilation, confused sexual identity, emptiness, and internal deadness may be transformed through erotic creations.

Is the label "perversion" adequate to describe these ingenuous and intricate inventions of the distressed and confused child hidden within the adult? I vividly recall, during my years of psychoanalytic training, that all these solutions, including the homosexualities, were defined by our teachers as "deviations from the (so-called) normal sexual act, and any such deviation was indelibly marked as a *sexual perversion* contrived by a *pervert*. However, the concept of "deviation" inevitably implies a "norm"—the notion of a drive with pre-formed qualities and ways of expression which, clearly, does not exist in human beings.

I still remember my surprise, as a young and inexperienced analyst during my first years in practice, at listening to certain analysands recounting that they had once again made love and that it had been more or less successful, only to learn some months later that in order to arrive at this comparative success one had to attach his partner to the bed with cords, whereas another required his lover to whip him on the buttocks or urinate upon him, in order to achieve orgasmic pleasure.

In fact I was to discover that the majority of my analysands who had, so to speak, *reinvented* the primal scene (as compared with its orthodox representation), regarded their sexual activites and object choices as being totally in accordance with their representation of themselves and in conformity with their erotic wishes, in spite of individuals, or society as a whole, who might judge their form of sexuality and object choice as "perverse" and therefore wrong. Thus, I came slowly to realize that the specific form of any given individual's sexual predilection can only be considered as a clinical problem in search of a solution to the extent that the analysand's sexuality creates conflict and psychic suffering.

I would like to emphasize at this point a *counter-transference hazard* of a conformist nature regarding deviant sexual practices. The polymorphous nature of adult sexuality has of course no need to be recalled. Our analysands describe an infinite variety of erotic scenarios, fetishistic accoutrements and disguises, sadomasochistic games and so on, that are regarded as private areas in their love lives and are not experienced as compulsive, nor indispensable as a means to sexual gratification. If some of our analysands can only attain a satisfactory erotic exchange by means of fetishist or sado-masochisitc scenarios, even though we might wish them a less constrained love life, we have no justifiable reason to believe that these individuals should abandon their sexual practices simply because we allow ourselves to judge their unorthodox sexualities as symptomatic. Most individuals experience their erotic acts and object choices as being in conformity with their desires, whether or not they are judged by others as "perverse". I reiterate the notion that sexual preferences only become a problem requiring analysis to the extent that they are not in conformity with the ego ideal of the individual in question and therefore become a source of psychic suffering. (An exception must be made here for those sexualities that are condemned by the law. I shall deal with this aspect later.)

With regard to homosexual orientations, there are additional counter-transference complications stemming from a heterosexist attitude revealed by a certain number of analysts, with the consequent risk of deafening their understanding of their patients' needs. (The same might also be said of a "homosexist" counter-transference evidenced by certain gay and lesbian analysts.) Whatever the personal predilections of the analyst may be, it is not for her or him to decide that their homosexual analysands would benefit by becoming heterosexual—or vice versa. It is true that a certain number of gay and lesbian patients discover, in the course of their analytic voyage, that they are "latent heterosexuals" and that hitherto unconscious terrors have rendered heterosexual relationships impossible. But this represents a very small minority; the majority of homosexuals, male or female, have no wish to relinquish their sexual orientation and become heterosexuals—any more than the average heterosexual would wish to become homosexual—and we can only approve of this standpoint in recognizing that one's sexual predilections and object choices are a vital substratum not only to one's feeling of sexual identity but also to that of subjective identity.

The only sexual predilections that I would qualify as "perverse" are limited to certain forms *of relationship* to the other—notably, sexual acts that do *not take into account the needs or desires of the partner*, such as sexual child abuse, rape, exhibitionism, and voyeurism, or necrophilia (frequently preceded by murder of the chosen partner). As you have probably realized, these sexual acts are identical with those condemned by law in the Occident.

Neosexualities

I come finally to what I have called the "neosexualities". This term is not a concept but rather a certain way of listening to our analysands as they describe and explore their sexual lives. After lengthy cogitation over the underlying significance of those acts and choices that are distinguishable from what might be termed the homosexual "norm", or the heterosexual "norm", with years of clinical observation I have came to understand that these unusual scenarios serve not only to repair fractures in the feelings of subjective and sexual identity in the individuals concerned, but also protect their internal objects from feelings of unconscious hate and destructivity toward them (in part linked to un-elaborated oral and anal drives characteristic of infantile incorporative and excorporative libidinal drives).

Thanks to the miraculous discovery of a neosexual creation, that which formerly appeared senseless becomes significant and a sense of psychic vitality prevails, even if only punctually, over the feelings of inner deadness. These same conflicts could have found less felicitous solutions in the form of psychotic or psychopathic modes of expression. In spite of the exigent conditions, along with the compulsivity and anguished affects that often accompany these unusual scenarios, their aim of *self-cure* in the face of menacing neurotic and psychotic conflict, leads us to conclude that *erotisation* is a powerful way of overcoming early psychic trauma, thus allowing Eros to triumph over Thanatos.

To resume the above considerations, I have proposed that "neosexuals", whether of homosexual or heterosexual orientation, have been compelled to reinvent sexual erotism and love relations and that the obligation to create such solutions is frequently allied to silent biparental transmissions or to erroneous communications concerning sexual identity, adult sexuality and the notions of what is the substance of "femininity" and "masculinity". Sometimes these parental (and often transgenerational) transmissions have led to the belief that all sexuality is forever forbidden. The construction of these new primal scenes therefore represents the best solution that the child of the past was able to find in the face of fear, confusion, and mental pain linked to every libidinal urge. Also it stands to reason that the solutions that have been found tend to last throughout the individual's lifetime.

Apart from the desires and anxieties of parents, we frequently discover in addition a series of traumatic events in childhood: stories of sexual abuse, the sudden disappearance of a parent due to abandonment or death, or again, experiences of hospitalization that the child had to undergo. In this latter respect I am reminded of certain sexual practices that are current today, such as "piercing" in which a ring is inserted into the glans penis, the clitoris, the navel, or the breasts. Robert Stoller, the renowned researcher into the field of sexual deviations, when he expressed the wish to better understand these latter-day deviations of a masochistic order was subsequently invited to speak to the members of an exclusive Club in Los Angeles reserved for men and women who sought partners for "S and M" practices. Many of the club members were highly cooperative with Stoller's (1991) research project and accepted the invitation to discuss at length their sexual practices and their understanding of their erotic proclivities. To his astonishment, Stoller learned that a considerable number of those who sought to be pierced or cut as an erotic turn-on had in childhood been hospitalized for considerable periods of time for serious, life-threatening illnesses, and had had, in consequence, to submit to continual injections and other painful piercing treatments in order to save their lives. It would seem that, separated from their parents, for many of these children the doctor or nurse with the needle came to represent reassuring parental figures, particularly since they usually showed great affection to their little charges and explained to them that the needles or the cutting of their skin were necessary to enable them to get better and one day to go home. This revealing observation appears to demonstrate that the capacity to *eroticize* terrifying or torturing experiences may well have saved these children from more tragic outcomes such as a psychotic, instead of a neosexual solution.

The capacity to eroticize unbearable experiences brings to my mind two analysands who demonstrated this strategy; the first was a talented French author who sought analysis because of writer's block and, after a year of intensive analytic work, revealed for the first time that he needed to seek out sexual partners who would agree during their love-making to strangle him almost to the point of suffocation. Just before losing consciousness he would give a signal to the girlfriend to stop the strangling and this very gesture was sufficient to provoke an ejaculation. In the slow reconstruction of his childhood he recounted memories of extreme anxiety and suffocation due to attacks of asthma and that these occurred regularly while he was being closely held by his adoring mother. He recounted also that she would frequently lie on top of him in an attempt to subdue an asthmatic attack. In reconstructing what he interpreted as his mother's desire to fuse with him, he was eventually able to perceive the similarity with his erotic scenario. One day he admitted : "Yes indeed, it's exactly the same exciting and death-dealing feeling that I lived through continually with my mother— but the big difference is that now *I am the one who is in charge*. It is I who command the suffocation and I who stop it when the excitement and the terror become too strong."

The other is the case of a woman psychiatrist in her forties who had been a constantly over-stimulated child due to sexual games throughout her infancy, instigated by both her father and her older brother. In her search for a lover capable of satisfying her sexual demands she complained that they all fell asleep after love-making whereas she, although she experienced an orgasmic climax, remained desperately desirous of further gratification and, in her inability to sleep because of her frustrated longing, would wake up her lovers and beg for a continuation of their love-making. Although she felt that her sexuality was, in a certain sense, addictive she, like the male patient, also proposed that her erotic conditions were satisfactory since *she* was now the one to control the constant demand for sexual stimulation.

These vignettes exemplify the imperious need in certain adults to make use of complex erotic enactments in an attempt to find solutions to traumatic events of the past linked to overwhelming sexual excitement or fear.

Once again we must recognize that when our analysands recount these complicated or unusual conditions for making love with consenting partners, although their accounts will lead us to search for the hidden significance of such scenarios, if these neo-sexualities cause no suffering to either partner and are not felt to be unduly compulsive, we have no reason to lead such analysands to envisage other erotic aims because of our personal value judgements. If such is our ambition it is our problem and not theirs!

This leads me to underline another aspect of today's sexual patterns: the sexual liberation over the last thirty years has had the effect, among others, of allowing us to observe that core gender and sexual identity, far from being fixed entities in the psychosexual organization are, on the contrary, frequently fluctuating. It is perhaps inaccurate to suppose that a given individual is necessarily either "heterosexual" *or* "homosexual". When a heterosexual analysand recounts homosexual dreams and fantasies or engages in occasional homosexual encounters, the analyst might, unawares, readily adopt a heterosexist attitude with a consequent risk of blocking his or her ability to follow and understand the fluctuations in sexual desire and orientation, just as another may remain deaf to similar fluctuations in gay and lesbian analysands who may also reveal hidden phantasies or avowed leanings toward heterosexual encounters.

In conclusion, having proposed that human sexuality is fundamentally traumatic from the dawn of psychic life and filled with problems and pitfalls thereafter, in spite of the difficulty in being a human subject, as well as being gendered and sexed with the subsequent imperious need to find solutions to the complexities of love relations, may I add that these dimensions nevertheless contribute importance and intensity to humankind's erotic love life. Perhaps the thousand and one solutions to the solicitations of Eros might all be envisaged as a symptomatic compromise.

In that case, might one not propose that the totality of human sexuality consists, basically, of *neosexuality*?

References

Freud, S. (1905e) [1953]. Three essays on the theory of sexuality. *S.E.*, 7: 8. New York: Norton

McDougall, J. (1986) *Theatres of the Mind: Illusion and Truth on the Psychoanalytic Stage*. London: Free Association Books.

McDougall, J. (1995). *The Many Faces of Eros*. London: Free Association Books.

Roiphe, H. & Galenson, E. (1981). *Infantile Origins of Sexual Identity*. New York: International Universities Press.

Stoller, R. (1991). *Pain and Passion*. New York: Plenum.

CHAPTER NINE

Father makes a difference
The development of the son

Leena Klockars

The father and the fatherhood

T he word father evokes equally strong associations in our minds as the word mother. However, the mental images of father are clearly different from those of mother. The concept and tasks of motherhood are generally related to good care, nurturing, maternal love and mother's lap. The images of mother are usually related to an infant, a small child. Mother is the symbol and ideal of intimacy and love. The images of father are related to our well-being more distantly and in a broader sense. Father is the symbol and ideal of security and protection. We have the concepts of Fatherland, the Name of the Father, the Father in Heaven, Our Father. They are the foundations of our security. Perhaps because of the lack of close, concrete links, the power of the mental images and phantasies of fatherhood is even greater than in the case of motherhood.

When we talk about fatherhood, we immediately associate it with motherhood. We may, in fact, ask whether there is fatherhood without motherhood or whether fatherhood is always at the same time related to motherhood, as motherhood is always related to fatherhood. Motherhood is never actually unclear. Even when idealized, motherhood is always concrete, known, even felt. Mother and child have shared a bodily relationship for a long time, they have existed one inside the other, even sharing sensations. The child has always been part of the mother's body, and this contact continues at least during the time of nursing. The bodies of the father and the child have never been part of each other, the child has not been part of the father's body, although the child is the father's flesh and blood and carries his genes. Fatherhood is uncertain, even its physical connection and genotype have remained unknown until quite recently. Although fatherhood is, therefore, above all psychic and social, it is also experienced as strongly corporeal and inherited, even if not as internal or immediate.

The father of the child is always on the mother's mind as well, as good or bad, desired or detested, but always there on her mind when she takes care of her child. In that way, the father is present inside the mother even during the nine months of pregnancy, together with the foetus. And through the mother's acts of nursing and love, the image of the father, too, is mediated to the child. In this way, the earliest fatherhood is mediated to the child through the mother, through mental images of the mother.

Fatherhood is culturally bound and the status and significance of fatherhood vary from one culture and age to the other. In recent Western culture, in particular, the functions of the mother and the father have approached each other and the father, too, has become associated with care giving and nurturing. The tasks of the father and the mother have been conceived as different partly because of the difference in the bodily contact related to the birth of the child. The relationship with the mother is usually regarded as dyadic or twofold, whereas the relationship with the father is triadic or threefold. The mother carries the baby in her womb, she tempts the baby away from autoeroticism to alloeroticism, to a shared life. The mother nurses the child, nurtures her, takes care of him, and shows her tenderness, sensuality, closeness and, therefore, the basics of physical and psychic love as well. Tähkä (1993) notes that our most highly developed feelings always have a feminine quality. The father's job is to beget the child, take care of his pregnant female, support the mother during her pregnancy, safeguard her labour, support her nursing, help her take care of the child, and create a safe shelter for the mother–baby couple. At first, the father is mostly in touch with the child via the mother. As the baby grows, the father's significance even as a direct contact with the child increases and the father creates his own dyadic relationship with the baby. The significance of the father changes from the supporter of the contact between the mother–baby couple first into the creator of a similar relationship and later into one who differentiates the mother-baby couple from each other.

The father introduces distinction, difference, separation and externality into the child's world. Infant observations make it apparent that fathers take care of their children differently from mothers, even when they perform similar care-taking measures. Fathers do the same things in a different way. Fathers take care of the child and play with the child differently, because they are different. They have a different size, their face, hands, speech, skin, and entire appearance are different from mothers'. The father tempts the child to a relationship that is different, new, and novel. The father tempts the child away from the symbiotic and dyadic relationship with the mother towards a different kind of dyadic relationship, away from sharing by bodily interiority towards sharing at an external and psychic level.

The birth of fatherhood

It is difficult to know when a man's fatherhood begins. Does it begin when the man's child distinguishes him and experiences him as his father or does it begin when the child is born or when his wife becomes pregnant, or even when the man finds the woman who will be the mother of his children? Or does fatherhood begin in the first images of copulation in a young man's mind, or even from his first ejaculation, or has fatherhood already begun to live in the son's mind in his early identification with his father, or perhaps even in the early stage of falling in love with his mother? Does fatherhood begin to live in the boy's mind when the love relationship between his mother and father is revealed to him, from the oedipal relationship with his parents? The mental images of fatherhood apparently have dyadic, triadic, and oedipal roots.

The roots of fatherhood run deep. Not to speak of the roots that reach from the nature of fatherhood unto the previous generation, and even unto the third and forth generation. When we study the family history of Oedipus, we note that Oedipus was a son who suffered from the lack of a father in the fifth generation already, and who damned his own sons to death, so that they killed each other and brought the line to an end. The patterns of fatherhood continue.

A man has many different reasons to wish to become a father. A man has a body, a penis, and sperm that loudly announce their desire to penetrate and impregnate, and he has a phallic desire to man, conquer, possess, and multiply. A man also has a desire to love and share his life with a woman, get a child with her and thus see his own manhood reproduced and continued. A man has a desire for a new object, a mental image of the child as a reciprocal human being and contact. A man has had his own childhood, which is why he knows what it is like and wants to re-experience and recreate a new father–child relationship, similar to, or perhaps better than, the one he had with his own father. A man has generativity, a desire to give something good to a child, to a future generation, he has a desire to take care and foster the continuity of life. A man has many desires.

A man also has fears about becoming a father. A man's fatherhood does not have the same gradually strengthening bodily basis as a woman's motherhood does. Fatherhood begins more suddenly than motherhood. Although a man is proud of his capability of impregnating a woman and begetting children, he also has to experience incapacity and envy towards motherhood. Kestenberg (1970) has described how a very small boy already wishes to have children. The future father may be afraid of losing his freedom or about the burden and responsibility of taking care of his child. Society does not protect fatherhood the same way as it protects motherhood. The burden of motherhood is accepted and it is taken into account, whereas the burden and responsibility of fatherhood are not generally discussed—even paternity leave is there to help the mother. Fatherhood is considered self-sufficient and powerful, but perhaps at the same time secondary.

At the psychic level, however, the most fearful thing is often the loss of the wife–woman for the sake of the mother–woman. Before the child the man has received attention and care from his wife that after the birth of the child become entirely directed to the new-born baby, and the man may well be left without them. A reciprocal two-fold relationship becomes a triangular relationship, where mother and child form a strong couple, unavoidably leaving the father outside in many ways. The relations between the three parties are not symmetrical, but different and unequal. The mother is the queen of needs, she is of vital importance to the baby and thus the man is the one who is left outside. Every new father has an oedipal experience in his childhood phantasies and memory images, the love of a little boy for his mother and the desire to be the most beloved person in the world for the mother. He has been frustrated in this wish and left outside his mother's desire, as mother has wanted to have a grown man by her side. In other words, the father has at some time, a long time ago, already been rejected by his mother–woman. And now, as a brand-new father he is again rejected by a woman, this time his wife–woman, and it is the baby that receives the breasts and tenderness of the wife–mother–woman. The father is left waiting for the moment when the mother will turn away from the baby back towards him and become a woman for him. Depending on the experience of the oedipal situation—and his other experiences of rejection, too—a man relates to the new situation in accordance with his past and his wishes. To remain separate and outside, the third party, perhaps even lonely, is a man's destiny, while interiority, dependence, and sharing are a woman's. Hägglund & Hägglund (1985, p. 111) talk about how a man's envy of the child-bearing mother is directed at his own wife, whom the future father may want to deprive of the reproductive joy and happiness of the mother–child relationship and get it himself. An unconscious wish to destroy the child is awakened in the man, who experiences the child as the mother's achievement. According to Hägglund and Hägglund, a man transfers this envy problem from one developmental phase to another, from envy between wife and husband to envy between father and son.

An infant reacts differently to its mother and its father. An infant reacts to its father in a very special way, differently from anyone else, and the father seems to have a highly special status in the small child's mind. Although the child's relationship with the father develops by the side of the mother–child relationship and has many similar, dyadic, and even symbiotic, characteristics, something highly different and significant seems to be involved in relation to the father. The relationship with the mother seems easier to take for granted, and it is familiar in its corporeality. The relationship with the father is strange and different, it involves curiosity and attraction, but at the same time fear and authority, too.

The importance and tasks of the father

We consider it the mother's task to take care of the small baby and we talk about the motherly functions. Similarly, we may talk about the father's tasks and the fatherly functions (Tähkä, 1993). Lacan (1964) talks about "the Law of the Father". The father's function is the name of the activity separating from the mother; the father then sets about to fulfil this function as a person. A father who wants to have too motherly a relationship with his child, one that is similar to the mother's relationship with the child, makes it more difficult for the child to see differences and feel limitations and protection. The Law of the Father may appear without an actual external father (Davids, 2002, Fonagy & Target, 1995), because the Law of the Father develops as an internal process as the mental image of the all-satisfying mother broadens in the child's mind to include the idea of an unsatisfying mother. When this happens, the mother, who does not always satisfy, assumes the task of taking care of the Law of the Father, the fatherly function, by helping the child bear her impulses, frustration, and delayed satisfaction. In other words, the actual absence of the father does not as such prevent the internal father and the Law of the Father from appearing, but it does make the process more difficult and thereby creates emotional and cognitive problems (Davids, 2002). By the side of and with the help of the father's authoritarian and limit-setting functions, the father tempts the child to a new world of its own, outside the mother's world. The child's ability to receive the father and the Law of the Father depends on the mother's ability to let the father come, to let him be different and to respect the difference of the father.

Separation from the mother is threatening to the baby. The mother's presence feels good and her absence feels frightening, everything that takes the mother's presence away is bad. At first, separation, difference and strangeness become bad things.

Therefore, even the father has to receive and adopt separation, strangeness, badness, and otherness as his characteristics by being different from the mother. Father is of Another Kind. A good father will bear, tolerate, and understand this, he will not try to be similar to the mother and he will not try to be Number One for the child or compete with motherhood. In this way, the father protects the child's mental image of a good, satisfying mother; the father protects the mother–child dyad. McDougall (1989) points out that the father's contribution as a person who takes care of the mother and satisfies the mother's emotional, narcissistic, and sexual needs is significant. This helps in that the mother does not need to find all her own satisfaction from taking care of her baby, but she can devote herself to taking care of the baby's needs. In this case, the baby is not left with the impossible task of satisfying the mother's needs. When the father acts as a symbol of strangeness, he accepts the role of a limit setter, and the Law of the Father becomes formulated for the child. The Law of the Father sets limits, but a law that does not set limits does not protect, either, as Lacan puts it. The Law of the Father protects the child. Although the Law of the Father breaks the child's mental image of a fully satisfying and possessed mother, it also sets the child free of his symbiosis with the mother and dyadic relationship with the mother. The child is allowed and, indeed, forced, to look outside the dyad to find new sources of satisfaction. Many researchers (e.g., Blos, 1985; Bollas, 2000; Campell, 1995; Fonagy & Target, 1995; Mahler et al., 1975; Stoller, 1979; Tähkä; 1993) consider it the father's task to help the child separate herself from the mother. And, of course, the mother to separate herself from the child.

At the beginning, the mother was the one who satisfied the baby, she was all-powerful, omnipotent, to the child. In spite of the symbiotic and dyadic relationship, the satisfaction has not been equal; the child does not fully satisfy the mother, who needs some other satisfaction as well. She needs the father. The father–man satisfies the mother, he is omnipotent in relation to the mother, i.e., he is the omnipotent to the omnipotent, the phallus. But this omnipotent father is in his turn satisfied by the mother. In other words, the omnipotent mother and omnipotent father are the real couple, the real dyad, and the baby is only the product of the couple's relationship, and not its creator. Although the baby is at first in a dyadic relationship with both mother and father, the baby remains outside their original, true dyad, in a triadic relationship with his parents. At the same time, the father becomes in the child's mind a mighty person by the side of the mother, the object of mother's love and desire, the idealized father.

In normal development, the first object of a daughter or son is the omnipotent, satisfying mother, who is bodily familiar to the child and takes care of his or her needs. Later, as the daughter develops (e.g. Klockars & Sirola, 2001), she changes the father into the object of her love and adopts the mother as her object of identification. For the son, the mother remains an object of love forever, though the mother is later abandoned during adolescence and the son chooses as the object of his love someone outside the family, different from the mother and from the son's internal image of the mother.

The parents take care of their child differently depending on whether the child is a boy or a girl. The parents also take different attitudes to a daughter and a son. During the so-called mirroring stage that is part of the child's development (e.g. Tähkä, 1993) the child finds his or her self in the parents' mirroring gaze. Mothers, for example, have been able to describe how they find it impossible to nurse their new-born child unless they know whether it is a boy or a girl. In this way, the child's identification with its gender begins at birth, as the parents unconsciously treat them as either girls or boys. Identification with one's own gender is therefore a consequence of through what kind of eyes the parents look at their child. Corporeality and bodily experiences naturally have an important role in sexual identification. Later, identification is greatly strengthened by the child's own observations of sex differences. This, however, only begins around the age of eighteen months, at which stage gender identity has already developed quite far.

The son's route towards the father

There are many reasons that awaken the desire for men's world in a little boy. To begin with, mother has always looked at her son as a boy and mirrored in her gaze masculinity and the boy's similarity to the father—man, thereby pushing the boy towards the world of the father. The mother's mental images of the son's father are mediated to the son ever since infancy. The mother's mental images of masculinity include the mother's mental images of other men as well: her own father, her brothers, earlier love relationships and all other men she has admired or detested. The status and value, idealization or nullification of men are visible in the mother's eyes and mediated by her images. The uniformity of the mother's images of men makes the boy's identification with men easier, although more binding, while their mutual difference makes it more difficult but perhaps also more versatile.

Second, a little boy may at a very early stage realize his mother's need and longing for another person, her incompleteness and insufficiency, a lack that the boy has been unable to fulfil. The mother's mental images of her own omnipotence or insufficiency have an important influence in the boy's conception of women. The mother's and woman's strength or weakness becomes mediated in this way. At the same time, the father–man's ability to be desired and needed or useless and insignificant also becomes transferred.

Third, when the little boy loves his mother he realizes the difference of his mother's love for him and for the father. The mother looks at the father in a different way. Although the mother brings pleasure to the child in many ways, she is usually careful not to bring too much pleasure and tensions in the area of the child's sexuality. The boy very early begins to differentiate different satisfactions, different relationships; he begins to see that the relationship between the mother and the father–man is different from his own relationship to his mother and father.

Fourth, the little boy is aided in this process by the father's presence, the attractiveness of the father–man and his desire and ability to be the object of idealization, the desirability of men's world. The father's admiring gaze mirrors the son's future as a man. The father becomes a rescue from the attractiveness of the mother and more attractive than the mother.

Fifth, the son experiences that he is bodily separate and different from the mother and as he continues to observe his environment he begins to take interest in what is new, external, and, until then, strange. The son is curious and reaches towards new sensations and experiences, and towards the father and the father–man too. While he searches for an explanation for his strangeness and difference, he finds the father–man both in his mental world and, usually, as a person.

The son's desire to join his father in men's world is largely awakened on the basis of the feelings that the parents (and nurturing grown-ups) direct at their son, both consciously and unconsciously. The mental worlds of the parents and their conceptions are mirrored and mediated to the son, who creates his own self and identity with the help of various internalization processes. The internalization processes describe the way in which the son, after the differentiation of the self and object images, is at first able to identify with the functions that the father represents (functionally selective identifications, Tähkä, 1993); after the individualization of self and object, he becomes able to identify with the father's admirable characteristics (judgementally selective identifications, Tähkä, 1993); later, the son strives further to share his emotional experience with the father (informative identification, Tähkä, 1993). The boy grows up to be a man by identifying with father–men.

The oedipal junction

The development of object relationships

The early *dyadic* relationship between father and son develops partly on the basis of the father's own early mental and memory images and partly through the mother on the basis of the mother's mental images of men, particularly in the way in which the mother encourages and allows time shared together by father and son in their masculine world. This early dyadic world of the son's relationship with his father includes a great deal of what exists in the son's relationship with his mother, but is yet essentially different, because the father is different. In this dyadic relationship the son absorbs the father's way of being in a relationship with his son, the father's functions, with the help of identification. According to Tähkä (1993), it seems to be important that the father, at least for some time, is also a dyadic, conflict-free love object to the son, because this facilitates identification. Simply because of his separateness and difference from the mother, the father becomes an admired and idealized identification object, and physical resemblance adds to the desire for identification. The mother still remains an idealized love object. The world of the parents' mutual difference, separateness, lacks, various interactive relationships, and sex differences starts in the child the development of thinking and symbol formation processes. The son is forced in his mind to process the difference between his mother and his father, the various relationships, lacks, and needs. He learns and is forced to make comparisons. What is essential is that the relationships with the mother and the father are the first and most central dyadic relationships and that they are different kinds of dyadic relationships and help the child to understand differences. It is also essential that these relationships are dyadic from the son's point of view, but not from the mother´s or father's. When the mother looks at her son, she always has the father in her mind, as the father has the mother, which is why, from their point of view, their relationships with the son are triadic from the start. In this way, the parents lead the son into a triadic world by reflecting out their own mental images.

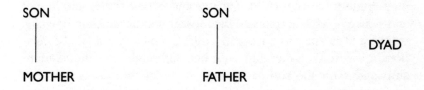

A *triadic*, threefold relationship between son, father and mother begins to develop when the son starts to build in mental images of the fact that these two most important people to him have actually allied with each other. This happens at around the age of eighteen months (Abelin, 1975). However, the child understands even earlier, at about the age of nine months (Abelin, 1975), that the parents somehow belong together and sleep in the same bed, for example. From the point of view of the formation of the thinking process and symbolization, it is crucial that such differences between these complex interactive networks and generations appear. Piaget (1947) talked about the egocentric child, who is unable to see herself as an outsider and is only able to comprehend her relationship and status with her parents with the help of the parents' mirroring contact. Fonagy and Target (1995) and Target and Fonagy (2002) stress the fact that the child does not perceive only the father's representation of the child in the father's mind, but also, specifically, the father's representation of the child in relation to the mother. What is essential here is how a third viewer, the second object in the child's life, the father, helps to represent the relationship between the other two with his perception and in this way represents the relationship first in his mind and by doing that helps the child to internalize it and to make a representation of it. According to the writers, the relationships cannot be represented in the mind unless there is some external element, so that the relationship develops into a second-order representation that promotes abstract thinking. The parents' mirroring contact is based on their own memory and mental images of their own triadic relationships with their parents. The parents' own experience and understanding of the differences between generations date back to their childhood and become visible in their attitudes to their own child. The transfer from a dyad to a triad has been either smooth or painful to them at its time and it is through the saturation of these experiences that they guide their own child. Fonagy and Target (1995) and Target and Fonagy (2002) emphasize the mother's importance in how she wants, and is able, to allow the child to enter into a triadic relationship with his father and with her. Although a triadic relationship opens for the son at the age of under two years, the true understanding and mastery of the triadic relationship only becomes possible much later. According to Tähkä (1993), a triad may become experienced only when additional internalizations that take place with the help of judgementally selective and informative identifications have made it possible. However, in infant observations, infants of only four or five months of age have already been observed to be capable of relationships of the triadic type (Fonagy & Target, 1995, Stern, 1995; Target & Fonagy, 2002,). The triadic relationship is a relationship between the son and his two beloved and idealized parents, and as such it does not yet involve competition or ambivalence in relation to anyone. From the point of view of the son, it is a family idyll, shared by all of them. There is room for everyone in the same bed, the boy feels, as long as he himself can be in the middle. The formation of a triadic relationship is important and does not yet mean the same thing as an actual oedipal situation (Burgner, 1985). As with dyadic relationships, there may also be several different kinds of triadic relationships in the son's life; what is essential, however, is that the triadic relationship that makes the deepest impact is the one where the two most important people to the son form a triad with him.

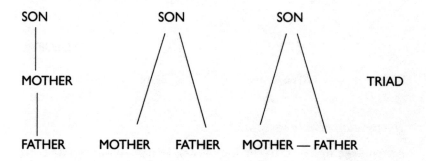

SON   SON   SON

MOTHER   TRIAD

FATHER   MOTHER   FATHER   MOTHER — FATHER

An *oedipal* relationship, the oedipal truth, is revealed to the son when he realizes that there is not actually room for all of them in the same bed in the same way, because mother and father have something that he does not have, they have a special sexual relationship with each other. It is not just that he is small and there is a difference between generations, but there is the love and sexual relationship between his parents and he is not part of it. Although the parents, particularly the mother, have satisfied the son's needs in virtually every other sense, they have not satisfied his sexually sensual needs. And yet mother and father offer that pleasure to each other, which is truly an experience of injustice and a shock to the son. The son's own gradual bodily development forces him to transfer his mental image of instinctual pressures, sexuality, and bodily sensations to the relationship between his parents. These primal scene phantasies, the son's mental images of the nature of sexual love, begin to take form at this stage. The son's whole world changes from an egocentric, satisfactory idyll into the multi-dimensionality of reality. The sexuality between the parents is both scary and desirable. The reformulation of object relations, the strong increase in sexual impulses and the development of the thinking and symbol formation processes form a junction, an oedipal junction, and the rails that arrive there and depart from there change the son's world. What is essential in an oedipal triadic relationship is the entrance of the parents' mutual sexuality into the son's world of ideas, or the existence of two different sexes and two different generations.

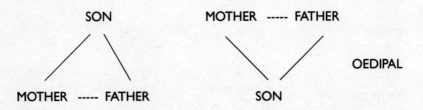

The development of sexuality

Around the age of three or four years, sexual sensations and the penis become central to the boy (Bollas, 2000; Kestenberg, 1970). There are neurological, bodily, and psychic developmental reasons for this. Sensations in the genital area become stronger and the boy will understand the central role of the penis in sexual difference and identification with a man. Sexual sensations become important and central and yet, judging from the reactions of the parents and the environment, confusingly forbidden and shameful at the same time. The penis brings great joy and pride, the boy touches it and feels it a great deal and is able to bring about the exciting and plea-surable erection of the penis by himself. The boy manifests huge pride after learning to pee in a standing position and later when he can pee very far, almost as far as his father and his friends, and certainly farther than girls and women. In this phallic–narcissistic phase, the penis brings great pride, boasting, and self-confidence. At this stage, too, deep fear is felt at the idea that the penis might be lost or injured. The importance of the penis to the boy lies largely in other things than gender or sexuality. In the boy's world, the penis means manliness, father's strength and activity. Fathers are different and do things differently from mothers, because their anatomy is different. Gender is an essential part of our identity, not only a part of our sexuality. The existence of the penis is an indica-tion of activity and masculinity and its loss would mean in the boy's mental images passivity, submission, and lack of strength, even castration. Later, during sexual maturity, the fact that it is the penis that penetrates the vagina and not vice versa concretely proves that the penis–man inevitably has a more active nature than the vagina–woman, who receives. (Davids, 2002).

The thinking and symbolization process

The child's thinking develops at the same time as his object relations and sexuality, and undergoes a tremendous change during the first three years of his life. As a process it is, of course, largely part of the neurological development of the brain. The child's linguistic development proceeds at the same time. Memory develops more slowly. The so-called implicit or bodily memory is functional right from birth, and causes the fact that a person can remember by his body and senses, although he is not able to bring his memory to words. It is only at the age of three or so that the development of so-called explicit memory makes it possible for verbal memories to become attached and conscious. Object relations and the stimuli and challenges given by the environment also have a significant influence in the development of thinking and language. Britton (1989) and Zachrisson (2002) explain how the realization of the oedipal triangle promotes thinking and how difficulties arise if its internalization is prevented. Britton talks about triangular space, the perception of three-dimensional space as a consequence of the perception of object relations. Many researchers (Fonagy & Target, 1995; Lacan, 1964; Rosenfeld, 1992; Target & Fonagy, 2002) emphasize the father's influence in the child's learning of symbols and language. The father and language both bring difference and separateness in the relationship between the mother and the child; they both represent a third, different element, as the therapist does in a therapeutic relationship. A symbiotic relationship without language is no longer enough, and father and language begin to represent the missing element, the symbol. Symbolization and reflection, the thinking of one's own actions and relationships, become possible with the help of language and a third, external element. At this stage, children in fact reach for elementary symbolic thinking; they are able to make comparisons and anticipate consequences, and they begin to understand the meaning of reasons and guilt. The development of the triadic relationship from different dyadic relationships is, therefore, important and essential to the development of thinking.

The oedipal son

The oedipal son is born at the junction of these three simultaneous phases of development. The oedipal son is alone and lonely. Infancy has been irrevocably left behind. The son cannot go back to the dyad with his mother or father, without submitting himself to regressive passivity. Although the dyad brings both physical and mental pleasure it cannot satisfy the awakened activity, sexual sensations and instinctual pressures. The sexual relationship that exists between the mother and the father is hidden, forbidden, and strange to the son. It is a mystery. When the son's open sexual behaviour is forbidden, he is shown that sexuality is secret. It becomes obvious that a world inside one's own mind is hidden and secret to the others. Although it leaves one outside and alone, it also helps one justify and keep one's own limits. The limits protect, although at the same time they exclude. The development of one's own mental world brings with it one's own, internal images, desires, and will. The omnipotence of the mother and the idealiza-tion of the father can no longer save the son from thinking, as mother and father no longer live or experience in his stead. The ambivalence between the father and the mother is demanding and problematic, but strong identification with the father–man takes the boy to the world of men, while the mother remains a necessary refuelling station for love and tenderness. However, as the father has become an object of identification, he has also become a rival for the mother's love and admiration. Even in this way, the son has been left alone. He would like to get and win mother herself as his love object, but he is at the same time afraid that he would then lose his father and be punished. To get his father's approval and love, therefore, he should submit to his father's will and desire, i.e., be passive, and not a rival. The son has an apparently impossible conflict.

The parents, too, look at their oedipal son through different eyes than they had looked at their earlier little child, the infant. The parents look at their oedipal son through their own oedipal experi-ences and mental images. The mother is forced to abandon her son to the world of men. If the father has been unable to become sufficiently aware of his own oedipal desires he remains uncertain in his relationship with women and continuously searches only for justification for his wife–woman. Then the son becomes a threat to the possession of the wife–woman, a rival to the father, and has to be sent away, as Laius sent away Oedipus, his son.

Hägglund and Hägglund (1985, p. 111) aptly describe the paradox; how the father can be attached to his son and at the same time let him go; how the father can both keep his wife and hand her over to his son; how the son can simultaneously destroy his binds to his father and keep them, and how the son can love a woman as a mother, mistress and mother–whore.

The oedipal situation gets solved and dissolves gradually, when the son accepts the special relationship between his mother and father and the sexuality it includes. At the same time the son accepts the fact that he is left outside it. Side by side with the painful experience of being an outsider, however, a belief grows in the son's mind that good and strong love exists and that he himself in the future, after he has grown up to be like his father, can achieve such love together with a woman who is like his mother. Hanging on to this hope and identifying himself even more strongly with his father, the son does not experience the situation as too submissive or humiliating, but as sorrow and difference as well as promise and joy. Ikonen (1986) describes oedipal love as a powerful emotion, the origin of great love, which influences all later relationships in life.

If the oedipal situation becomes too shameful and humiliating to the son, he may react with too much bravado, bombast, or phallicism. Difference—sexual differences and differences between generations—then become symbols of superiority and supremacy. In the son's mind, the father's strength has turned into power, even violence. Ikonen (1998) talks about a phallic defence, aimed at replacing the mental images of reciprocity and sexual love by the idea and desire of superiority, use of force, and violence. If excessive, this leads to a situation where phallic pleasure becomes more important that the pleasure received from reciprocity. According to Ikonen, contempt of what has been lost, violation of limits and use of violence become symbols of freedom and power. Sexuality, too, becomes a means of power and violence. When not excessive, however, phallicism has essential and necessary positive effects on the boy. In terms of self-esteem and activity, the son accumulates important new experiences, activity becomes a good thing and too much passivity is experienced as submissiveness.

The lack of a father

As concepts and mental images, father and fatherhood are highly social and cultural, and as such, they become mediated to the son even when he does not have an actual father close by. Other people then carry out the father's functions in the boy's mind, those who protect and limit and are different from the mother. At the same time, however, it is clear that the longing and need for a father is also always in the son's mind. The lack of a father causes the son sorrow, extra psychic work, and emotional and cognitive difficulties at every stage of his development. This does not mean, however, that the son could not develop into a sufficiently balanced and happy person and a future father.

As became apparent in the description of early developmental stages, the importance of the father is obvious particularly at the time of separation from the mother. The father brings difference and separateness into the son's life; the father looks at the son through manly eyes and mental images. According to researchers (Burgner, 1985; Campell, 1995), sons who grow up without a father more often remain stuck in a dyadic, passive relationship with their mother, and it is more difficult for them to reach the necessary, healthy phallicism. The appearance of the triadic and oedipal developmental phases and working through them is easier for the boy if his everyday life includes a father–man to whom he can surrender the mother. Second, the father's role as the person who sets limits and prohibitions is important to the son; when there is no father, this task is left to the mother and the son himself. According to researchers (Burgner, 1985), this entails the risk that either limits and prohibitions are not set sufficiently or that they become too strict and demanding, because the son has to set them himself from the point of view of a small child afraid of authority. The desire and obligation to break limits that is part of youth is more natural when they have been set by a father–man. Third, the father is very important to the son as an object of identification, building the basis of the son's developing identity, although the identity searched for is separate from the father and possibly even completely different. As the developmental phases and psychic tasks of development are repeated in the son's life, the son needs a fatherly and masculine object of identification throughout his life. The lack of a father causes sorrow even in adulthood.

The later stages of the father–son relationship

The oedipal stage has been both demanding and even humiliating for the son, but at the same time, it has been a phase that has structured his ego and built new structures. The elements of the son's own separate identity have been formed and the search for identity can begin. If the parents were mainly experienced as good, triangulation was successful and the father became an identification object it is possible for the son to accept being left outside and experience relief and joy from the love relationship between his parents.

Sons must break away from their mothers and fortify their masculine identity. Sons are forced to tolerate competition, games, winning, and even losing. In a game, it is acceptable to be violent and beat others, even women: those witches have to be overcome one way or the other. There is no return to the early relationship with the mother. It is a problem to the son's development if the mother continuously devalues the father–man and asserts the superiority of the mother–woman. Identification with the mother lessens the son's possibilities of later appreciating masculinity and identifying with it. The absence of the father, for its part, makes it more difficult for the son to stay away from the mother and become attached to the masculine world of the father.

In childhood, the mother's omnipotence and the idealized father were important motivators and protectors of the son's growth and development. The mother's omnipotence was destroyed with the help of father idealization. This involved idealization of the father's might and strength, the father's phallus, with which he protected both mother and son. Although the father's protection also meant limit setting, which the son defied and contested during his oedipal and phallic stages, the protection and the limit setting were at the same time necessary for the son in terms of identification. A similar series of events is repeated during adolescence. In early adolescence, as the desire and fear of breaking away increases, the mother's power again enters into the son's world and has to be fought against with the help of idealizations concerning the father's masculinity and might.

However, early adolescence also brings a final disappointment of the parents' omnipotency, as they become powerless, unfair, and ordinary in the son's mind. New models for identification are found outside the family, in manly models and idols and, particularly, in the circle of friends. When the father fails to achieve perfection in the son's mental images, he seems to limit the son's own use of power too much; the father becomes devalued and nullified. Together with the devaluation of the father, even the father's power, his phallus, becomes nullified. The phallus now belongs to youth, the sexuality and vigour of youth. The idealization of the father is killed and the internal mental image of the father is murdered. The father is dethroned: "the King is dead, long live the King!" With the defiance of youth, the son now takes over the reins. He reaches his own sexuality, conquers his own woman and finds his own sexual relationship with his own woman. In this way, the son has finally won the mother–woman from his father, which he was unable to do during the oedipal stage. Now the son is omnipotent and mighty; he has taken his father's phallus; he has murdered his father in his mind.

Adolescence represents another junction in the son's life. Blos (1967) calls adolescence the second individualization, because the oedipal conflict normally gets solved in the crisis of adolescence, although it is of course never solved fully or finally. The psychic separation work of the oedipal stage changes into independence work during adolescence. The son must find his own identity, even though it will be transformed several times during the later phases of his life. The internally impressive and powerful father ideal is left on the background to serve as structures for the superego and moral; however, the son breaks away from the father ideal as an ego ideal and replaces it with his own, new, personal ego ideal. In spite of all his desire to be separate, the presence of the father and even the father's acceptance and getting the "father's blessing" for the son's own separateness are very important to the son.

While the son has been growing up and reached adolescence, the father has become middle-aged and grown old. Although the father has been so very important to the son and to the son's relationship with his mother, he has usually also concentrated strongly on working life and his own professional identity. Depending on the family situation and the father's situation, the father–man's conflict in dividing his time and interest between his work and his family may be equally strong as the mother–woman's. The father may take part in the son's everyday life actively and with plenty of time or he may keep on the side and follow the son's development from there. Commitment and interest are essential to the father in terms of his fatherhood, but to the son, they also mean time spent together.

As I pointed out at the beginning, motherhood and motherliness are always concrete and object-related, even when they are idealized. Fatherhood and fatherliness are more distant and more broadly related to the well-being of objects; idealized, they refer to the safeguarding of our well-being and to our basic security. Thus, a grown-up man may experience fatherliness and fatherhood by taking care of a great deal of other things besides his own son and family. Duties elsewhere than at home may also represent fatherliness to the father. A man's desire to be a father includes his desire to be generative on a larger basis, to conquer and possess, fertilize, and multiply. A man may experience fatherhood by taking care of things as a political leader, building a military career and being in charge of safety, or even by donating his sperm anonymously. In that case, it may be difficult even for the man himself to distinguish idealized fatherhood from the concrete, close fatherhood that every son longs for in his day-to-day life.

In his middle-age, a man faces the same dyadic, triadic, and oedipal problems and conflicts he has faced earlier in life. Once the children have grown, the father–man tends to search in his wife–woman the dyadic warmth that has remained in his idealized mental image and which he had to give up as a child when he had to break loose from his mother. Now dependence has become acceptable again. A man may experience the triadic relationships with his grown-up son as difficult and disturbing, athough at the same time he wants to keep them going; he experiences oedipal jealousy of his wife–woman's motherly feelings for her adult son, as the son just does not seem to be getting independent enough for the father–man, who would like him to leave his mother to him.

Every father gets old. Every man gets old. A man past middle-age will look back as well as ahead, measuring his accomplishments as a human being, and also as a man. Professionally, he has usually already reached his peak; physically, he has been losing strength for a long time already; the children have moved away to live their own lives; even his wife has become conventional. Masculine power and defiance no longer have a place in the man's life unless he expressly sets out to get them for himself. The man may be satisfied by what he has achieved, that he is alive and in reasonably good health, that sexuality still brings him pleasure, that he did well professionally or that his son has found his own fatherly place in society. The man may have become a grandfather, an idealized grandfather for his son's son, so that the chain of good fatherhood continues. The man may even be satisfied with the fact that everything did not go as he had thought in his youthful dreams; everything became conventional, but yet good enough. Or the man may be dissatisfied with his past and still try to change it. It may yet be possible to do even better professionally; it may yet be possible to maintain physical youth by strenuous exercise; it may yet be possible to seek strong sexual pleasure, perhaps even to have more children, even a new son.

The death of a man's father is an important, significant and unique event. In his the preface to the second edition of *The Interpretation of Dreams* (1900a) Freud writes that the book was: "my reaction to the death of my father, that is, to the most important event, the most poignant loss in a man's life." Although the man's own father may have been old and weak for a long time already, in the man's mental images the father has still represented shelter and protection, and the death of the father means their final loss; now he alone is his own and his family's shelter and protection.

The fact that he himself gets old brings in the man's life once again the same feelings of loneliness, externality, and lack of strength as he had experienced at the oedipal junction in his childhood. The man's ability to accept and understand that with his own fatherhood and fatherliness he has been able to shelter and protect his son's development and life and even influence his son's ability to be a father to his own son, however, makes it possible for the man to achieve wisdom and peace of mind in his old age. The conflict between the idealization of childhood and adolescence and the sufficiently good achievement of old age now has to be solved and accepted for good.

Acknowledgements

I would like to acknowledge the financial support of the Students Mental Health Service in Finland and Signe and Ani Gyllenberg Foundation.
My thanks to Kaisa Sivenius for her translation.

References

Abelin, E. (1975). Some further observations and comments on the earliest role of the father. *International Journal of Psycho-Analysis*, 56: 293–301.

Blos, P. (1967). The second individuation process of adolescence. *The Psychoanalytic Study of the Child*, 22: 162–186. New York: International Universities Press.

Blos, P. (1985). *Son and Father*. New York: Free Press.

Bollas, C. (2000). *Hysteria*. London and New York: Routledge.

Britton, R. (1989). The missing link: parental sexuality in the Oedipus complex. In R. Britton, M. Feldman, & E. O'Shaugnessy (Eds.), *The Oedipus Complex Today: Clinical Implications* (pp. 83–101). London: Karnac.

Burgner, M. (1985). The oedipal experience: effects on development of an absent father. *International Journal of Psycho-Analysis*, 66: 311–320.

Campell, D. (1995). The role of the father in the pre-suicidal state. *International Journal of Psycho-Analysis*, 76: 315–323.

Davids, M. F. (2002). Fathers in the internal world. In: J. Trowell & A. Etchegoyen (Eds.), *The Importance of Fathers* (pp. 67–92). The New Library of Psychoanalysis, 42. East Sussex: Brunner-Routledge.

Fonagy, P., & Target, M. (1995). Towards understanding violence: The use of the body and the role of the father. *International Journal of Psycho-Analysis*, 76: 487–502.

Freud, S. (1900a) [1955]. The interpretation of dreams. *S.E.*, 4–5. London & New York: Hogarth.

Hägglund, T.-B., & Hägglund, V. (1985). *Lohikäärmetaistelu.* . Helsinki: Nuorisopsykoterapiasäätiö

Ikonen, P. (1986). On the impact of the Oedipus complex. *The Scandinavian Psychoanalytic Review*, 9(2): 145–159.

Ikonen, P. (1998). On phallic defence. *The Scandinavian Psychoanalytic Review*, 21(2): 136–150.

Kestenberg, J. (1970). *Children and Parents: Psychoanalytic Studies in Development.* New York: Aronson.

Klockars, L., & Sirola, R. (2001). The mother–daughter love affair across the generations. *The Psychoanalytic Study of the Child, 56*: 219–237.

Lacan, J. (1964) [1978]. *The Four Fundamental Concepts of Psychoanalysis.* New York: Norton.

Mahler, M., Pine, F., & Bergman, A. (1975). *The Psychological Birth of the Human Infant.* New York: Basic Books.

McDougall, J. (1989). The dead father. *International Journal of Psycho-Analysis, 70*: 205–220.

Piaget, J. (1947) [1950]. *The Psychology of Intelligence.* London: Routledge & Kegan Paul.

Rosenfeld, D. (1992). Psychic changes in the paternal image. *International Journal of Psycho-Analysis, 73*: 757–771.

Stern, D. (1995). *The Motherhood Constellation: A Unified View of Parent–Infant Psychotherapy.* New York: Basic Books.

Stoller, R. (1979). Fathers of transsexual children. *Journal of the American Psychoanalytic Association, 27*: 837–866.

Target, M., & Fonagy, P. (2002). Fathers in modern psychoanalysis and in society: the role of the father and child development. In: J. Trowell & A. Etchegoyen (Eds.), *The Importance of Fathers* (pp. 45–66). The New Library of Psychoanalysis, 42. East Sussex: Brunner-Routledge.

Tähkä, V. (1993). *Mind and Its Treatment. A Psychoanalytic Approach.* Madison, CT: International Universities Press.

Zachrisson, A. (2002).Gåtans svar är människan; om Oidipus och psykoanalysen. A Paper read at the Scandinavian Psychoanalytic Congress, 31 August, Oulu, Finland.

CHAPTER TEN

Dreams in the therapeutic relationship

T. Eskelinen and P. Folch

I n this paper we base our study of dreams in the domain of the analytical session. This is where dreams are narrated and dramatized, but it is also where dreams are generated to a large extent, and where they return to, according to the vicissitudes of the patient–analyst relationship. The emotional experience that the patient has in the session is loaded with implications that activate the contents of his internal world at its various levels: in physical sensations, in the forms of social interaction, in reverie and in nocturnal dreams.

The dreams are transformations of unconscious thought, thought that in wakeful hours is expressed in reverie, and while sleeping in dreams. We use the term "reverie" in the sense employed by Bion (1962), referring to the unconscious processes of linking experiences that come from different levels of the personality differentiating it from day-dreaming, which is a more conscious mental activity geared mainly to satisfaction of desires. We are referring to a continuum of elaboration of emotional experiences going from dreams during sleep to reverie during the waking hours. The setting is conceived so as to facilitate the expression of these processes. During the session the analyst's interventions influence the patient's reverie and, in our opinion, can modify something in the dreams when they are told at the end of the session. For the analyst the reverie would mean receptivity at all levels of his personality, sensual, emotional, and rational and of his thinking unconfined by limits imposed by desire, which directs the mind towards the desired or towards reassuring defence. This helps him to understand the complexity of his patient's experiences and how he deals with them. However, anxiety in the face of the new, unknown, for both the patient and the analyst, mobilizes the defences.

When a patient tells us his dream, he creates a special atmosphere between himself and the analyst. Besides the apprehension of mystery and inscrutability—hence catastrophic anxiety—that announcing the dream denotes, the patient has the expectation of the analyst being able to contain his anxiety and approach the uncanny, unknown aspects of the dream and understand something of it. Encouraged by the setting, the patient feels moved to continue dreaming, but this time while awake; and, in fact, his associations and the style in which he comments upon them might unfold the opaque, suggestive texture formed by condensations and displacements and other dream mechanisms.

The patient's dramatized story of the dream has no clear plot; or even if it has at first, it is liable to be modified as the relationshp in the session develops. All dreaming is a continuous process and its images and its drama are far from being static. The emotions and the unconscious fantasies which animate the dream images and dream drama are *per se* directed towards what is unknown if the analysis is to thrive. And the opposite is true: both the analyst and the patient alike tend to struggle against the anxiety that the unknown awakens by sticking to the already known, thus repetitive, aspects of the dream. The observation of the interactive experience in the session becomes the nodal point in understanding what is being experienced. The incidents of the dramatization, how the analyst takes on the role the patient gives him (*role responsiveness*, see Sandler & Sandler (1998)), how he confirms or denies it by his attitude, his silences, or his comments are also important in understanding his dreams. The patient also switches between his role of narrator and that of actor. Meltzer (1984) wondered if the character who takes part in the dream is the same as the one who recalls it in the session. In order to represent some of the complexity of his experience, the dreamer, like Pirandello in his *Six Characters in Search of an Author*, succesively attributes different aspects of his internal world, of his internal drama, to the characters in his dream.

Dreams and the analytical session are spaces that correspond to each other. They are spaces of reciprocal representation, but they are also settings where the unspoken, the unknown can be dramatized and formalized—all that which occurs throughout the session, with the words spoken and unspoken. When this verbal and extraverbal interaction abounds, the dream's hermetic quality might give way to a progressive elucidation. The continuing drama is the key and the means of understanding of the shadowy, ambiguous, suggestive work of the dream. In effect, this form of internal communication, this way of thinking, which is the dream, in its dense ambiguity not only blurs and hides that which Freud called the latent thoughts of dreams, but also it suggests them, it evokes them without specifying them, stimulating multiple possibilities. The dream's succesive dramatization of the differents aspects of the "dream thinking" evokes the analyst's resonance, draws him into dreaming the patient's dream and helps him to understand some of the complexity which is condensed in the dream image.

Ella Sharpe (1972) in describing the poetical–literary expression of dreams brings us closer to that integrating function of the activity of dreaming which encompasses the subject's disparate experiences: past and present, external reality and psychic reality, partial objects and total objects, etc. The condensation into one single image or movement of different layers of sensorial, emotional and cognitive experiences, of the dreamer's own story, brings the work of dreams closer to the workings of poetry. We should not forget that Freud's term "condensation" is expressed in German with the word *Verdichtung* —which means "thicken". And *Dictung* or *Dicht* means poetry. The poet condenses multiple experiences in an image that strikes the reader and has the power to evoke memories of things that seemed to have been forgotten.

Dreams lead to dreaming. In the atmosphere of the setting the patient feels encouraged to go on dreaming, awake this time. The analyst may well be inspired by the way the patient tells the dream. He can observe the use that the patient is making of his own narration. The transformation of the story into a drama now takes place with the assumption of roles on the part of the patient and the analyst. The patient's intra-psychic drama becomes an interpersonal drama in the session which enables the analyst to combine what he observes with what he feels, when perception and resonance (Joseph, 1993) can feed his reverie, so that the most favourable conditions for interpretative clarification are produced. This new drama, which is developing in the analytical situation, has a retroactive influence on the dream. It recomposes the dream, modifying the course and the content of its narration.

The coexistence of the dream's clarifying and defensive elements makes us think of the formation of compromise that Freud (1900a, pp. 596–597) found in the structure of dreams, like the structure of neurotic symptoms. The formation of compromise is the result of the dialectics between the thirst for knowledge and the need to ignore, in the balance between the two poles of covering up and discovering. Depending on which of these two is predominant, the dream will lead to the creation of false symbols, or, on the contrary, to the generation of symbolic meaning and to the unravelling of the patient's own truth. However, the most onerous defence does not lie in the formation of the dream, no matter how abstruse that may be. Rather, it is in attacks on the ability to dream, on dream's meaning, on its capacity to make connections. This sometimes makes the patient forget his dream altogether, and at other times impedes its development and leads to the patient diverting emotional experiences to events outside the transference, to sensorial phenomena and hallucinosis.

The following clinical vignettes are set out with the intention of illustrating different parts of these considerations about dreams. We have chosen material from two patients who have been in analysis for several years. We are going to describe how both patients lived out their dreams in the session and how something in the dreams that the patient claimed to have had during the night seemed to have changed according to the patient's experience with the analyst in the session. One of these two patients, S, has a rather limited relational life, although he has overcome depersonalization anxieties. He lives in a regressive equilibrium. Depressive anxieties and feelings of persecution sometimes overwhelm him. His dreams are not very complex but have a strong emotional charge. They are sober in their description and often make S feel surprised and perplexed.

The other clinical vignette comes from a turning point of the analysis of a woman patient, X. Her dreams were usually rather elaborate, but she remained a distant observer of them. In the three dreams she describes in one session and their analysis in the transference situation she moves nearer to the emotional experience of a complicated oedipal situation which seems to be at the root of the pathology in her social relations that had been brought to a dead end.

Clinical material

S, a borderline patient, came to analysis overwhelmed by a phobic organization of his external conduct and obsessive control of his internal world. However, this control had not stopped his superstitious, hypochondriacal meticulousness from sliding down into a marked delusion. This meant he suffered from an intense fear of mental imbalance, or madness. His relationships beyond his family circle were very limited. His sex life was exclusively masturbatory, with incestuous, voyeuristic, and scatological elements. He couldn't stop his imagination from being threatening. If some idea *"got into"* his mind, it became real simply because he had thought it. He did not believe completely in his fantasies, but he felt impelled to behave as though they were facts.

Analysis alleviated the feeling of being overwhelmed by these symptoms, and this allowed S to take on different forms of employment and to broaden his relational life slightly.

The session we are going to feature comes from a period of the analysis, already in its sixth year, when S was able to approach his relationship with the analyst more openly. He could object to the analyst's interpretations. He began to be interested in his feelings, his imagination, and thinking. Intense sado-masochistic elements of his object relations were appearing in the transference, more and more clearly. Often these were denied and acted out in a poorly covered-up way in the relationships he began to have with certain domestic animals.

The day before the session we are going to describe, he had left the session fearing that he would find dead a pet he had acquired a few weeks earlier. He had kept it starving. He felt guilty for having treated it badly. The relationship with the animal had been one of total possession. S had used it as a means of revenge for all those situations in which he had felt subjugated by people who, in his mind, had taken advantage of his problems and passivity. He had been talking about the feeling of resentment that these experiences had forged, and the satisfaction and pride his fantasies of revenge produced in him. Although the resentment was idealized, he sometimes felt pain that the thing in his life that he saw as being the most destructive was the very thing that gave him the most composure and security. He was also disturbed by the pet's strange behaviour. It ate pieces of wood and it injured itself on the bars of the cage, as if it had gone mad.

At different times, the patient had been able to recognize that he dramatized his relationship with the analyst in his relationship with the pet. He felt the treatment to be a shameful dependence. S said the analyst was abusive for pointing out the difficulties he was dealing with: such as, for example, the pet's self-destructive behaviour as an expression of his self-destructive madness, with his torturous dilemma of whether to stay in pathological isolation or to dare to leave it.

> S began the session by saying he had had a terrible, gloomy dream, but he didn't know if it was worth talking about. In any case he wanted to talk about what had happened the previous afternoon . . . it was a ridiculous, embarrassing thing. When he had got home from the session, he had found the pet dead . . . so he had to think about whether he should take it back to the shop where he had bought it, but he didn't want them to think he was trying to get anything out of them. He thought he would seem ridiculous, like a dejected child. He felt discouraged. He sat down to eat and stuffed himself with pastries, and afterwards he felt as if he had rid himself of the pet.

> The analyst said that his treatment of the pet, far from being ridiculous, in fact reproduced the painful feelings he had about his personal relationships. He had tried to alleviate his pain of loss with the pastries, as if at a funeral banquet.

> The patient smiled and said that at funeral banquets the cannibals eat the dead body. Then he returned to talking extensively about his doubts.

> The analyst felt pulled in several different directions. On one hand, the announcement of the dream had given way to something very specific:

the death of the animal, which dramatized so many aspects of the patient's way of dealing with his internal object. This probably kept the analyst from considering something more immediate between himself and the patient. But he questioned what had happened in the previous session. When the patient arrived home, was the session already dead, and did the things dealt with in it no longer have any meaning? Or perhaps he didn't dare to say openly that the lack of clarity of the interpretations made them meaningless? What is for sure is that the analyst, shaken by the description of the death, decided to deal with less painful aspects—the bulimic reaction—and not to tackle what later seemed to be the focus of the patient's anxiety: on the one hand the death and loss and, on the other, his fearful questioning of the analyst for giving him inconsistent interpretations. The patient didn't protest too loudly but he was caught in what seemed almost sterile doubts. Did his ironic response that the cannibals eat the dead body express some slight awareness that some of his doubting was almost munching over and over again doubts that become dead by their repetitiveness? However deadening was his repetitive doubting, it seemed to explore whether or not he dared to ask for explanations of the analyst in the session or in the pet shop. On the other hand, aside from his demand for clarification, the patient seemed also concerned that he felt he had not paid enough attention to the work done in the analysis.

The patient continued by saying that when, after much prevarication, he did go to the pet shop, he felt ridiculous. The shop assistant told him, "Look, the poor creature died, and that's that."

The analyst reminded S of his fears that his eagerness for control, dramatized with the animal, had proved deadly and that he had felt ridiculous about his need to share the responsibility with the people who had sold it to him, because they might have sold him a sick animal, or perhaps, in analysis, he had been given bad interpretations. He also indicated how S transformed his need and interest in understanding into torment, torturing himself with his sterile doubts just as he had tortured the animal, which then had gone mad.

The patient recounted a few anecdotes that showed more positive, less rigid aspects of his daily life, and a little later he began to talk about the dream.

I was in a house, and there was an old man there who looked after it . . . suddenly someone started knocking at the door over and over again; I asked the man why he didn't open the door, and he told me that he wouldn't open it because it was the Devil knocking . . . yes, yes [anticipating the analyst's surprise], it sounds like a fairy story like the one about Little Red Riding Hood or something, but that's the way it was, the Devil was knocking at the door and the man told me that he was in human form, that he had taken on the appearance of a man, but it really was the Devil. . . . I suffered a lot during the dream, I had an unbearable sense of foreboding that stayed with me after I woke up . . . and I suppose you might laugh because of the way I tell it, but it really was absolutely terrifying . . . above all because it seems inevitable that the Devil will burst in on me.

In his interventions, the analyst likened the figure of the Devil with the uncontrollable strength of the patient's resentment, which he wanted to rid himself of. But when he experienced it in the session, he felt anxious that the old analyst who looks after the house and his mind might not be able to withstand the attacks of what he feels as a diabolical irruption.

The patient seemed sad and receptive, and after a brief silence continued the story of the dream.

He said that in the house he found a young man and a young woman. He didn't know how they had got in. The woman was a classmate of his from a pre-University course, whom he had liked a lot; she was very attractive. The youth was a stranger to him, and the girl, with the passing of the years, had become fat and had gone to seed. The atmosphere of the dream had changed. When the analyst asked him if the Devil had faded away, it seemed hard for the patient to say that he had calmed down during the course of the dream itself . . .

Probably he had found something attractive in the analyst's interventions, and this had moved him to remember the dream and/or to re-create it in the session.

The analyst said that the dream had changed a great deal from the disturbing terror of the beginning...

The patient said that indeed, the initial feeling of foreboding had changed. (It wasn't clear if he was referring to the beginning of the dream or the alarming beginning of the session.)

When referring to the young man who accompanied the girl, the patient said he didn't know who it was, he was a stranger, "...you're not going to believe this, there wasn't really a dramatic change in the dream . . . I don't know, as I've already said the girl was past it, she wasn't young any more . . ." S said this with a sad and worried air, as though he thought that the analyst saw things with too much optimism.

The analyst told him that in fact the second part of the dream wasn't too easy to face. When he had been able to put aside his resentment and he had been able to think of an attractive woman, he had seen that the years had gone by, that something that had previously been attractive to him had now sadly faded, that he had let beauty slip through his fingers. As for the young man who accompanied the girl, he seemed to represent S himself, unknown to himself, and his still unknown chance to be sensitive again to what he once found attractive. Away from his monotonous control of his terrifying anxieties and torturous doubts, he felt himself a stranger, afraid of new experiences that were accompanied by the uncertainty of the new, and by sorrow for having abandoned his attractive objects.

S's initial vacillation about whether or not to talk about the dream had been put aside for a moment by telling the story of what had happened the day before, his consternation over the animal's death. He had felt incapable of recounting the dream. He had announced it as being serious and sinister. Surely he was calming himself with the first few exchanges of the session, and with the way he dealt with the episode of the animal's death. The dream had terrorized him because its condensation and displacement were too discrete to quell his anxiety. Once he had ascertained that the analyst coped with his recounting of the pet shop episode, and remained receptive, he was able to talk about the appearance of the devil in his dream. Yet the patient seemed nowhere near realizing that the specific fact of the animal's death served to express, via displacement, the more immediate experience of the previous session, the interpretations that had disappeared into thin air and were emptied of meaning.

The attack on the experience gleaned from the animal's death an opportunity for the movement of fleeing and re-encountering. It was a transformation of a violent immediacy that causes unbearable anxiety to a painful, but more tolerable distance. The animal's death fitted the bill in representing the agony about the interpretations, but at the same time it was a way of bringing that agony back to life. The transformation was, in a certain way, an unconscious waking dream—or, rather, the repercussion on the patient's conscience and conduct of an unconscious waking dream, which had been dramatized on the way to the pet shop and in the pet shop itself. Once there, the issue of blame and guilt had come up. Had the animal died because of S's cruel negligence, or because the shop had sold it weak or ill? Recounting these doubts came to transfer this issue to the analyst. The patient seemed to question that something in the analyst's interpretations had not been clear enough to remember them. He felt these thoughts so disturbing and danger-ous that they should not appear in the session or be discussed in it. They transformed into tormenting doubts that the analyst, the old man in the dream, might not be able to stand.

But even though the dream was not recounted, it was being dramatized in the first exchanges of the session, and in its very course, the reality of the session started to be a corrective experience of both dream and waking dream, reverie. The analyst pressed on to deal calmly with the things that had caused terror in the patient. The analyst's reverie had led the way to re-establishing the situa-tion in a far less fatalistic light. So the patient extended the recount-ing of the dream to include the appearance of the young couple, instead of the devil.

To our understanding the patient goes on dreaming in the session, in tune with the analyst's interventions. When the analyst coped with his doubts and demands, the patient was able to dream of rejuvenation; the analyst is not as moribund as the dead animal; and the patient does not feel his mind invaded by destroyed objects or diabolical doubts. In their place there is an attractive woman and a young man, surely evoked by the attractive things the analyst had been able to evoke by his previous interventions. In a fraction of second he imagines an attractive couple, a relation which is funda-mentally different of those of controlling and tormenting. However, the woman is no longer so young, she's a bit past it, and this brings a painful feeling—not so sinister any more—of the passing of time. And there persists a feeling of the difficulty of repairing the neglected object, and doubts of his ability to change. The man who is with the attractive woman is unknown to him; S does not know this kind of relationship. He seems quite pessimistic that this man could be himself.

We now move on to comment briefly on a second case. We will focus on three dreams described at different points of one session. We leave aside much of the interaction between analyst and patient.

X is a university teacher who came to analysis because she found herself in a dead-end in her relationships, especially with men. These relationships had caused her so much suffering that to all intents and purposes she had withdrawn from having a social life. She often had relationships with married men of her father's age. She was frigid, but she stuck to a belief that her simulated enthusiasm made men feel virile. Deep down she knew it to be false.

She made a point of showing suitably courteous behaviour; she treated the analyst with respect and often behaved protectively towards her. She was well-spoken, and sometimes explained the meaning of her more arcane vocabulary to the analyst, who was not a native speaker of the language used in the sessions. However, she was easily hurt, and then her protective tone cracked. Sometimes, after a problematic session, she cried at home, screaming insults at her analyst. The following day she came to the session feeling embittered, determined to give up the analysis because "it doesn't do me any good."

From the very beginning of the analysis she had expressed desperate loneliness, having no hope of having what she called "a real relationships".

We will now focus on three dreams in a session from a Friday close to the summer holidays. In the previous session, X had described how her mother spoke about her father. According to her mother, her father was incapable of any sensuality; his supposed "virility" was a bluff. When X recounted a dream towards the end of the session, the analyst made a rather hasty interpretation of the dream's content, not elaborating enough the whole experience in the session.

The Friday session began with X recounting a dream:

In the dream, X was at a horse show in the Spanish Riding School of Vienna. There were some lovely horses and attractive riders. One of them was particularly attractive, with a very well developed body. His horsemanship was perfect; as was the green cape he was wearing (the analyst had been wearing a wide green skirt the day before). He rode like the best trainers. Then he jumped over the horse's head, sat on the floor and doubled over like a puppet.

One of the spectators said, "It's Nembutal."
X corrected him, saying, "No, it's *Clerambutal*."

X explained that sometimes she took a Nembutal to sleep. She knew it was strong, and it knocked her out. Then she referred to the "Clerambutal scandal". A large number of cows had been killed by an overdose of Clerambutal, which some farmers had given them to make them grow more quickly. Several people had had heart problems after having eaten meat from the cows treated with this substance.

The analyst remembered her dissatisfaction with her hasty interpretation at the end of the previous session. She saw the mention of the Spanish Riding School of Vienna as a direct reference to her. She wondered if the day before she had wanted to show that she could deal with a difficult situation in a fast, omnipotent way. Then she worried that the patient might never be able to have a real, solid, relationship with a man if he had to be so perfect and idealized. The she realized that this concern had covered her disquiet with her own self, because it moved her attention from her hasty interpretation to the patient's relationships with men. She felt reluctant to go on.

Realizing this, the analyst intervened to say that the patient had felt that the analyst had been "showing off" her professional capacity in the previous session and that she had felt it to be dangerous. Yet, aparently she seemed to present it as something fantastic. The analyst asked her if she could remember having any impression that her comments were unconvincing.

The patient quickly said that she didn't remember anything in particular from yesterday's session, and that what's more, she didn't believe that the rider in the dream was representing her analyst, but rather her father, who was an attractive man who wanted to be seen as dashing and perfect.

The analyst reminded X that in the previous session she had talked about how her mother saw her father; that his virility was a bluff. She also indicated to X the way in which X was trying to make her, the analyst, feel comfortable, by saying that the rider wasn't her, it was X's father. In this way she seemed to want to avoid the discomfort she felt when trying to face up to her critical thoughts about the analyst in yesterday's session. But it was in the dream that she expressed this criticism. The analyst also told X how in this way (saying that the "bluff is my father's") she was allying herself to the analyst to talk about her father's defects, just as she had done with her mother.

Here there was a long interchange. X seemed in some way more present than usual. She seemed to see two main points of the interpretation, her difficulty in facing her criticisms and expressing them directly and using them to create a particular triangular situation in which two people form an alliance to speak ill of the third.

Then there was a long silence.

Then X said, speaking slowly, as if with great care, that she had had another dream:

> We were in Alba and Eric's beautiful house. [This was couple who were both older than X. Alba, the wife, was a friend of hers and occasionally a colleague at work. The husband, Eric, had recently had an affair with X.] They had come back from a long journey, which Alba described in a lively and interesting way. I felt very jealous; they had everything and I live alone. But then Eric came up behind me and put a parcel for me on the table. It was a present. I had to hide it from Alba. I had a hard time covering it up with pieces of paper, so that Alba wouldn't realize.

After a brief silence, the patient said she had remembered another dream.

> I don't know what it was, but there was a soft noise. I saw you [the analyst] with some other people. You were wearing a plain black dress, rather austere, with a white blouse and a curved neckline—like housemaids used to wear. You said that we had to look into something. You moved a wooden panel away from the wall, and a horrible smell of rotting flesh came out. Then you took out the body of a man, pallid and half putrefied. But once he was out of there, he came back to life. You hugged him and said, "Thank God, my brother is alive and well!"

X established a link between this dream and her meeting with her mother the day before. Her mother, desperate, had told her that she was on the verge of madness; the nightmares of her childhood had returned: one more step and she would fall into the abyss. Her mother had added that she felt alone and unloved, as she had when she was little. She recalled her wedding night, which passed off without any physical contact with her husband.

X added that she could not say anything to her mother that seemed in the slightest way critical of her. She had never been able to do so. Her mother would break down immediately.

The analyst thought that the two dreams might have been changed by the experience of the session: the patient had experienced the analyst as somebody who was able to describe X's fantasies and states of mind from new points of view—this was shown by the allusion to new and interesting journeys; they were journeys through her internal and external world. These descriptions had awakened in her interest and admiration, but also unbearable jealousy and envy. To cover these feelings she had remembered or created the defensive end of her second dream about the present from her friend's husband. That is to say, she need not be jealous because she and the man had a secret tie. But she had to hide it.

When she spoke about her mother, mulling over her "childhood nightmares", she seemed to be quite aware that she was talking about herself, and her anguish at feeling alone, not relating in a more real way with others, or with the analyst in the analytical task. It would seem that the analyst's interpretation had broken through her usual defence of displacing her problems on to other people and regarding them from a safe distance. That is what she was doing at the beginning of the session; when she shifted on to her father the ironic view of the analyst expressed in the dream. Nor had she been successful in her usual tactic of pairing up with someone to criticize someone else.

The last dream seemed more clearly representative of the elaboration X was making of the relationship that was developing in the session. Was there something that smelt bad, from the previous session? Was it that the analyst's weak and hasty interpretation, when it remained aparently unnoticed, unthought about and unspoken, began to stink because X could use it secretly against the analyst? It seemed a splendid present against any envy or jealousy! As the analyst went on speaking, X seemed to get quite interested in experiencing the analytical work as a real possibility to face her own problems that contaminated her relationships.

At the end of the last dream some hope was expressed, regaining some warm and affectionate family ties. The analyst remembered how X, desperate, had once told her that both her parents' families had broken off their relationship, which was difficult to keep up because of their different socio-economic levels. But was this really the reason? Or was it because they found it difficult to put up with the " childhood nightmares"—envies, jealousies— which had never been confronted directly?

As in the case of the other patient, we consider that the second and the third dream had changed in the session from what they had been experienced during the previous night. In the second dream a couple have the potential to inspire interest, although it immediately becomes riddled with jealousy and envy. In the third dream, the analyst ,trying to contact with these unspoken, hidden feelings seems to bring about some hope for warmer and less desperate relationships.

Final comments and suggestions for discussion

By extending the function of dreaming to this continuous activity of unconscious waking dreaming, reverie—understood as the "digestion" of emotional experience—it might seem that we had deposed nocturnal dreaming from the pre-eminence it was given by Freud.

But our intention is to indicate quite the opposite, as follows.

(a) The exceptional quality of nocturnal dream allows us to unveil a process of affectation and elaboration of the continuing course of dream experience in the session.

(b) When the external reality is "closed down", nocturnal dreaming, more than waking dreaming, allows us to visualize, on the borderline of the preconscious—unconscious snippets of the patient's internal world, his way of expressing it or of concealing it; an internal world that is inter-objectal, a continuous interaction between the Self and the internalized objects.

(c) Via this approximation to the world of dreams we also realize how much is unreachable; what dreams cannot help us to clarify. Freud referred to this when talking about the navel of dreams (der Nabel des Traums), where dream melts into the darkness of the unknown.

(d) The exploration of nocturnal dreaming in the session has also shown us the through-line between it and waking dreaming, their confluence, and their reciprocal repercussions. Nocturnal dreams prepare us to modify our capacity of dreaming when we are awake, and the flow of our imagination modifies our memory of the nocturnal dream experience.

By saying that a condensation of the night-time dreams' images is unfolded in the session in the form of drama, we are alluding to different aspects of the transference:

(a) Transference from the patient's mental space to the space of the therapeutic relationship.
(b) Transference from one character of the dream to another, and to the analyst.
(c) Transference from the repetitive drama of internal history to the indeterminate nature of the patient–analyst relationship, with the hope that the representation will be able to shift from a rigid, predetermined script to new possibilities.

Finally, and from a technical point of view, our thoughts can be summarized as follows:

(a) By being receptive and able to dream the patient's dream, the analyst can come to recognize how the dream becomes lived out in the session and the different roles the patient lives out and attributes to him.
(b) Recognizing his inevitable incarnation in one role or other of the dream will allow the analyst to "dream", in his wakeful receptiveness, the meaning of the dramatization taking place, and indicate it to the patient. This helps him to formulate the interpretation in a way that facilitates the patient's emotional understanding.
(c) The analyst's ability to dream and process his own somatic, emotional, and cognitive responses to the patient's storyline, narrative style and extra-verbal behaviour, will help him to choose which point to focus on in his next intervention.

But there are also some evident limitations here. This dream shared between patient and analyst also has its navel, its hidden darkness. This is where unconscious experiences of both parties intermingle, inspiring discomfort and uncanny dread, and this is why they are so difficult to approach.

References

Bion, W. R. (1962). A theory of thinking. *International Journal of Psycho-Analysis*, 43: 306–310.

Bion, W. R. (1992). *Cogitations*. London, Karnac.

Freud, S. (1900a). The interpretation of dreams. *S.E.*, 5: London: Hogarth.

Joseph, B. (1993). A factor militating against psychic change: nonresonance. In: M. J. Horowitz, O. F. Kernberg, & E. M. Weinshel (Eds.), *Psychic Structure and Psychic Change. Essays in Honor of R. S. Wallerstein*. Madison, CT: International Universities Press.

Meltzer, D. (1984). *Dream Life*. London: Clunie Press.

Sandler, J., & Sandler, A. M. (1998). *Internal Objects Revisited*. Karnac.

Sharpe, E. (1972). Mécanismes du rêve et procédés poetiques. *Nouvelle Revue de Psychanalyse*, 5: 101–114.

CHAPTER ELEVEN

A brief inquiry into the value of man

Pentti Ikonen

I n the following discussion on the value of man from the psychological point of view, we shall limit ourselves to pursuing no more than one or two threads in a wide and complex texture.

It is a clear psychological basic fact that what we love is valuable to us. We see its value. We need not question it. We want the object of our love—be it another person, another living or lifeless creature, or even a state of affairs—to exist and continue existing. Its value to us is self-evident. It is only when we do not like something, when it bothers, annoys or disturbs us in some way, that we begin to question its value. Why does it exist? Of what value could it possibly be? We may say that it has a negative value. In fact, it should not exist at all, at least not as it now does.

Let us formulate our starting point in simple terms: love awakened in us reveals the value of the object of our love to us. We neither add nor attach any value to it: the value within it is revealed to us.

However, a person may also have value because with his or her help we may be able to get something that we like or that is important to us. The other person, with whose help we obtain it, has instrumental value. Another person's intrinsic value is based on an immediate experience of his or her value, whereas her or his instrumental value is based on our knowledge that with his or her help we will be able to get something or other.

An enormous quantity of intrinsic values is attached to so-called worldly goods. We experience these intrinsic values immediately with no need for justification. At the same time, we continue to observe how people use one another in order to acquire these "worldly goods". Then the other person has instrumental value to us to the extent and length of time that we are able to use him or her in order to acquire worldly goods for ourselves.

Another person may have instrumental value to us in a much less obvious way as well. A person may have such value to us for example because her or his value lies in that he or she represents similar opinions, lifestyle or tastes as we do in some matters that are important to us. We then experience that person as a support to ourselves, perhaps even as the champion of our cause. Her or his value turns out to be instrumental when for some reason or other we cease to agree on these matters. The person's value collapses in our eyes, because it had been based on that he or she had served as an advocate of our opinions.

There are fields of life where it is particularly difficult to see a person's intrinsic value and instrumental value as separate things. Such fields include family relationships, erotic life, one's relationship to oneself and the field we call the supreme values. For a small child, the parents are both a necessary means of survival and the most valuable part of the world. The whole question of intrinsic or instrumental values does not even arise. It is only little by little that the parents' value becomes evident even when they cannot serve as means to the ends the child would wish to use them for. This happens when the parents cause the child some disappointment, or when they cannot or do not want to help the child fulfil his or her wishes or protect her or him against various discomforts or chagrins, pain, sorrow, insults, etc., but the child nevertheless wants them to exist and continue to be close to her or him. The parents have intrinsic value to the child, because the child loves them for their own sake. Our parents usually maintain their instrumental value for us for as long as they are able to help us in some way. We often understand this help as the parents' love or natural desire or duty to their children for as long as both parties are alive, even if we at the same time find this unacceptable.

Children, too, have instrumental value to their parents in many ways: they continue the family line, provide support in old age, carry out the parents' own wishes and dreams, etc. After many disappointments, when the children fail to fulfil these expectations, the extent to which the parents see the intrinsic value of their children, i.e., the extent to which the love required to see it has survived in the parents, becomes revealed.

Within the field of erotic life, the relationships where one's partner mainly has importance as something other than as an object of erotic love often become objects of criticism and ridicule. If the partner is a means to achieving money, a job, social status, or any other benefit, there will always be those who raise this instrumentality as the object of their criticism. If, on the other hand, the partner can serve as no means to anything, even that will be criticized. "Why go out with someone who is no good for anything?" In both cases, the things that can or cannot be achieved by means of the partner do not actually belong to erotic life. In the first case, the partner is a means to achieve them, in the other, no good as a means to achieve them.

The same division into intrinsic and instrumental value may take place within erotic life. The partner's value then lies mainly or exclusively in the extent to which he or she is able to satisfy the other person's erotic or sexual desires. If the partner is unable to satisfy them, his or her intrinsic value as a person and her or his instrumental value in matters erotic and sexual become revealed as clearly differentiated. Erotic love does not necessarily include the kind of love that reveals the other person's value as a person.

When erotic love is awakened, the intrinsic value and the erotic value of the love object have not become differentiated. In being in love, they are merged, and the beloved person's intrinsic value gains tremendous additional power from her or his erotic instrumental value. To be sure, the erotic and sexual feelings based on a young person's intense sexual curiosity may be aroused regardless of the intrinsic value of the object and may even benefit from being eclipsed by it, just as the erotic and sexual feelings of a cynical libertine are usually disturbed by an observation of the object person's intrinsic value. In general, however, it is almost impossible that erotic love should be awakened without some degree of realization of the future beloved's intrinsic value as a person. As the relationship continues, the partners' intrinsic values and instrumental values become differentiated, but if the relationship continues successfully, they become united again in a new way. The relationship is then based on the fact that the intrinsic value of the beloved has become illuminated to both loving parties through the power of the other's erotic value.

What has been said above is a kind of basic formula for why erotic love can be seen to both greatly illuminate and seriously blur the value of man; why erotic love can either reveal a person's intrinsic value in all its greatness or turn him or her into a mere instrument of desires and passions. This should bring a contribution to the discussion where women in particular protest against being only considered sexual objects, i.e., a means.

People also tend to forget their own value and consider themselves as only a means to achieving certain things or accomplishing something. The desire for possessions, power, or glory, for example, may direct itself to a great variety of things: material, sensual, sexual, social, moral, mental, or spiritual. In these cases, a person has value to her/himself only in so far as he or she is a good means to achieve them. The person's intrinsic value has been eclipsed by his or her instrumental value.

Even the values characterized as supreme often eclipse man's value as such. They usually come accompanied by the announcement that a person has value only in so far as he or she is prepared to submit her/himself as a means to fulfilling or defending these supreme values—even at the cost of his or her own life. It is only as this type of a means that the person has value. History, and the history of ideas in particular, reminds us of this. It suffices to see that even in these contexts man's value is being sought for through something else, as if a person's value lay in that she or he is at a high intellectual, artistic, ethical, or spiritual level, for example. As if that person did not have any value as such. As if even at this level she or he had value only as a means.

The above might be considered no more than idle talk, if we did not in some part of our conscious mind continue to be in touch with what Kant in his time put into words as follows: another person must never be treated primarily as a means or an obstacle to our own pursuits but as a value as such. The protests that have arisen and continue to arise in different fields of life are a further sign of this: in work and in social life, in family and love life, in the life of science and arts, and in spiritual life. It is my view that through seeing this, we see something of the great tragedy of humankind. Man's value as such is sacrificed for his or her value as a means.

The value of man as a means is not in any way objectionable or unimportant as such. The value of the means depends on what it is used for, how well it works and at what cost. We only reach the difficult, critical point when man's value as a means becomes greater than man's value as such. Then even the best and most supreme things turn against themselves and begin to cause destruction, disasters, and suffering. Our world today is full of shocking examples of this. The world is also full of everyday, almost unnoticeable, but no less powerful examples of a similar disproportion between man's intrinsic and instrumental values in our relationship with each other and with ourselves.

No rules or codes of conduct exist on how we can sufficiently take into account man's value as such, both our own and other people's. How do we know when we are about to ignore man's intrinsic value for the benefit of something else? Where and how do we draw the line between man's value as such and as a means? Drewermann (1977) has written a study of Antoine de Saint-Exupéry's book, *The Little Prince*. The Finnish title of the book translates, "It is only with the heart that one can see rightly". As sugary and perhaps utopian as it may sound, the title is still touching. It is with the heart that we see man's value as such and the line that distinguishes it from man's value as a means. The title of the book may be read so that it says the same thing I said at the beginning of this study: love reveals the intrinsic value of its object. The beloved is not loved because he or she is a means to something else, but as her or himself. She or he as such, as him or herself, is a valuable object of love.

At this point I would like to take up a passage in the *New Testament*, although my reading may be somewhat out of the ordinary. When St Matthew weighs the works of love in his vision of the Last Judgement, he puts the following words into Jesus' mouth: "inasmuch as ye have done it unto one of the least of these my brethren, ye have done it unto me". Who are "the least of these"? It is often thought that they are people who are disadvantaged in some way, marginalized outcasts of society. But we might also interpret it to mean that they are people who are no good as a means to anything. What is done for them is done for themselves, their value as such. The same thinking may be applied to sinners, the publicans, the prodigal son, and the lost sheep. They cannot serve as spiritual representatives of the congregation, and the love and acceptance shown to them is not shown for any spiritual merit, but for themselves. In that sense they, too, belong to "the least", although that aspect of the matter usually goes unnoticed.

It is another matter altogether that although we cannot turn any of the "the least" into an instrument for anything at all, we can turn the "works of love" we direct at them (such as helping them) into instruments of earning some merit for ourselves. In that case it is no longer a question of them or their value, but of ourselves and various other things.

Love reveals the intrinsic value of the object of love to us. However, love is not an attitude that is at the disposal of our conscious will. That is why we spoke of "works of love" and not love. The same goes for all, even the least, degrees of love. They are not determined by conscious will, either.

Is it then even possible for us to see man's intrinsic value — another person's and our own value as such—unless some degree of love has revealed it to us, unless it has become obvious to us regardless of our will? I would assume that there is another way, one that is not independent of our will to the extent love is. I refer to respect.

We may outline the question as follows: love teaches and enlightens us about the fact that others and we ourselves have value as such and that it is possible to see this value immediately, when it is revealed to us by love. Respect, again, means that we assume or attach to another person or ourselves value for itself, regardless of whether we are able to see it at the moment or not. We, so to speak, wish to believe in its existence, although we cannot see it. Or, to put it even more prudently: we want to behave in such a way that we do not by our behaviour deny the possibility that value exists, but, quite the opposite, we want to assume or attach value. We want to trust what love teaches us of intrinsic value. It is no longer independent of our will, but it may often feel naïve or valiant.

What destroys or hinders our love destroys and hinders the possibility of intrinsic values becoming revealed to us. Instrumental values, which are based on "what follows what" type of knowledge, by contrast, we can easily see and learn to see even more of them. The destinies of instrumental values follow the destinies of our intelligence and knowledge. The destinies of intrinsic values—and therefore of the value of man as well—follow the destinies of love and respect. When we inquire into the value of people and things, we ought to inquire into our love and its destinies: what awakened love and what destroyed it, what opened ways for it and what hindered it? Of this, psychoanalysis has a great deal to say.

Acknowledgements

My grateful thanks to Kaisa Sivenius for translating this chapter into English.

Reference

Drewermann, E. (1997). *Vain Sydämellä Näkee Hyvin (It Is Only with the Heart that One Can See Rightly)*. Helsinki: Kirjapaja.

CHAPTER TWELVE

The religions of health and beauty

Mikael Enckell

V ery likely there are some robust natures—my father would probably have considered them dull—who think they are hale and hearty and who consequently hardly ever worry about illness or even think of it for long periods. Gloating or envious, we may presume that the merciless circumstances of life will sooner or later catch up with them, too, and bring them back into line. They seem not to be particularly numerous either among authors or among those who have joined the medical profession.

Still, we can distinguish common features of kinship in all these three kinds of people: in the robust, "imaginary healthy", in the hypersensitive, nervous authors, and in the—mostly—skilful, doctors. I mean that all three, even if they go their separate ways, are passionately engaged in gaining control of the powers that, often unfamiliar and beyond the horizon of our ability to see, are unpredictable threats against our lives and our well-being. The robust, by means of denying illness—sometimes with their lives at stake, for example after a heart attack—refuse to submit to their symptoms with the humility their own interests dictate. And the imaginative author, by constantly dealing with all kinds of possible illness, in actual fact rejects the reality of an enemy that threatens us all from a more or less unfamiliar direction. As far as doctors are concerned, we need only remind ourselves that at hospitals it is said that doctors constitute a clientele that is particularly difficult to treat. We can then understand how anxiety-ridden they become when a central defence method, medical treatment, can no longer keep the danger at a distance from themselves.

Foreboding at the prospect of various illnesses and approaching death, even if at the moment no illness even exists, is a particularly obvious and malignant special case of the anxiety and uneasiness that the universal, inevitable uncertainty of life conjures up in us. Of course we see it, too, in the sense of insecurity that is an integral part of all our human relations, evoked by our distinct, or sometimes indistinct, awareness of how little we basically know about those close to us, ourselves included. It is true that we imagine for a long time that we really know our parents, our children, and those we share our intimate lives with, but the fact is that we know them to a considerably less extent than our need for security demands. Both are mistaken to a great extent and at times this fact, painful or joyous, is surprisingly clear.

These uncertainty factors are, on the whole, enemies, saboteurs of the peace and harmony we seek. And now I would like to defend the thesis that there is an unmistakable parallel between the authors' and the doctors' ways of dealing with these basically insurmountable factors in life. Considerably simplified and stylized, the common pattern might be described as follows: Afflicted by accidents and adversity each person tries, by drawing close to real or fictitious fellow beings, to get to know the Adversary, but via someone else and under the cloak of the scientific or aesthetic illusion and thus under the protection of the dangers that are "real." Only the individual perspective of a personal fate can act as an intermediary for the understanding of detail that gives us the feeling of a genuine response in this connection. We are always waiting for the individual case, the individual details, in order to attain the feeling we long for, the feeling that we understand something of someone else's world of experience. This is a lucky, satisfactory situation limited to a concern for only two: he who understands and he who is understood. Here the pattern from all deep intimacy between people is repeated, modelled on the prototypes: the meeting between the two lovers or the mother and her child. Often the two contracting parties alternate in this intimate interplay of the two roles that complement each other.

For this reason, we shall come closer to the conceptual network between literature and medicine as they are reflected in Marcel Proust's life and work. In Proust's case, as opposed to what probably was the case with Anton Tchekhov, it is rather a question of the invalid's perspective than of the doctor's. The first, born of the recent marriage between the Catholic doctor Adrien Proust and the Jewish stockbroker's daughter Jeanne Weil, Proust faced a threatening environment from the time of his birth in 1871 in a Paris surrounded by the Germans. Its people were starving and shaken by the Communard insurrection, soon to be bloodily defeated.

As an infant, the boy was generally regarded as unfit for life, and his difficult start survived in the minds of mother and son from then on, contributing to the legendary strong bond between them. When Marcel was barely two years of age his brother, Robert, was born. He was to follow his father's example, becoming a doctor, a surgeon, and a professor of medicine, extroverted and successful. The relation between the brothers has consistently been characterized as good, even if as adults they were not particularly close to each other.

At the age of ten, on a walk in Bois de Boulogne during a visit to his grandparents' home in Auteuil, where he was born in 1871, Marcel had a serious choking fit. This was the first attack of the serious asthma that would later make him an invalid for the rest of his life, and would also actively contribute to his premature death at the age of fifty-one. He wrote himself of how upsetting this traumatic experience is for a child who has always considered air and breathing as natural and often even enjoyable. Here he is confronted with the terrifying fact that they are no longer that—a surprising drowning on dry land that in the future would be only inches away.

Thus, the misgivings from Marcel's infant period recurred, affecting everyone in the family. In every respect he became hypersensitive and sickly, spending weeks in bed. For months at a time he was absent from the classes he had begun at the Lycée Condorcet at about the same time as the asthma debut. At this school, with its high standard, he was inspired by the philosophy teacher Darlu and he established important friendships with gifted youths like

Jacques Bizet (the son of the composer) and Daniel Halévy. His mother watched over him, put him on a milk diet, rationed his relations with friends she feared were detrimental to his development, and, for example, for the sake of his health sent him wholesome wines at the garrison where he was doing his military service.

In many ways he contributed himself to this closeness to his parents *vis-à-vis* his health and his intimate life. For example, he asked his father for advice concerning details of his sexual habits. Even if his father in his capacity as an internationally famous hygienist—one of the creators of the *cordon sanitaire* for the prevention of the cholera epidemics of the period—could be seen as an authority in the subject, Marcel's frankness seems surprising to a Finnish observer.

There is a dividing line, a chasm, between the various members of the Proustian family that makes it seem to disintegrate into two factions. There is the medical side stressing health, with the two doctors, Adrien and Robert, identified as heterosexual and masculine, socially and erotically active and successful. There is the side engaged in literature, identified as the feminine part of the family: Jeanne and Marcel. The latter is the invalid, constantly craving affection, mainly homosexually oriented, literary, socially and sexually devoted to the role of the observer, the chronicler of an inner reality that he nevertheless supplemented with an outer reality and an historical process. Mother and son were united in their literary ambitions by the common project of together translating Ruskin from English to French, texts that were to have great significance for the development of Proust's aesthetic idealism.

Of particular interest are the differences of opinion concerning concepts of the ideal between the two factions of the family. On the one side there are the rational, pragmatic doctors with their sights set on what promotes health and the social good. On the other side there is the philosophical–literary perspective on the conditions required for literary productivity and its goals. Proust writes as follows:

> Happy years are wasted years. We must wait for suffering in order to be able to work. Happiness is beneficial for the body but it is grief that develops the powers of the mind. But let us welcome the physical pain that grief affords us as the price for the spiritual

knowledge it gives us. Let our bodies decompose since every piece
that is released from it is linked to our work. . . . [1938, pp. 58–59]

Is this not a resolute polemic against the well-meaning
hygienic–medical treatment programme whose aim is to promote
good health but which totally disregards the nucleus of our
emotional life, conflict, and pain?

In these and related polemics it is essentially a matter of differences between our respective perceptions of reality and the ensuing
consequences. It is, however, not only that among ourselves we
have different ideas about what our reality is like. For example,
reality seems different to the famous hygienist Adrien Proust on a
trip to Egypt and Persia to research the infection routes of cholera
to Europe than to the asthma afflicted and often bedridden Marcel
Proust, engaged in configuring the inner realities that have formed
just his own life. Besides this we, together, have several perceptions
of reality at the same time and we give priority to one or another
depending on the inner and outer situations we happen to find
ourselves in when we speak and write to each other.

Let us expound our thinking further, beginning with the fact
that we all have several perceptions of reality existing parallel to
each other. From these we choose and discard depending on the
circumstances that are guiding us. On the top layer we have the
prevailing social ideas, the reality shared with others and interpreted conventionally. For the most part this dominates our practical lives and seldom provides a reason for speculations about the
true nature of reality. Under this often comparatively uncompli-
cated reality, however, other considerably more mysterious conceptual patterns live and work. Periodically, sometimes more often
than we realize, these influence our moods and our conduct, for
example in day-dreams, dreams, magic and superstition or, less
often, in the strange hall of mirrors of the psychotic state.

We might imagine such a layer of reality in our soul as a woven
fabric consisting of the traumatic experiences we have encountered.
Because of the dominating intensity they possess and the effects
they have had and have—both forward and backward in time,
retroactively—they contribute enormously to the formation of the
image of the individual's life where they were found. In any case
this is true for the individual himself, even if the traumata did not

occur during the early stage of the general character formation in childhood.

From this layer of more or less straightforward, trauma-linked recollections, Proust for the most part drew his life-work, and seen from this angle it is significant that he did not start his work on the novel (*A la Recherche du Temps Perdu*) until the time of his mother's death in 1905. Her presence and his thoughts about it—the focal point of the novel's first section—must have played an important role in the choking fits he suffered from the eleventh year of his life. Her definite disappearance thus triggered the creation of an imaginary world where she was always present, but where at the same time her presence was continuously threatened by his awareness of her actual absence.

Thus we can see *Remembrance of Things Past* as both a traumatophilic and a trauma-vanquishing mausoleum erected over the loss of his mother, where the loss itself represents a reunion with her. The text reports in profusion vestiges of the feelings of abandonment and jealousy he felt. It can be said that the painful experiences Proust incessantly returns to are a kind of "delayed" or "lingering" versions of the original, sudden, chaotic trauma: pain as trauma in slow motion. And already carried a bit further towards more distinct, more clearly defined ideas.

While medical thought, in the Proustian family upheld by Adrien and Robert, represents technological thinking which, when it has established a functional disorder, goes on to recommend a technique to "take care of" it, Marcel's literary thought concentrates on what we inevitably experience. For better or for worse he lives in a world of sensations, what we are blessed with and what we cannot escape.

In Proust's novel there are several collisions between Marcel's thought and the medical attitude. What is perhaps the most extensive survey of doctors and their various idiosyncrasies is presented in the description of his grandmother's illness and death from uraemia, for the most part described from the angle of his mother's last illness in September 1905. At the same time it is one of the most explicit narratives in the novel of the reunion with human helplessness in the face of the inevitable. This is sometimes reflected in Marcel's agitation, anxiety, and guilt feelings, sometimes in the extremely varying reactions on the part of the doctors about what later on becomes more and more obvious: the impossibility of maintaining a belief in a happy outcome. This is to say that here we meet something essential to the traumatic situation: nothing any more can avert what seems to you the very worst that can happen. And you have nothing to successfully defend yourself with.

In this respect, it is a matter of a special kind of literature, a literature of texts that not only crystallize around intolerable experiences, but whose main task is also to search them out again as time goes by, to ponder over them and be mirrored in them. Another and even more obvious example of this kind of literature is the work of last year's Nobel prize winner. Imre Kertesz's entire authorship is based on his concentration camp experiences. When he says that his native land is rather Auschwitz than Hungary, or that that camp was the best thing that has ever happened to him, he is indicating his point of departure, what lent substance and goal to his inner life.

Like so many basic and incomprehensible revelations about human life, this is at once an absurdity, a paradox, and a truth. A zealous psychotherapist with his sights set on recovery might call this literary position deplorably "masochistic". Since the author in question is trying to find experiences that were primarily difficult, painful, or intolerable, the term seems to be correct. But if, as is all too often the case, we introduce a predominantly negative connotation, the characterization then seems misleading and downright counter-productive. For what intellectual, artistic or otherwise innovative achievements have not had as crucial prerequisites and points of departure an intense interest in what has once been suffered? If not all, then at least a large number.

Here, we are touching on one of the points where, in the course of striving towards well-being and happiness, therapeutic thought finds itself on an obvious collision course with reasoning that reflects our forced or even voluntary interaction with the accidents of life and our own history. Few authors have with more conviction and intellectual force castigated the rationalistic progressive optimism that we inherited from the Enlightenment and the liberalism of the nineteenth century than Dostoyevsky. In *Notes from the Underground*, which starts with the wonderful sentences, "I am a sick man. I am a spiteful man. I am an unattractive man. I believe my liver is diseased," the author goes on:

And why are you so firmly, so triumphantly, convinced that only the normal and the positive—in other words, only what is conducive to welfare—is for the advantage of man? Is not reason in error as regards advantage? Does not man, perhaps, love something besides well being? Perhaps he is just as fond of suffering? Perhaps suffering is just as great a benefit to him as well being? Man is sometimes extraordinarily, passionately, in love with suffering, and that is a fact. There is no need to appeal to universal history to prove that; only ask yourself if you are a man and have lived at all. As far as my personal opinion is concerned, to care only for well being seems to me to be positively ill-bred. Whether it's good or bad, it is sometimes very pleasant, too, to smash things. [1956, p. 36]

From the above it is clear that we are dealing with two different kinds of thought: one socio–medical–technological, where the goals are self-evident and seldom questioned, and one existential–literary where scarcely anything at all is self-evident in principle. Everything can be the object of doubt and objections. Like all other forms of human thought, both of these are also basically imperialistic in nature; they both strive to extend themselves as far as possible and hardly admit directly that their approach is limited with regard to validity. Every human thought is by its nature and its essence fundamentalistic and, in order to be induced to retreat to a position within the limits of reasonable applications, must be refuted by a new thought, a different opinion that is just as legitimate.

Let us now adopt a similar way of looking at things: every thought and every opinion is like a tool, usable in some connections but not in others, where it ought preferably to be replaced by something else. If this is so, then such a limitation probably applies also to this relativizing point of view, doesn't it? Where then do we find a barrier against this relativizing mandate?

We can see this kind of barrier being formed by the actual emergence and early developmental history of the thought itself. That is to say that as one of its necessary prerequisites and necessities of life it, the thought, has the illusion of unrestricted omnipotence. Without this illusion it withers and shrivels, ceases to captivate its thinker, dies and disappears before it has really matured and materialized.

In order to understand better the inner, inevitable hubris of productive thought, I think we ought to look at the real roots of ways of thinking, the inner and outer reality configurations of the various religions. We do not perceive significant thoughts as if we ourselves had brought them about. They "turn up", we are somehow inspire,d and then attribute them to divine influence. We get a free ride on them, so to speak, into the land of their birth: the kingdom of omnipotence and timelessness.

And there Marcel Proust also resides by virtue of the seven-volume work, *Remembrance of Things Past*, which, in almost three thousand pages, creates a world not less universal or eternal than Homer's and not even inferior to the Bible in the matter of potentialities for creating worlds. More than any other literary work of the twentieth century, Proust's novel invites the reader to enter a world created by the author and re-created by the reader. The consistency with which this project is carried out lifts it high above the many notable books of the century.

Graham Greene wrote:

> Proust was the greatest novelist of the twentieth century, just as Tolstoy was of the nineteenth. . . . For those who began writing at the end of the twenties or the beginning of the thirties there were two whose influence was inescapable: Proust and Freud, who complemented each other. [quoted from White, 1999, p. 2]

To this the commentator Edmund White adds the following assessment:

> Assuredly Proust's reputation and prestige overshadows Joyce's, Beckett's, Virginia Woolf's and Faulkner's, Hemingway's, Fitzgerald's, Gide's, Valéry's and Genet's. [*ibid.*]

And his superiority rests conclusively on his ability to create a world, which in turn is dependent not only on the breadth of the novel but also on its style, as the German philologist of the period between the wars Curtius stated in an essay on Proust's style in *The Criterion* (1924). In it, the outer world and the inner reality reflect each other continually and incessantly, and so give the personality a backbone of eternal life. Just as forgetting is a prerequisite for successful recollection so variations and changes are the starting points for the experience of the essential return; for Proust the manifestation of Beauty above others.

And this aesthetic and literary victory over change, forgetting, and death is brought home partly at the expense of more short-sighted satisfactions and with a disregard for a largely prescribed life due to health considerations. The hygienist and the doctor recommend a sound way of life and appeal in this way to our desire for a long, basically eternal, life. Proust met an early death, but transported himself and the reader into an adventure that was certainly momentary and gliding by, but also recurring, of the eternities that lie at the bottom of our most intense impressions and experiences. Perhaps with some simplification we can here distinguish a front line between two religions—the religions of medical health and aesthetic beauty.

References

Curtius, E. R. (1924). On the style of Marcel Proust. *The Criterion*, April: 311–320.
White, E. (1999). *Proust*. London: Weidenfeld and Nicolson.

CHAPTER THIRTEEN

Descartes' *cogito* as a model of reality

Johannes Lehtonen

The French philosopher René Descartes (1596–1650) has been one of the most influential figures in the history of philosophy and the sciences. The long-prevailing view of a dichotomy between mind and body in western thinking derives from Descartes' differentiation between the laws governing the external physical world and the private facts of the subjectively experienced mental life (*res extensa* and *res cogitans*). In her introduction to the latest Finnish edition of his writings, Alanen (2001) describes Descartes' work as an ambitious endeavour to establish a scientific explanation of the world ruled by natural laws and to lay down principles of thought that would lead to a certainty beyond question. Descartes' influence has been greatest in the field of philosophy of the mind. His achievements in mathematics and optics were also considerable, as was his thinking in moral philosophy, but his physiological investigations did not lead to any definitive findings.

Descartes' most important insight was his affirmation of the irrefutable certainty of the sense of being that can be attained through the process of thinking, which he epitomized in the famous axiom *cogito ergo sum*. In *Discours de la Méthode* (1637) Descartes reached that conclusion by way of doubting the trustworthiness of all knowledge. Only knowledge a person is himself able to recognize as valid, as opposed to what is externally learned, is of consequence. Even modest knowledge, provided that it is personally appropriated, brings greater satisfaction than extensive formal learning. It is crucial to search for knowledge that one can understand and perceive personally. To show off by using the wisdom of others makes no sense. It is necessary to develop one's own method of thinking, which can be trusted. Significant is only what one has made one's own and knows to be true through one's own thinking. Although no grand insights may ensue, anything found by one's own thinking is significant when it is certain, and it can be used as a basis for seeking further truths. For that reason, humility, or concentrating on personally attested understanding, can give great joy.

In presenting his method of thought, Descartes argues that anything can be doubted. The senses are deceptive and can lead to incorrect observations. False deductions can be made, and thinking may be delusive. Nothing is absolutely certain. After describing convincingly and in detail the systematic uncertainty entailed in the making of observations and in thinking, and drawing attention to the fact that there is always room for doubt, Descartes asserts that the person who doubts everything is oneself. From that, *I think, therefore I am* follows inevitably. Descartes' method of thinking is thus primarily one of doubting, which in itself, however, can no longer be doubted. Doubting does not put an end to thinking. Doubt, on the contrary, is proof of the existence of thought, and therefore of the continuity of being. To think or not to think is an impossible question.

Descartes' method of thinking demonstrates that by systematically following the demands of critical thought, by abandoning everything that is certain, and thereby stepping into the void, the doubter can find his very self. In the insight "It is I who think", sense of being and, consequently, sense of self, reach to the level of intelligibility, since the two are connected in the process of thinking. Descartes' acceptance of the vacuum resulting from systematic doubt led him to the discovery of a personal sense of being. For him, the basis of thought revealed by the *cogito ergo sum* principle meant the achieving of both personal and philosophical certainty.

Its importance for philosophy, and science in general, unquestionably results from the fact that its logic is immediately and universally recognized: it has both a personal and a scientific resonance.

Cogito accepts empirical uncertainty

It is important to distinguish between everything connected with the objects of *cogito* and the constitutive elements of the thinking process. Systematic doubt about the certainty of knowledge concerning the objects of thought is what gives *cogito* its cogency, and indicates simultaneously the limited nature of human knowledge, a tenet that underlies all Descartes' thinking. By the systematic use of critical doubt he opened up a new way of thinking, which gave freedom to cognition as a means of investigating the nature of the world and the self.

Exposing the structure of the existing world to free scrutiny by following the rules of cognition required, however, that knowledge be released from its existential bonds. The problem of whether knowledge and doubt, if followed without let or hindrance, could result in a threat to human self-understanding, had to be resolved. Only then was it possible for thinking to become a method that could be freely used in the study of existence and its conditions. Thereafter, uncertainty and the discovery of hitherto unknown lacunæ were not merely the permanent lot of the investigator, but characterized the very essence of thinking and illustrated the nature of knowledge by calling attention to its limits. None of this lessened the significance of scientific findings; rather, paradoxically, it underscored their value.

What, then, is the origin of the freedom of critical thinking that became possible for Descartes? After such a decisive insight, critical awareness could no longer question the certainty of existence; more precisely, Descartes' assurance of *his own sense of being*. The limitations and uncertainty of knowledge, and the fickleness, even the illusory nature of thought, could not shake the foundations of that sense of being. Scientific and critical thinking, indeed rational knowledge in general, were freed from their conditional state and became fully permissible, something that had not been possible before Descartes' perception. The increase of knowledge lost its critical significance for religion and for the theological premisses of existence. Descartes loosened the bonds and scientific enterprise became free of religious control, as has been pointed out by Georg Henrik von Wright (1987) in his discussion of the *cogito ergo sum* dictum.

Sense of being as the basis of cogito

When the focus is shifted from the objects of investigative thought to the constitutive grounds of Descartes' conclusion, another important perspective is revealed. In the certainty that in thinking, originally doubting, I must exist, because the one who doubts is myself, thought and the sense of being are united. It is impossible to refute logically the validity of Descartes' claim. He who doubts everything is *himself* the one who doubts and thinks, and thus unquestionably exists; otherwise his doubting would not exist. From the certainty of doubt and from the impossibility of thought that does not exist may arise, however, the notion that Descartes' formula is simply cognitive in nature and concerns nothing more than the contents of cognitive thinking. But this is not the case. Descartes' conclusion is impressive precisely on account of the fact that it unites cognition with the sense of being, however elusive that sense may be.

Cognitive assertions like "This is my hand" or "This is my body" are not sufficient to confer trustworthiness upon the sense of being. The certainty of existence requires more than just cognitive deduction. The famous proof of the existence of the external world presented by the philosopher G. E. Moore may serve as an example and indirect illustration of that. At the end of a long lecture, he raised first his right hand and then his left in order to convince the audience of its reality (Moore, 1939), thus manifestly coupling cognition of existence and sense of being. Descartes was more explicit, however. His insight "It is I and no-one else who exist(s) in my thinking" did not conceptualize the sense of being by using concrete metaphors. By creating a bond between the personal *me* and the enigmatic *sense of being,* he attributed a personal cast to the latter and thereby conceptualized their relation in purely psychological terms.

Cogito and dualism

That the probative force of the axiom stems essentially from the sense of being is something that appears to have received scant attention. Descartes' philosophy has usually been regarded as an expression of the dualistic relation of mind and body, which implies the division of reality on the one hand into natural-scientific and objective explanations of the world, and on the other into individual, subjective, inner psychological, and intentional, in the last resort, mental existence. Descartes was certainly a dualist in that he differentiated between *res cogitans* and *res extensa*, but in his *cogito* dictum he used no auxiliary arguments. In itself, the insight did not postulate two different substances, nor did it entail denial of the meaning of physical substance. Although in scientific debate the physical nature of phenomena is often considered to be the ultimate model and only true proof of reality,[1] Descartes' conclusion about the certainty of the sense of being, revealed in the process of thinking, shows that thinking is an equally authentic proof, and therein lies the deepest significance of his enthymem.

Descartes deduction has been understood, especially by psychosomatic and neuro-biological reseachers, to mean the expulsion of the mind from the body. For this reason it has been subjected to criticism and even described as Descartes' error (Damasio, 1996). He accepted, however, the mind–body connection and believed the pineal gland to be the site of their interaction, but that was not pivotal for his philosophy. The all-important feature of his axiom was the uniting of cognitive thought and sense of being, which gave to thinking a scientifically assured existence, with its own principles, within and not outside the physical world. It also freed the mind from the limitations of physical *description,* but made no statement about its nature, as he later clearly explained (Descartes, 1641).

The perspective of developmental psychology

After establishing the irrefutability of his personal existence Descartes went on to say:

> From that I knew that I was a substance, the whole essence or nature of which is to think, and that for its existence there is no

need of any place, nor does it depend on any material thing; so that this "me", that is to say, the soul by which I am what I am, is entirely distinct from body, and is even more easy to know than is the latter; and even if body were not, the soul would not cease to be what it is.

And in *Meditations* (Descartes, 1641) he asseverates: "I am a thing that thinks."

Such thoughts were, of course, retrospective, and they do not supplant or alter Descartes' central insight. From a psychoanalytical point of view, the reassuring quality of the enthymem can be seen simply as an indication of a developmental step. The certainty of the sense of being it implies seems to originate in the special thing-like nature of the undifferentiated experiences that dominate infantile psychological life before the symbolic function becomes available. Their source is in the bodily sensations and affects which ultimately constitute the sense of being. Because it unites cognitive thought and sense of being, Descartes' *cogito*, rather than implying some kind of mind-substance, supplies a prime example of the connection that may arise between verbal and thing presentations, which is basic for achieving the developmental level of conscious presentations and symbolic functioning (Freud, 1915e, p. 201).

Via the sense of being, Descartes' description of the nature of the mind thus contains an affective component that endows thinking with the certainty of existence. A differentiated image of the self, as something distinct from objects, is an achievement that a child becomes gradually capable of towards the end of its first year of life (Mahler *et al.*, 1975; Stern, 1985; Tyson & Tyson, 1990). Affects connected with the early sense of being are different from categorical affects related to differentiated object relationships. Sense of being as an affect is of a more fundamental order. Among the many researchers in the field, especially Veikko Tähkä (1993) has emphasized the significance of the developmental step from undifferentiated psycho-physiological affects to coherent and differentiated object-relational affects.

A sense of the continuity of being begins to mature in the mind of the child between the ages of six and eight months. Anxiety when meeting a stranger is usually regarded as the external manifestation thereof, signifying the ability of the infant to experience the presence and absence of the securing mother in a personally unique way (Spitz, 1957, 1959). Stern (1985) uses the concept *emergent self* for the first developmental phase, which leads to the crystallization, at the age of approximately three months, of the core self. Piaget (Wolff, 1960) characterized the first level in the development of thinking as the sensory–motor phase, which he divided into several sub-phases. Spitz underlined the coenæsthetic nature of the first organization of the self.

"The body ego" (*Das Körper Ich*, Freud, 1923b) is an umbrella concept which can be regarded as covering the earliest developmental stages of the ego. From the point of view of the body ego, the key to understanding this early development is its connection with the bodily experiences, instinctual functions and satisfactions of the infant. These experiences are realized via the body surface, either in the skin or in the mucosa of the mouth and the alimentary tract. Freud (1923b) depicted the body ego as the psychic projection of the body surface. I have suggested (Lehtonen, 1991, 1997) that the body ego, as the first organizing principle of the human personality, becomes psychologically manifest in the primary organization of dream experiences, i.e., in the dream screen (Lewin, 1946). Through the tie between the dream screen and the body ego, the emergent psychological life of the infant becomes anchored to the nascent unconscious ordering of the infant's mental (or protomental) experiences and the formation of the matrix for dreaming and, therefore, thinking.

The physical reciprocity involved in the care of the child by the mother provides the emergent self with many kinds of observations and experiences. The interactions gradually lead to primary models of psychological functioning within the care-taking relationship. In one way or another, the impressions created in the infant are linked to experience of the body, particularly its surface, and they have vital significance for the continuity of the physical and psychological existence of the baby. These experiences, *in statu nascendi*, are not yet expressible in words, though they are available for verbal communication later, when the bodily core of affective experience is acknowledged. Those early life experiences remain unconscious and pre-verbal, as well as undifferentiated with respect to their origin, i.e., the infant is unaware as to whether they are instigated from within or without. As Winnicott put it "In absolute dependence the infant has no means of awareness of maternal provision" (Winnicott, 1963, p. 87).

Towards the end of the first stage of body ego development, primary identification with the mother-object begins to be consolidated by the mutual identification of infant and mother (Hoffer, 1966). The identification is intensified in parallel with the emergence of the first autonomous self-experience, when the organization of the core self begins to detach itself from the maternal environment. Primary identification can be seen as a threshold phase from undifferentiation towards differentiation, and it forms the step that creates coherence and leads the infant to an integrated personal unity (Salonen, 1989, 1997). Distinct mental images and cognitive categories of thought thus become truly meaningful only after the sense of being has become stable and so strong that changes in the child's circumstances and its dependence on the mother and other external factors are no longer a threat to an enduring sense of being. Winnicott thought the experience of continuity was critical at this stage of development of the self. When the sense of being gains in strength and staying power, the mind can continue its development towards individuality and differentiate into a true self from the *psyche* part of the undifferentiated psyche-soma (Winnicott, 1949).

In the developing child, the good primary body affects are delimited by experiences of hunger, abandonment, and the absence of care and satisfaction. When such negative body affects are dispelled by adequate care, the integration of experiences of satisfaction and absence of care will follow. Good and bad experiences become fused and the sense of being becomes more stable. In these experiences mind and body are inseparably linked to one another because affects, which arise via bodily experience, are tied to the body's biological processes, especially to those that are connected with vital body processes, as Damasio (1996, 2000) has also emphasized. Affects motivate attempts to repeat good experiences that will assure continuity and preserve relationships that provide satisfaction and support the sense of being. Bodily and affective events thus combine to shape the developing individual into a unity which cannot be understood by using *only* natural scientific categories of the body, or *only* descriptions of affective, and other mental functions.

The psychological understanding of the mind´s relationship to the body is also corroborated by the findings of neuro-biological research. Damasio (2000, pp. 270–271) has shown that several areas in the brain, like the periaqueductal grey, the anterior cingulate, and parts of the neo-cortex, participate in the inception of the earliest elements of a sense of being. He has characterized such experiences as "the feeling of what happens". He stresses the central importance of affects in the creation of the proto-self and the core consciousness. He attributes to them a crucial role in the regulation of brain activity and in guiding behaviour from the very beginning of individual development, all the more as the possibilities for unfettered choice increase. From this perspective, the ineradicable certainty of the thinking process, which was Descartes' special insight, is confirmed rather than discredited by the findings of modern neuro-biology, because there would be no sense in attempting to discover the neuro-biological basis of the feeling and thinking processes if the latter were mere epiphenomena.

The first years of Descartes' life

The great philosopher's mother, Jeanne Brochard, died on the 13th of March 1597, when René (born on the 31st March 1596) was not quite one year old. Descartes was brought up, together with his elder brother and sister, by his grandmother, Jeanne Sain, who became very close to René. His father, who took care of René's education in the best French schools of the period, remarried when René was four.

Descartes thus experienced the greatest loss possible for a small child, the death of his mother, at a very early age. He had presumably just attained a self-experience and sense of being separate from the continuity of his mother's presence. Without trying to draw any far-reaching psychological conclusions from these few biographical details, it is probable that Descartes' intuition, which was to change western philosophy and the scientific *Weltanschauung*, was in some sense the after-effect of his experience at the time of his mother´s death. We may suppose that he had just reached the early stage of his separate self: his sense of being in any case survived a loss that must have shaken the foundations of the small child's life. Could it be that it was that early bereavement which motivated him, many years later, to formulate the great philosophical theorem that made him famous? His mother's death did not completely destroy the one-year-old René's sense of being, which remained with him, no doubt largely through the support of his family. He made it his task as an adult to explore the cognitive and scientific grounds for the preservation of a sense of being when confronted by every possible source of doubt, a principle that was at the heart of his method of thinking.

Descartes' implacably scientific frame of mind and his strictly critical observations of reality, casting doubt upon everything that *seemed* to be, suggests that in the later phases of René's growth and development his father played an important part, particularly with respect to his personal ideals. Chasseguet-Smirgel (1983) has drawn attention to the significance of a father's influence in the acquisition of thinking that is based on the acceptance of order as opposed to chaos. She calls it a universal law and regards it as formative for the development of, and respect for, the abstract reality principle, which creates the preconditions for an understanding of the intrinsic meaning of facts and the need for scientific coherence, both of which were precious ideals for Descartes.

According to Gammelgaard (2002) there is a wavering stage in the development of the mind that precedes attainment of a stable self. Before achieving self integrity, the coherence of the self may for a time come and go, causing much uncertainty and suffering because of the still unstable relation between consciousness and the unconscious. Mastering it calls for extreme effort and the use of all the subject's strength and creativity in order to maintain the unity of the sense of self. It seems possible that, for Descartes, conscious and systematic doubt, which led to the certainty of his sense of being, was a great psychological relief, i.e., I do indeed exist. I did not disappear or get lost when my mother died.

The correspondence between Maxime Leroy and Freud on the subject of Descartes' dreams

Some support for the idea that there is a connection between his early life experience and his philosophy may be found in Descartes' dream material, which Maxime Leroy sent to Freud for analysis

(Freud, 1929b). Descartes' detailed descriptions of his dreams evince his conscentiousness also with respect to his internal mental life. Freud was of the opinion that the examples of those dreams that had been sent to him contained elements that were closely connected to the dreamer's day consciousness, in which matter he was surely right.

It seems, however, that Freud did not have access to Descartes' biographical data. Some elements in these dreams are suggestive of a severe, possibly catastrophic, threat that was mastered with great difficulty, especially the very beginning of the account of the dreams (Editor's note on Freud's letter to Maxime Leroy, Freud, 1929b, p. 200):

> Then, during the night, when all was fever, thunderstorms, panic, phantoms rose before the dreamer. He tried to get up in order to drive them away. But he fell back, ashamed of himself, feeling troubled by a great weakness in his right side. All at once, a window in the room opened. Terrified, he felt himself carried away by the gusts of a violent wind, which made him whirl round several times on his left foot.

In the dreaming that followed, he attempted to make his devotions, and the threat was about to be resolved by the appearance of a melon (probably a breast symbol), but he was removed from the melon by a new gust of wind. The last section of the dream sequence allowed him, nevertheless, peace with the aid of reading in the dream a passage from Ausonius, beginning with *est et non*, which was preceded by a contemplation of the theme *quod vitæ sectabor iter*.

It is probable that the early traumatic experience of losing his mother gave rise to a vivid sense of imminent danger that found expression in this dream of being carried away by the gusts of a violent wind, perhaps an allusion to a danger of death. Also the potential pacifier, the melon, was unavailable to him because a further gust of wind drove him away from it. With his trust in authority, represented in the dream by Ausonius, he was, however, able to contemplate his condition, which he did in Hamlet-like fashion—*est et non*[2]—and sought for a direction in his life—*quod vitæ sectabor iter*. The sequence of these dreams also shows Descartes' fidelity to his internal experience, which he maintained, despite serious threats, mastering them by his inherent mental capacities, together with the teachings available to him.

Conclusions

From the point of view of developmental psychology, the separation of thought from bodily experience is thus unwarranted. If we recognize, however, the affective aspect of the sense of being that is involved in Descartes' *cogito ergo sum*, and especially its origin in the bodily sense of being, its significance is brought into relief. *Cogito ergo sum* becomes possible when the world of primitive affects, as part of the original sense of being, related to the absolute dependence of the infant on the mother-object, is transformed into an independent and integrated existence in which the sense of being is gradually united with the process of thinking, or, in metapsychological terms, the connection is formed between thing and verbal presentations, leading to an increasingly distinct existence, a transition from absolute to relative dependence (Winnicott, 1963). Descartes' dictum cannot be questioned, nor can the fact that sense of being is integral to it. In addition to its philosophical and scientific meaning, *cogito ergo sum* implies, rather than a separate thinking substance, the cardinal developmental event of acquiring the capacity to experience the self as differentiated from the surrounding world, as a symbolic category of existence having personal "me-contours", which is, at the same time, also a condition for authentic human relations. This was developmentally important for Descartes, because he had to struggle to detach his self-image from the mother-image that had become associated with death. This conclusion is supported by the content of his dreams, which he memorized for consultation with friends in attempting to understand them, and which later became the subject of a correspondence between Freud and Leroy.

By becoming conscious, the experience of the sense of being finds a conceptual place with other, more familiar, thought categories and patterns. Although Descartes' assertion, by giving autonomous status to thinking in its wider meaning, may in one sense be considered dualistic, it also clearly unites the worlds of affect and thought. Descartes' perception, taken as it stands, thus does not divide the world completely into a mind that is fully independent of the body and a body that functions solely according to the findings of natural science, having no aspects pertaining to the mind. The experience of thinking is not realized *per se*, but within the sense of being, as his enthymem clearly indicates, and that connects it to bodily functions. The connection is also pertinent in the other direction: the affects that arise through bodily functions and satisfactions, and the dawning capacity to think, once they have gained some autonomy, begin to regulate the behaviour of the child and influence his or her relation both to the self and the caretaking environment. Mind and body (brain) are inter-relational. Philosophically, that implies that neither is *alone* sufficient as the basis for a theory that will cover both the biological and the personal self. We need more inclusory models.

Notes

1. Henrik Enckell has presented the view that all scientific models may be seen as potentially equal, since they can all be regarded as metaphors of the reality they attempt to explain (Enckell, 2001).
2. *Est et non* may also point to an earlier stage of development, which Spitz (1957) linked with the infant's capacity to express *yes* and *no*.

Acknowledgement

I am grateful to Antony and Elisabeth Landon for the translation.

References

Alanen, L. (2001). The Life, scientific work and philosophical thinking of Descartes (in Finnish Descartesin elämä, tieteellinen työ ja filosofinen ajattelu). *The Works of René Descartes I* (pp. 7–27). Helsinki: Gaudeamus Yliopistokustannus University Press.

Chasseguet-Smirgel, J. (1983). Perversion and the universal law. *International Review of Psycho-Analysis, 10*: 293–303

Damasio, A. R. (1996). *Descartes' Error. Emotion, Reason and the Human Brain*. New York: Putnam Books.

Damasio, A. R. (2000). *The Feeling of What Happens. Body, Emotion and the Making of Consciousness*. London: Vintage.

Descartes, R. (1637) [2001]. *Discours de la Méthode*. (pp. 117–168). Transl. T. Aho, L. Alanen, S. Jansson, T. Kaitaro, M. Reuter & M. Yrjönsuuri. Helsinki: Gaudeamus, Yliopistokustannus University Press.

Descartes, R. (1641) [2002]. *Meditationes de Prima Philosophia*. Finnish translation from C. Adam & P. Tannery (Eds.), *Oeuvres de Descartes I–XII* (pp. 19–84). Paris: Cerf 1897–1909, transl. T. Aho, L. Alanen, S. Jansson, T. Kaitaro, J. Kaukua, M. Reuter & M. Yrjönsuuri. Helsinki: Gaudeamus Yliopistokustannus University Press.

Enckell, H. (2001). Psychic reality and psychoanalysis: A look through the theory of metaphor. *Psychoanalysis and Contemporary Thought, 24*: 231–252.

Freud, S. (1961). The unconscious. (1915e). *S.E., 14*: 159—215. London: Hogarth Press.

Freud, S. (1961). The ego and the id. (1923b) *S.E., 19*: 1–59. London: Hogarth Press.

Freud, S. (1961). Some dreams of Descartes. a letter to Maxime Leroy. (1929). *S.E., 21*: 197–204. London: Hogarth Press.

Gammelgaard, J. (2002). Det Ubevidste: Indhold og Genese (The unconcious: content and genesis). *Presented at the Nordic Psychoanalytic Congress, Oulu 1-4 August 2002.*

Hoffer, W. (1966). Infant observations and concepts relating to infancy. In: W. Hoffer (Ed.), *Early Development and Education of the Child* (pp. 75–90). London: The International Psycho-Analytical Library/The Hogarth Press.

Lehtonen, J. (1991). The body ego from the point of view of psychophysical fusion. *Psychotherapy and Psychosomatics, 56*: 30–35.

Lehtonen, J. (1997). On the origins of the body ego and its implications for psychotic vulnerability. In: V. Volkan & S. Akhtar (Eds.), *The Seed of Madness: Constitution, Maternal Environment, and Fantasy in the Organization of the Psychotic Core* (pp. 19–57). New York: International Universities Press.

Lewin, B. D. (1946). Sleep, the mouth, and the dream screen. *Psychoanalytical Quarterly, 15*: 119–134.

Mahler, M., Pine, F., & Bergman, A. (1975). *The Psychological Birth of the Human Infant*. New York: W. W. Norton.

Moore, G. E. (1965). Proof of an external world. 1939. Transl. S. A. Kivinen. In: G. E. Moore, *Etiikan peruskysymyksiä* (pp. 83–116). Keuruu: Otava.

Salonen, S. (1989). The restitution of primary identification in psychoanalysis. *Scandinavian Psychoanalytical Review, 12*: 102–115.

Salonen, S. (1997). Humiliation and dignity: Reflections on ego integrity. In: V. Volkan & S. Akhtar (Eds.), *The Seed of Madness. Constitution, Environment, and Fantasy in the Organization of the Psychotic Core* (pp. 59–79). Madison: International Universities Press.

Spitz, R. A. (1957). *No and Yes.* New York: International Universities Press.

Spitz, R. A. (1959). *A Genetic Field Theory of Ego Formation.* New York: International Universities Press.

Stern, D. (1985). *The Interpersonal World of the Infant.* New York: Basic Books.

Tyson, P., & Tyson, R. L. (1990). *Psychoanalytic Theories of Development: An Integration.* New Haven: Yale University Press.

Tähkä, V. (1993). *The Mind and Its Treatment. A Psychoanalytic Approach.* Madison, CT: International Universities Press.

Winnicott, D. W. (1949). Mind and its relation to the psyche-soma. In: D. W. Winnicott, *Through Pediatrics to Psychoanalysis* (pp. 243–254) [reprintedLondon: The Hogarth Press, 1987].

Winnicott, D. W. (1963). From dependence towards independence in the development of the individual. In: D. W. Winnicott, *The Maturational Processes and the Facilitating Environment* (pp. 83–92) [reprinted London: The Hogarth Press, 1979].

Wolff, P. H. (1960). The developmental psychologies of Jean Piaget and psychoanalysis. In: *Psychological Issues,* Vol. II, No. 1, Monograph 5 (p. 181). New York: International Universities Press.

Wright, G. H. von (1987). *Science and Human Reason* (in Finnish *Tiede ja ihmisjärki*) (p. 58). Helsinki: Otava.

CHAPTER FOURTEEN

The conceptual space of psychoanalysis

Simo Salonen

P sychoanalytic understanding takes place in a conceptual space that was created by Freud's scientific vision. Instead of being exhausted by time, the creative potential of this space still generates lively discussion and informs psychoanalytical thought. In fact, it is striking to realize how often new psychoanalytic discoveries and contemporary theoretical formulations are traceable to Freud's original insights, as if they had already been, implicitly, embedded in his scientific vision.

The metapsychological points of view form the classical dimensions of psychoanalysis. Within these dimensions the analytical material, often intricate and anxiety provoking, attains a position and meaning in the analyst's mind as well as in psychoanalytic discourse, without the analyst necessarily being aware of it. I am not going to consider these dimensions in greater detail, but I will focus on the conceptual whole constituted by them. In defining this whole as the conceptual space of psychoanalysis, I am going to outline a frame, within which it is justified to speak of psychoanalytic understanding.

Freud's original creation

I will take two characteristics of Freud's mind as my starting point, namely his capacity for spatial thinking and his pervasive urge for intellectual integrity which constitute his achievement as well.

Nunberg's description of Freud's mode of thinking illuminates my first point. In his introduction to the *Minutes of the Vienna Psychoanalytical Society*, Nunberg writes :

> ... For many years I had the opportunity to watch Freud during discussions in the meetings of the Society. When a speaker's remarks aroused his particular interest or when he was trying to make his own point especially clear, he would lift his head and look intensely, with extreme concentration, at a point in space, as if he were seeing something there. This tendency to see what he was thinking is reflected in his writings. They contain many pictorial elements, even when dealing with highly theoretical concepts. If his doctrines were considered fantastic speculations by some, we may say that he first looked and then believed, and did not first believe and then see. Only a man with such a vision could discover and see the laws governing the intricate labyrinth of the human mind. . . ." [Notes omitted] [Nunberg & Federn, 1962, pp. xxvi–xxvii]

Freud's entire life work illustrates his capacity to visualize what he had observed in psychic reality within an abstract space. This space then came to form the shared frame of psychoanalytical understanding.

What makes an individual like Freud transcend the scientific conventions of his time and create a radically new paradigm? Perhaps it depends not only on the genius of an original mind, but also on the personal experience in the critical phases of early psychic development when the child begins to conceptualize reality for the first time. Ostensibly, many creative individuals have experienced traumatic events in their early childhood, the overcoming of which presupposes exceptional courage and vision. Hardin's (1987, 1988) study of Freud's early years illustrates this notion.

Winnicott (1971) derives creativity from an early illusion shared by the infant and its mother. He denotes this illusion as the potential space forming the foundation not only for human creativity, but also for cultural achievements in general. Winnicott also visualises the psychoanalytic situation from this perspective. He compares it with children's play.

Green (1978) makes an important addition to Winnicott's original idea, arguing that potential space cannot be understood only as a shared experience between the infant and its mother, but a third element, the infant's father, has also to be taken into account. The psychological presence of the biological father frames from the very beginning the creative illusion shared by the mother and her child. For this reason, the illusion is not an arbitrary one akin to a delusion, but is delimited by reality. According to Green, removing radically the image of the father will result in a psychotic construction. The setting represents this third element in the psychoanalytic situation (Green, 1978).

Accordingly, human creativity is not a limitless phenomenon or infinite in nature, but it is outlined by the imperatives of reality. Concerning scientific creativity, this viewpoint is essential. Does this not imply that scientific insights have to be submitted to methodological reality testing?

Another characteristic of Freud's mind is also worth mentioning in this connection, namely, his intellectual integrity, which was painfully achieved through continuous self-scrutiny and thoroughly tested by his lonely struggle to maintain his creation. Clarity of vision is not inevitably an inborn capability, but the ego's late achievement in its struggle with those drive instinctual forces that tend to blur this clarity. As a matter of fact, the problem of the ego-split and the fetish preoccupied Freud's mind in his later years (1927e, 1940e). In offering a very simple way of avoiding the threat of castration, a fetishistic solution may easily attract the scientist more than a sound perception of reality. When human helplessness, shame, and guilt constitute the object of inquiry, as in the case of psychoanalysis, one is particularly tempted to resort to intellectual compromises, endangering scientific reasoning and conceptual clarity (Rangell, 1974; Salonen, 1986).

Although Freud worked in close association with many creative colleagues interested in sharing his thoughts, his personal contribution was, however, superior. Therefore, psychoanalysis was identified with his person for a long time. The potential space of psychoanalysis existed only in relation to him, not apart from his person. Over half a century after Freud's death, psychoanalysis can no longer be simply identified with him or any individual analyst. On the contrary, it now represents an autonomous therapeutic and scientific tradition shared by analysts and their patients.

In considering the importance of analytic training in the transmission of psychoanalysis to the following generations, Innes-Smith (1989) emphasizes the viewpoint of the inheritance of scientific traditions. What is inherited is a potential space making a specific self-reflection possible. According to him, the analysts are guardians of this space. Actually, psychoanalysis can hardly survive without attentive guardianship, either as a clinical setting or as a conceptual space under constant pressure of drive instinctual forces and the inherent human reluctance to be aware of them.

A limited scope

Psychoanalysis represents a demarcated approach to human nature, not a general *Weltanschaung*. This limitation also applies to its method, i.e., the psychoanalytical setting and its rules.

Viderman projects transference into the focus of the psychoanalytic experience. He illustrates the analytical situation by Plato's classic parable of the cave.The prisoners enclosed in a cave can only infer the conditions outside by following the shadows reflected on the walls without having any opportunity of directly perceiving reality. By analogy, the technical rules of psychoanalysis and its special affective atmosphere enclose a "cave", i.e., the analytic space. The setting cannot be arbitrarily modified without the situation itself being destroyed. [Viderman, 1974, p. 473]

> ... Neither the analyst nor the analysand can modify the analytic rules of the game without seeing the entire construction fall apart, thereupon leaving room for radically different reference systems. Neither one nor the other can turn round to perceive the hidden face of the instinct. We see only the reflections, from which the interpretation must imagine a reality as alien to what is brought to our knowledge as are the shadows to reality, of which they are the projections on to the walls of the cave. [*ibid.*]

According to Enckell (2002), the psychoanalytic situation forms the stage for the unconscious psychic processes to evolve as a *metaphorical process*: in other words, it creates a frame for understanding psychic reality inaccessible to direct observation.

By committing themselves to this limited scope, both the analysand and the analyst consent to the fact that their common experience might greatly surpass all that they are able to anticipate or comprehend beforehand. Whereas the analysand is obligated to follow the rule of free association, the analyst is confined to the principles of intellectual integrity, i.e. he is obliged to scrutinize all that will be met via his own associations and affective responses without adhering to his favourite subjects. The goal of psychoanalysis can be attained only through truthfulness and by following the rules agreed on. In framing the wishful fantasies of both participants, these rules prevent the omnipotent manipulation of realities during the periods of treatment when inner helplessness tends to blur one's vision.

Thus, the analytical situation is constituted not only by a shared creativity between the analyst and analysand, but is also defined by transference and its detailed analysis. These two elements are, however, not sufficient for characterizing the entire situation. A third aspect is still required. Psychoanalysis is not only a creative scientific discourse, but, in addition, it seeks and has always sought solutions to human conflict. The atmosphere of the analytical situation is characterized by a particular hope grounded in scientific knowledge. This hope is related to an opportunity of discovering an inner solution to unconscious drive instinctual conflicts.

The conceptual space expanded by psychoanalytic theory helps the analyst to tackle unconscious resistance to change and visualize it within wider perspectives. The situation is analogous to the difficulties in navigation. When no other points of reference can be found, one's position can be calculated by the celestial bodies and their known constellations. On the other hand, theory is also a projection of the vast clinical experience accumulated over a whole century. As long as psychoanalysis maintains its creative vision and is capable of genuine transformation consonant with clinical observations, it will survive as a scientific tradition.

The horizon of the psychoanalytical situation

In his film *The Great Dictator* (1940), Chaplin has a surrealistic flashback: he is a combat pilot in the First World War. After wrongly perceiving the horizon, he continues the flight upside down. In looking at his watch, he accidentally drops it. The watch falls to hang from its chain, straight upwards! The pull of gravity has momentarily unveiled the illusion that was based on an erroneously chosen horizon. In the same way, the horizon of the psychoanalytical situation can be ambiguous and difficult to interpret. Also, the psychoanalytical process may be progressing seemingly well, until some unexpected minor point like Chaplin's watch dispels the illusion.

Modern pilots orientate themselves by an abstract horizon that is shown by an electronic instrument. A genuinely internalized theory can be compared to this kind of automatic device that shows an abstract horizon (Halgrimsson, 1993). In fact, the task of psychoanalytic study is to provide for the reliability of this device, a task that has become more and more complicated owing to the fact that psychoanalytic theory has been evolving along divergent lines. It is no longer self-evident that the readings of the instrument of orientation are comparable across various schools. In considering whether the future of psychoanalysis centres around one theory or many, Wallerstein (1988) is inclined to the latter alternative. In my opinion, psychoanalysis would, however, lose something essential by giving up a shared conceptual space. An ideal frame is needed where the now divergent lines of thought can possibly converge again in the future.

Following Freud's view (1912e), the psychoanalytical attitude has been compared with a mirror, reflecting the analysand's inner constellations. Although this analogy may be misleading in bringing an optical device to mind and perhaps in not sufficiently recognizing the analyst's active role, it is, however, relevant for understanding the metaphorical screen on which the transference is reflected in the analytic situation. How should the analyst understand his role in creating such a mirror?

Psychoanalysis has from its inception considered psychic phenomena against the background of human sexuality. We have definitive knowledge about the phases of the libido development. We also understand how the human mind becomes organized into a structural whole through the inescapable drive conflicts and the inner solutions found for them. The recent advances in psychoanalysis, Veikko Tähkä's (1993) extensive life work included, have substantially increased our theoretical understanding and our readiness to treat severe psychic disorders. With all this progress, the focus of psychoanalytic interest has also tended towards the earliest modes of psychic experience. Unfortunately, this has in part taken place at the cost of the analysis of intra-psychic conflict. When the Oedipus complex is considered to belong only to a phase of early psychic development, there is a great temptation to underestimate its importance as the nodal point of unconscious psychic processes in the analytic situation.

In his study of Leonardo Da Vinci, Freud (1910c) analyses the late works of the master. According to him, they reflect a true resignation of the inescapable realities of life, including death. Freud designates these realities "Necessity" after the Greek goddess of fate, Ananke. In describing the Oedipus complex, Freud actually discovered the code of the individual's relation to genital reality. This group of equations offers the key to understanding how inborn drive instinctual potentialities are actualized in each new generation. Through oedipal solutions, the child's ego will establish an inner congruence with human reality, coded also in its genetic endowment. McDougall epitomizes this painful moment in a touching way:

> ... what he [the child] wishes were true will never be true; that the secret of sexual desire lies in the mother's missing penis; that only the father's penis will ever complete her genital, and he will for ever be alienated from his primary sexual desire and his unfilled narcissistic wishes. [1980, p. 74]

An aspect of sorrow belongs to adult love life, too. It is related to the painful recognition of the course of time and the finitude of life. There is no category of time in the pleasure seeking unconscious and perhaps no concept of death either. They are attributes of the individual's bodily existence that remind us of Freud's mighty Necessity and challenges the ego to search for inner solutions to drive instinctual conflicts.

Perhaps it was not a mere chance that the pilot in Chaplin's film glanced at his watch before realizing that the horizon was upside down. In searching for a reliable horizon in the psychoanalytical situation, we encounter the time dimension, which forms an aspect of genital reality. Might not this reality be concealed beyond the analytic screen on which transference is projected? If this is true, the analyst's role in the analytical situation is to represent genital reality, and the intra-psychic solutions that are consonant with it. Psychoanalytic theory then serves this function as a shared frame of reference.

References

Chaplin, C. (1940). *The Great Dictator* (film).

Enckell, H. (2002). *Metaphor and the Psychodynamic Function of the Mind.* Kuopio: Kuopio University Publications, Serie D. Medical Sciences 265.

Freud, S. (1910c). Leonardo Da Vinci and a memory of his childhood. *S.E., 11*: 63–137. London: Hogarth.

Freud, S. (1912e). Recommendations to physicians practising psychoanalysis. *S.E., 12*: 111–120. London: Hogarth.

Freud, S. (1927e). Fetishism. *S.E., 21*: 152–157. London: Hogarth.

Freud, S. (1940e). Splitting of the ego in the process of defence. *S.E., 23*: 275–278. London: Hogarth.

Green, A. (1978) [1986]. Potential space in psychoanalysis. In: A. Green, *On Private Madness*. London: Hogarth Press and Institute of Psycho-Analysis.

Halgrimsson, O. (1994). "Forgotten" theory. *Journal of Clinical Psychoanalysis, 3*: 407–428.

Hardin, H. T. (1987). On the vicissitudes of Freud's early mothering. I: Early environment and loss. *Psychoanalytic Quarterly, 56*: 628–644.

Hardin, H. T. (1988). On the vicissitudes of Freud's early mothering. II: Alienation from his biological mother. *Psychoanalytic Quarterly, 57*: 72–86.

Innes-Smith, J. (1990). The self-analysis of the training analyst. *Psychoanalysis in Europe, Bulletin, 34*: 5–17.

McDougall, J. (1980). *Plea for a Measure of Abnormality*. New York: International Universities Press.

Nunberg, H. & Federn, E. (Eds.) (1967). *Minutes of the Vienna Psychoanalytical Society*. New York: International Universities Press.

Rangell, L. (1974). A psychoanalytic perspective leading currently to the syndrome of the compromise of integrity. *International Journal of Psycho-Analysis, 55*: 3–12.

Salonen, S. (1986). On conceptual clarity in psychoanalysis. *Scandinavian Psychoanalytic Review, 9*: 57–66.

Tähkä, V. (1993). *The Mind and Its Treatment. A Psychoanalytic Approach.* Madison, CT: International Universities Press.

Wallerstein, R. S. (1988). One psychoanalysis or many. *International Journal of Psycho-Analysis, 69*: 5–22.

Winnicott, D. W. (1971). *Playing and Reality.* New York: Basic Books.

Viderman, S. (1974). Interpretation in the analytical space. *International Review of Psycho-Analysis, 1*: 467–780.

CHAPTER FIFTEEN

On the conditions of understanding

Reflections from the patient´s point of view

Henrik Enckell

Introduction

I n the history of Western thought, the problem of understanding has been most thoroughly investigated in the context of written texts. The logical starting point for the investigation seems to have been a pragmatic one; when one reads or has to apply a text one does not fully understand, one needs guidelines as to how to interpret it. The reflection on the conditions of understanding, called hermeneutics, has its roots in antiquity, but there are two periods in modern history during which this strand of philosophy has been especially prominent and vital. The first was initiated in the eighteenth century Romanticist tradition by Friedrich Schleiermacher, while the second was started by Martin Heidegger and brought forward during the second half of the twentieth century by authors such as Hans-Georg Gadamer, Jürgen Habermas, and Paul Ricoeur. Moving from its earlier concern with the interpretation of texts, hermeneutics during this last period became involved with more general aspects of understanding.

The relation between hermeneutics and psychoanalysis has been a reciprocal affair. Paul Ricoeur published a book on Freud in

1965 (English translation 1970), while Jürgen Habermas published his major application of psychoanalytical thought in 1971. Both authors used the psychoanalytical model for their own purposes: Ricoeur's work forms part of a broader reflection on the interpretation of symbols, while Habermas saw in psychoanalysis a model for the emancipation of self-understanding, applicable also in the social sphere. Psychoanalysis, for its part, turned to hermeneutics somewhat later, most notably through American authors such as Spence and Schafer, but in a subsequent debate on the suitability of hermeneutics as a theoretical model for psychoanalysis a wide range of authors participated (see, e.g., Steiner, 1995).

In this chapter I will start out from a specific hermeneutic debate concerning the nature of understanding, a debate in which the psychoanalytic model was used as an example. I will then turn to some contemporary thoughts on the psychoanalytical relationship, the curative factors pertaining to it, and the status of object and reality in psychoanalysis. My aim is to investigate the relevance of hermeneutics for the explication and understanding of these current psychoanalytical ideas, as well as to examine *what kind of* hermeneutics these ideas imply.

The conflict of interpretations

As stated above, hermeneutics is an answer to the problem of understanding: when we do not grasp the meaning of a text, we have to reflect on how to make it open up to us. In his book on Freud, Ricoeur (1970) narrows down the pursuit of understanding to the reading of *symbols*. Symbols are not just any representations, but a device with one obvious meaning through which a concealed one might come to light. Since we do not reach the second, latent, meaning immediately, we need an interpretation. There seems to be a widespread consensus on this matter in Western thought—the divergence emerges in the "spirit" of interpretation, i.e., in the way of relating to the object to be read. Ricoeur states that *two* hermeneutics exist. One is characterized by *suspicion*; the thinkers in this tradition believe that fundamental human strivings are concealed behind different *disguises*. The "true" aspirations of man do not show in themselves, but have to be inferred through various distortions. For these authors, interpretation is a "tearing off of the masks". Marx, Nietzsche, and Freud belong, according to Ricoeur, to this tradition, and an example is Freud´s way of relating to dreams and symptoms as these are not to be taken at face value, but have to be "demystified".

The second hermeneutics is one of *faith*. Authors in this tradition do not "suspect" their objects, but are convinced that these will "speak" if they are listened to. Marx, Nietzsche, and Freud believe that the authentic meaning lies "behind" the human artefacts, while the thinkers belonging to this second tradition think the true meanings will unfold "in front of" the objects under the condition that these are related to in a spirit of attentiveness. If the first hermeneutics is one of suspicion, this second one is one of "revelation". Phenomenologists of religion belong to this latter group.

Both hermeneutics state that their objects have a double meaning, but they differ in how they think the second one should be reached. An analogical difference can be discerned in another dialectic Ricoeur sets out to investigate.

In the reflection on the objects to be interpreted, Ricoeur distinguishes two "directions". The first one is an "archeology", i.e., a theoretical stance according to which the meaning to be searched lies in a *temporal past*, beneath the current "layers". Thus this reflection goes "backwards". The other reflection goes in the opposite direction, as it sees its goal in the future, and is thus called a "teleology". The difference is one of conceptualization—one reflection sees its investigation as a way to the more original strata, while the other sees its route as a way forward, to a meaning that will unfold or be created.

Accordingly, Ricoeur discerns two dialectics in hermeneutics. On the one hand we have the hermeneutics of suspicion and the archeological conceptualization. On the other we have the hermeneutics of revelation and the teleology of reflection. Although Ricoeur sees a hidden teleology in Freud´s psychoanalysis, he makes it very clear that he sees Freud as belonging to the former traditions, i.e., the traditions of suspicion and archeology.

This reading of Freud is supported by the major hermeneutical debate in the 1970s. While Gadamer (1975) saw understanding as the result of a dialogue with the text in which the interpreter has to be open to the possibilities of the textual work, Habermas (1971) regarded this as a dispossession of the interpreter´s *critical* mission. According to Habermas, one has to take into consideration the power of distortion; the interpreter should—in the spirit of Enlightenment—attempt an "emancipation" of understanding. The debate between Gadamer and Habermas reflects the dialectics pictured by Ricoeur, and the two former explicitly claim that Freud belonged to the same tradition as Habermas (who used Freud´s model in the explication of his "emancipatory project", a project reflecting both suspicion and archeology). Gadamer and Habermas thus line up with Ricoeur´s reading of Freud.

As already mentioned, in the following I will delineate some contemporary psychoanalytical ideas about the psychoanalytical relation and process. I will do this in order to explore the question of whether Ricoeur´s, Gadamer´s, and Habermas´s reading of psychoanalysis is pertinent to this modern conceptualization of how, and under what conditions, the analysand gains understanding.

The psychoanalytical relationship; a contemporary view

As my starting point in the exposition of a modern view of the psychoanalytical relationship and process I have chosen the theory of Veikko Tähkä. There are several reasons for this choice. In his major book (1993), Tähkä presents a comprehensive, yet focused, view of the main psychoanalytical issues. Though he draws on different sources, Tähkä´s contribution is an original one, which in this instance implies an unusually well thought out picture of the workings of the mind. Furthermore, Tähkä integrates the most important contemporary perspectives (i.e., the developmental, structural and object-relational points of view) in psychoanalysis. In addition to this, Tähkä very consistently follows the principle that every psychic mechanism and developmental step has a *reason* to be investigated, thus following what is perhaps the most fundamental ideal in psychoanalytical science. Accordingly, for the purposes of this paper the choice of Tähkä seems to be a motivated one.

The transferential relationship

Tähkä divides the psychoanalytical relationship into three perspectives: for the analysand, the analyst is a *real*, a *transferential* and a *developmental* object. The first of these perspectives will not be described here.

As a transferential—i.e., past—object, the analyst represents a failed developmental line. For Tähkä, psychic development is identical to a growth in representational means. When everything goes well, the subject acquires mental devices—i.e., representational structures—which he can put to use in everything that goes with his relational being. When everything has gone well, the subject has, thus, representations at hand—mental structures with which he can represent the other (as well as all that goes with him) flexibly enough.

When a developmental line—for some reason or other—has failed, the representational growth has (in this part of the personality) become prematurely interrupted. In this line, the subject has, accordingly, only a limited set of representations. As one´s ability to feel is determined by the representational structures at hand, a limited set of these devices comes to imply a specific and circumscribed way of experiencing the other. In the transferential relationship, the subject´s way of experiencing the other is without alternatives, due to the fact that the alternatives require representations never acquired.

The transference represents a closed representational system. Due to the restricted mental devices, the subject´s interpersonal strivings become channelled into a repetitive craving in which the object also finds a repetitive role, specific for this subject.

According to Tähkä, the attempt to fulfil transferential wishes never leads to a resumption of development, but only to a fortification of cravings which, in the end, will come to nothing (due to the fact that transferential wishes are always ambivalent, and thus impossible to fulfil). As such, the transference never leads anywhere. In an analysis, the actualized transference nevertheless may prove useful as it tells the story of a developmental failure. In the transference, the analytical pair can detect the history of an interrupted developmental line.

In sum, the transference is a repetitive relational configuration showing the limitations of the representations at hand. As such, it represents a developmental failure and an interruption of representational transformation and growth. In itself, it only fortifies a certain set of cravings.

The developmental relationship

As stated above, Tähkä sees psychic development as identical with representational growth. This development requires an object; the generation of representational structures (facilitating a psychic elaboration) is dependent upon an outer object supplying the conditions for this development. During childhood, the primary caregivers are the objects in relation to whom the child acquires new mental structures. After the closure of adolescence, a subject naturally builds new representations, but the growth of structures which supply *new* possibilities for psychic elaboration has come to a close. According to Tähkä, psychoanalysis (or one of its applications) is the only possibility for establishing a relationship in which an adult subject may have his developmental potentialities revitalized.

The analyst becomes, spontaneously, a transferential object for the analysand, and this relationship reflects, as already mentioned, a representational closure. The developmental object, in turn, is the one in relation to whom the analysand resumes a representational growth. While the adult representational world is closed (just like the transferential one), the analyst as a developmental object is the one in relation to whom the representational closure is "opened up". This "opening up" marks the start of the "analytical" use of the analyst.

Thus, for the psychoanalytical process to be initiated, the analyst has to become—beside a transferential object—a developmental one. The conditions for this depend on the degree of mental structuralization of the patient. Due to space limitations the differences between different structural categories and their implications in this matter cannot be discussed here.

To sum up, the developmental relationship implies an opening up of the potential for representational growth. Later on, I will argue that this growth may be seen as the enhancement of understanding of the patient, an understanding which becomes actualized in relation to an object approached in a specific way.

The developmental illusion

The new approach of the patient, the opening up of the potential for representational growth, i.e., the initiation of the developmental relationship, is thus identical to the basic condition of the analytical process. Part of this opening up has, by Riitta Tähkä (2000; also Chapter Four, this volume), been identified as *a developmental illusion*.

In interpersonal relations, illusions are topical since they form the basis of the sense of *meaningfullness*. This can be seen in, e.g., *the transference illusion* (i.e., the illusion that the analyst conforms to the patient´s unconscious manuscript). Only through the initiation of the transference, parts of the analysand´s personality (i.e., the parts whose development have become interrupted) become actualized, and thus *real*. Naturally, this is a condition for making some aspects (i.e., the aspects which are manifested in the transference) of the patient´s experiential world part of the analytical process. The transference illusion makes important areas in the experiential realm real, and thus meaningful.

The transferential illusion is, however, a closed one. As was mentioned above, the basis of the transference is a restricted representational set through which the analysand establishes his relational experience, and the transference illusion is a consequence of the fact that the patient is able to represent his object only through this set. The transference illusion and wish is imposed on the other; in itself, it reflects the end of representational work or change, a fact manifested in the repetitiveness of the transferential experience.

While the transference illusion is part of the transferential relationship, a condition of the developmental relationship is a "developmental" illusion. This illusion is *the first representation and actualization of a possibility, i.e., the possibility of resuming a development that has once been interrupted*. In other words, the developmental illusion is the first representation of a potentiality for representational growth.

While the transference illusion represents the past, the developmental illusion is the representation of something totally new, i.e., the representation of a possibility never acquired, grasped, or actualized. The implication of the developmental illusion is that it may be possible to start an itinerary that has never been followed in relation to the primary caregivers but that has now opened up in relation to the analyst.

This represented possibility is called illusion since it is a phenomenon not placeable in the outer reality, nor in the inner. Its "realness" cannot be proved, or disproved. In fact, in this area the question of realness should not be posed. This can be seen in the shying away from the illusion in question: fearful of the risks of entering the possibilities of the illusion, the analysand may say that the analysis is not "for real", that this is "just work" for the analyst. Comments like these can be neither refuted nor affirmed, but only understood as manifestations of the patient's wish to defend himself from the risks of approaching the analyst as a developmental object.

Riitta Tähkä emphasizes the difference between transferential and developmental illusions; it is important for the analyst to realize that the latter is not the repetition of a closed wish, and that it is not a manifestation "behind" which some concealed wishes may be found. The developmental illusion is a response to the analysand's experience of being understood in a new way, and it is not to be 14interpreted as something hiding something else, but simply understood and shared as the phenomenon it is—i.e., as a new approach implying a representational opening up.

It is also important to realize the risks—for the patient—of entering the realm of the developmental illusion. The condition of the illusion is the experience of being understood. If the patient gives in to the developmental illusion, he approaches the analyst as an object upon which this very experience is dependent. Fundamentally, the developmental illusion implies a *new* approach by the patient, an approach in which he opens up the potential for representational change and growth, and all this is dependent on the experience of being understood in a new way.

The hermeneutical project: a general view

As stated in the introduction, the problem of understanding has been thoroughly investigated in the context of written texts. A classic in this field is Hans-Georg Gadamer's *Wahrheit und Methode* (1960, English translation 1975).

Gadamer describes the hermeneutical project (i.e., the project of understanding) through the process of reading a classic. The reader may share the tradition of the work, and this implies a common ground—the reader shares, so to say, *some* of the elements through which the world of the text is organized. On the other hand, the world of the work is a foreign one due to the fact that the classic speaks from a distant age. Although the work shares some organizing elements with those of the reader, it nevertheless speaks from a different stance.

The reader, naturally, starts out from his own time—a time that has supplied him with certain elements with which he builds his world. Now, when the text belongs to the tradition of the reader (and thus shares some elements with him), the latter might have the feeling that the book *speaks to him*. It speaks to him, but from a different stance, and this difference poses a problem. In order to understand the text, the reader has to "open up" to it, and this implies putting his own *preconceptions* to the test.

The experience of being spoken to thus makes the reader open up to the work. This does not mean an abolition of the preconceptions, but an implicit suspension of their rigid hegemony through a *use* of them. This use involves putting them to a test, subjugating the preconceptions in an interplay with those of the text. Now, the elements the reader shares with the classic are partly in what might be called a "dormant" state. In the dialogue with the work—as the preconceptions are put to use—the reader may have the experience that his dormant elements are being actualized *through* the work. Due to the fact that the text speaks from a distance, it opens up something new for me, and by doing this it reveals something about *myself*. In this process, preconceptions are not put aside, but are involved in an interplay through which they are tested against those of the work, and this implies a *new* use of them. Through this, preconceptions become understanding; my own world becomes more fully representented or actualized through the perspective of the text.

Symbol and metaphor

As stated above, Ricoeur started his hermeneutical project with an investigation of the symbol. In this period, he seems to have focused on this linguistic device as a model through which the process of understanding could be examined. After his investigation of the symbol, Ricoeur (1978) turned to poetics. In doing this, he left the symbol for the metaphor.

Even though the metaphor is a subgroup of symbols, in some respects it functions in a specific way. It seems clear that Ricoeur (just as in his works on the symbol) uses his investigation of the metaphor in an attempt to conceptualize some essential aspects of the process of understanding. It seems that, through the metaphor, Ricoeur is examining the same process as Gadamer.

For the poet—as well as for any person—the metaphor is a device used to represent reality. In conformity with many other authors, Ricoeur makes it clear that metaphors could be called "optical instruments"; we look through them in order to see. Compared to just any representations, the living metaphor differs in its inventory power. Fundamentally, the metaphor is a linguistic device in which meanings are *created* (an emphasis to be seen also in the subheading of Ricoeur's book on metaphors: *Multi-Disciplinary Studies on the Creation of Meaning in Language*).

In the metaphor, we have two sets of representation—words or larger wholes—which do not immediately fit. Due to the unconventional combination, the ordinary meanings of the words break down. However, in the fruitful *use* of the metaphor, one looks through the first set of representation at the second one, and vice versa. Looking through the new perspective, one comes to see correspondences not apprehended before. New bridges are built between the representational fields that seemed so far apart at first. Fundamentally, in the metaphor a *new meaning* is born out of the ashes of the old one; this is accomplished through the "work" done between representations.

In the philosophy of language, one distinguishes between the meaning of a word and its reference. The meaning is something taking place *in* language, while the reference is the thing "out there" which the meaning hints at; the reference is the reality. *Through* the meaning one comes to the reference.

This is all clear in reading ordinary descriptive prose, but what is the reality of metaphors? Or, more generally speaking, what kind of reality opens up in reading a poem? Or, more generally still, through fiction?

It should be clear that the metaphorical reality is not the one addressed in scientific discourse. One could say that the ordinary reference breaks down in metaphors, just as ordinary meaning did. Some authors say that the poem, accordingly, does not have *any* reference—or that the poem is "closed", or refers only to itself—but Ricoeur (1978) strongly argues that a new, or second, reference is opened up in the metaphor. Analogous with the new meaning rising out of the old, destructed, meaning, a new reference or reality might be said to open up in place of the abolished one.

According to Ricoeur, the metaphorical reference is the *possibility*. One could say that the contents of this reality both exists and does not; this reference can be described precisely through the dialectic of being and not-being. *In itself*, the reference of the metaphor does exist, but it is characterized by being *a reality of potentialities*.

One can thus say that the metaphor implies a series of dialectical tensions. In the dialectic of the words, a new meaning is created. This meaning opens up a new reality. This reality is a potentiality. Accordingly, the metaphor represents the widening scope of language, *and in the end it is the outpost of possibilities*.

Metaphor and understanding

Essentially, the living metaphor leads to understanding. There are two ways of thinking about this. First: in the metaphor, one looks through one word (or one set of words) at another one. Due to the unconventionality of the combination, the perspective is new. Through the novel perspective, one comes to see something new.

Second: in the living metaphor, work is done between its different components. This work leads to a widening of the representations in question. Through novel representations one sees something new. By looking through the unexpected perspective and the newly created representations, one *understands*.

Metaphor and the psychoanalytical process

Psychoanalysis is a science that investigates the work of *mental* representations. These are not primarily words, but thoughts, feelings, memories and perceptions. In order to conceptualize the work done in psychoanalysis, it seems reasonable to rely on a framework in which the concepts of understanding and representation are firmly established as well as interconnected in a long tradition. This is the reason for a psychoanalyst to turn to hermeneutics.

As seen above, the psychoanalytic relation can be divided in different aspects. The basis of this differentiation is the stance, or function, of the object. In part, the analyst is a transferential object. As explained above, this object is the reflection of a mental configuration the transformation and development of which has come to an end. For some reason or another work between representations has ceased in this region, and this leads to the repetitiveness of the relation. The transference is a metaphor (which can also be seen in the identity of terms: *meta-phoros* and *Über-tragung*) in structure, but a *dead* one: as nothing takes place between the mental fields, the same grouping of representations is found again and again (Enckell, 1999). In this respect the transferential relationship represents an *interrupted* development and a *closure* of representational work.

During the psychoanalytic treatment a developmental object may be born, and this object is the one in relation to whom the analytical process *per se* is initiated. In this relation, *the approach of the analysand is a new one*, differing in its conditions from the ones in the transferential relationship. While the latter relation starts out from the impossibility of representational work, the former implies a *potentiality for novelty, i.e., a readiness to let oneself be set in representational motion in relation to the object*. This can be seen as an approach towards an object in relation to whom the analysand is able to let different representational domains influence each other. In this approach, the analysand "opens up", discovering a new capacity to join a metaphorical movement. The result of this is a potentiality for representational transformation and growth.

The metaphorical movement of the developmental relationship is connected to the "developmental illusion". The developmental illusion implies a *readiness* to metaphorization, a metaphorization that becomes possible in relation to an object, *and only in this relation*. In the "opening up" a possibility is created, i.e., *the possibility of a relation in which a metaphorical movement can be actualized*.

Gadamer said that the process of understanding is initiated when the preconceptions of the reader are "put into play". The preconceptions are the categories through which one understands, but to understand something new they have to be "tested". This may happen in the reading of a classic; when the reader belongs to the tradition of the text, he shares some of the elements speaking in the work. On the other hand, as there is a distance in time between reader and author, the work speaks from a *different* stance, from a "horizon" of its own. Due to the combination of difference and sameness the reader has the experience of being spoken to, and, more specifically, the text seems to speak of the reader himself. Precisely this experience makes the reader approach the text in an opening up of the preconceptions—the representational categories are put into play in relation to the world of the work.

Analogically, the analysand may create the developmental illusion when he has the experience of being spoken to in a new way, this novelty implying a new understanding. A condition for the new understanding of the analyst by the analysand is the combination of sameness and difference (just as in the case of the literary work). The analyst speaks of the experience of the analysand (and has the ability to do so as he shares the representational structures giving rise to this experience), but he does so from a different perspective (i.e., from the perspective of his own representational setup). Precisely this experience of being understood in a new way opens up the possibility for the analysand to create a developmental illusion, and so approach the analyst as an object in relation to whom representations can be put into play.

As hinted at above, this can be viewed from the perspective of metaphorization. The linguistic metaphor creates a meaning, and through this meaning it opens up a novel reality. The ontological status of the metaphorical reality is the potentiality. Analogically, one can say that also in the analytical process a reality is actualized, i.e., *a reality of possibilities*. The precondition for this reality to unfold is an analytical relation in which a developmental illusion can be established. What follows is representational work in which mental fields influence each other, thus enlarging the representational world.

Broadly speaking the developmental relation leads to an enhancement of the understanding of the patient. By putting his preconceptions—his representational categories—into play, the analysand opens up to a world which thus becomes understood in a new way. This opening up is, at the same time, a self-realization. Accordingly, the self becomes realized in a relation towards an object situated in a position different from the one of the analysand. From this position the analyst can supply his understanding—an understanding that may put the metaphorical movement of the patient into play. *This is the power of understanding: the potentiality to set in motion an approach of the patient through which the latter may become himself.*

Hermeneutics and modern psychoanalysis

In the introduction, I presented the discussion conducted when an interchange between hermeneutics and psychoanalysis was initiated. In the work of Paul Ricoeur, two oppositional pairs (reflected also in the debate between Hans-Georg Gadamer and Jürgen Habermas) were presented. First, we have a hermeneutics of suspicion, and one of revelation; this opposition reflects the "spirit" in which an interpretation is conducted (i.e., the spirit of demystification on the one hand, and the spirit of listening on the other). Second, we have an opposition of reflection. On the one hand there is an "archeology" of meaning (according to which the latent or "second" meaning lies in a hidden "beforehand"—i.e., the reflection leads to the past). On the other hand we have a "teleological" conception of reflection (according to which the reflective movement is directed forwards—the meaning unfolds in the future). Although Ricoeur discerns a dialectic in both of these oppositions, and although he says that psychoanalysis implies all of these aspects or movements, it becomes clear that Freud—according to Ricoeur—*primarily* represents a hermeneutics of suspicion and an archeological reflection (an interpretation to which Gadamer and Habermas quite clearly subscribe).

When we consider the picture of modern psychoanalysis presented above, a shift seems to have come about; the hermeneutics inherent in this contemporary psychoanalysis appears to be somewhat different from the one presented three and four decades ago. While a hermeneutics of suspicion may be relevant in the encounter with the transferential illusion (which also implies an archeological conception as the transference originates in the past), the developmental potential is clearly to be met with another attitude. As Riitta Tähkä states very clearly, *the developmental illusion should only be shared and understood for what it is,* as this is not an illusion "behind" which one could find some repressed material important to lay bare. The same point is made by Stern *et al.* (1998) in their conceptualisation of the generative moments in the psychoanalytic process. The analyst facilitates a representational movement not solely by a "tearing off of the masks" (although this may—at least in some cases—be an important step in the overall process), but essentially in listening to, sharing, and supplying his understanding of the developmental illusion. The result of this may be a representational process implying a meaning, and an understanding, to come. This seems, clearly, to imply a hermeneutics of listening or revelation, and a teleological reflection.

Finally, one may ask if the conceptual instruments informing the past and the contemporary views reflect the change in inherent hermeneutics.

As mentioned in the introduction, when he wrote his book on Freud, Ricoeur was involved in an investigation of the symbol; in fact, the whole enterprise of reading Freud was part of an attempt to discover how to conceptualize and understand symbols and their interpretation. As also hinted at above, Ricoeur's definition of the symbol is very clear: the symbol is a representational structure with a double meaning. The two meanings are placed like a chain: through a first meaning one comes to a second one, i.e., the latent meaning is revealed only through the manifest one. According to Ricoeur, the structure of the symbol becomes clear only in the act of interpretation. Parenthetically, this definition makes a clear distinction between symbol and representation as the latter does not usually imply a *double*, but only a simple, meaning.

In contrast to the symbol, the metaphor is a figure in which we have *two* manifest words from the outset. In this linguistic device there is not a ready-made hidden meaning behind a manifest one, but an evolving meaning that comes about through the work done between words which do not fit. A *new* meaning is born out of the metaphorical interaction, and this meaning was not there before it was constructed.

The symbol seems to be a concept that fits a psychoanalysis where the emphasis is on *repression*; behind the repressing censorship we find the latent meaning. The metaphor, on the other hand, seems better to fit a psychoanalysis focusing on the new approach of the patient; the metaphorical movement is a generative one, and it seems to be able to encompass a general view of representational growth—it represents the *generation* of meaning, and the rise of a reality of possibilities.

Ricoeur turned to the metaphor after having investigated the symbol. One might ask if the transformations in psychoanalysis reflect this same change. Can one say that the representational structure of metaphor is more pertinent than the symbol to modern psychoanalysis? This must remain an open question, but the picture here outlined may point in this direction.

References

Enckell, H. (1999). Transference, metaphor and the poetics of psycho-analysis. *Scandinavian Psychoanalytic Review*, 22: 218–238.

Gadamer, H.-G. (1975). *Truth and Method*. London: Sheed and Ward.

Habermas, J. (1971). *Knowledge and Human Interest*. Boston: Beacon Press.

Ricoeur, P. (1970). *Freud and Philosophy*. New Haven: Yale University Press.

Ricoeur, P. (1978). *The Rule of Metaphor*. London: Routledge.

Steiner, R. (1995). Hermeneutics or Hermes-mess?. *International Journal of Psycho-Analysis*, 76: 435–445.

Stern, D., Sander, L., Nahum, J., Harrison, A., Lyons-Ruth, K., Morgan, A., Bruschweiter-Stern, N., & Tonick, E. (1998). Non-interpretive mechanisms in psychoanalytic therapy: the "something more" than interpretation. *International Journal of Psycho-Analysis*, 79: 903–921.

Tähkä, R. (2000). Illusion and reality in the psychoanalytic relationship. *Scandinavian Psychoanalytic Review*, 23: 65–88.

Tähkä, V. (1993). *Mind and Its Treatment. A Psychoanalytic Approach*. Madison, CT: International Universities Press.

CHAPTER SIXTEEN

On the idea of a new developmental object in psychoanalytic treatment[1]

Jukka Välimäki

The basic premise of psychoanalysis was already present in the early cathartic form of psychoanalytic treatment. Psychic illness was seen as caused by emotional forces relegated to the unconscious, outside the realm of consciousness. This state of affairs was viewed as the consequence of active psychic functioning, through which the conscious area of the mind ("ego-consciousness") protected itself against these forces, which Freud understood at the time to be made up of memories of traumatic, mainly sexual experiences. Already, at that period, the concept of the ego represented both consciousness and the agent of defensive operations.

The principle of treatment was to have the patient remember his traumatic experience, to abreact the dammed up affective energies attached to the trauma, and to make the facts of the trauma part of his consciousness (Breuer & Freud, 1895d). The period of the cathartic treatment principle ended in 1897, when Freud abandoned his hypothesis suggesting that the essential causes of adult neuroses could be traced back to early sexual experiences of seduction.

Development of the concept of the ego and psychic change

Making something conscious in the form of remembering was, thus, the central curative factor in psychoanalysis from the beginning. However, the development of theory of the ego remained in the background during the so-called second phase of psychoanalysis from 1897 to 1923, when the emphasis was on the investigation of unconscious wishes and instinctual drives and in the ways in which they seek expression past repression via their derivatives (Sandler *et al.*, 1997). On the other hand, precisely this emphasis and the birth of drive theory meant generally, from the point of view of psychoanalytic treatment technique, increased significance of the ego as the "organ" capable of expanding its area of consciousness and, through this, strengthening control over the strivings of the unconscious so much so that the central aim of psychoanalytic treatment could be crystallized as making the unconscious conscious (Freud, 1919a).

Freud's work "The ego and the id" (1923b) gave the ego a central role in the totality of psychic functioning, complemented by the new theory of anxiety (Freud, 1926d) and the ego's position in it as the regulator of psychic equilibrium. American ego psychology from the 1940s to the 1960s could be considered the terminus of the growing significance of the ego. The works of Anna Freud (1936) and Hartmann (1939) are recognized as milestones of the start of this theoretical development. Ego psychology represented, from a clinical point of view, also the development of theory on the fundamental agent of psychic change, that is, the ego. The essential addition from ego psychology to Freud's structural model was Hartmann's (1939, 1964) and his colleagues' theory of the autonomous ego functions, which was based on a conception of primary and secondary autonomy in the ego development. The former emerges in the individual mainly outside of psychic conflict, and the latter involves capacities of the ego, which, having once served to resolve conflict, can develop and become an autonomous part of the conflict-free area of the ego. Thus, more and more, the therapeutic effectiveness of psychoanalysis could be believed to lie, in the last analysis, in the ego's (further strengthened by its autonomy) reality-sense and in its capacity to carry out reality-adaptation once the repressed and symptom-causing mental contents had been brought to its awareness through interpretations.

* * *

The key figure of ego psychology, Heinz Hartmann, was one of the few analysts who did not recognize empathy as a practicable tool in psychoanalytic treatment (Tähkä, 1993). In his effort to distinguish psychoanalysis from the Central European *Verstehende Psychologie*, represented, for instance, by Karl Jaspers, Hartmann (1927) had many reservations about the role of both understanding and empathy in psychoanalysis, considering the goal of psychoanalysis to be, in lieu of understanding the mental, the explanation of its causal relationships.[2]

Wallerstein (2002b) states that the focus of Hartmann's interest was psychoanalytic theory, and that it was in fact Kurt Eissler (1953), who was responsible for adapting the theory of ego psychology to clinical practice. Eissler's model of psychoanalytic technique is described by Wallerstein as rigorous and austere, "embedded as it was in the abstract theorizing on Hartmann's natural science vision of psychoanalysis" (*ibid*. p. 153).

Accordingly, the significance of empathy (and the object relationship aspect it represents) was considered slight in the original ego psychological approach to technique and in the theory of psychic change. The confidence in the triumph of the ego's autonomy and reality adaptation following the making of the unconscious conscious through interpretations was seen as crucial.

Rise of the role of empathy and counter-transference

During the latter part of the 1950s, more began to be written about the positive significance in the analytic process of emotional attitudes arising in the analyst. On the one hand, there was talk about empathy, on the other hand, there was discussion about counter-transference as an indirect route to understanding the patient. I am delineating this development following the idea (Tähkä, 1970, 1993) that the emotional attitudes arising in the analyst, necessary and useful for the analysis, can be divided into two groups: empathic responses, that is, entering into the patient's self-experience and complementary responses, which are temporary identificatory responses and incitements to action provoked in the analyst by the patient's (positive or negative) need for an object. Tähkä states it was Helen Deutsch (1926), who introduced the concept of "complementary attitude", meaning by it a temporary emphatic identification with the object of the patient's wish. Complementary responses can be included in the concept of counter-transference in the broad sense, but Tähkä has emphasized the need to detach complementary response from the concept of counter-transference and to define counter-transference as only those emotional attitudes of the analyst that are detrimental to treatment.

Empathy

In his article, Greenson (1960) states that at the time of writing, very little had been written about empathy in psychoanalytic treatment. Out of articles written before the 1950s, he mentions two articles by Freud, and articles by Ferenczi (1928), Sharpe (1930), and Fenichel (1941). Greenson notes that each touches only briefly on empathy. Tähkä (1993) particularly mentions a paper by Deutsch (1926) and one by Fliess (1942) from the period before the 1950s.

Kohut wrote his article "Introspection, empathy and psycho-analysis" in 1959, an article in which he placed a combination of introspection and empathy at the very centre of psychoanalytic technique and as its scientific tool. Perhaps the article by Kohut, written before he founded the self-psychology school of thought, was also a reaction to the ego psychological view of empathy as of questionable significance in analysis. In fact, Schafer (1959) also wrote at that time a wide-ranging article emphasizing the importance of empathy for psychoanalysis. Loewald (1960) claims that the scientific model of the researcher and his subject of study and scientific neutrality had been taken as a model for the patient–analyst relationship and he goes to great pains in his article to point out its flaws. In his textbook of psychoanalytic technique, Greenson (1967) both emphasizes the importance of empathy and analyses its nature. He sees it as a fundamental prerequisite for psychoanalytic therapy.

*   *   *

Thus, empathy became established as part of the treatment method of insight-oriented ego psychology. Empathy is understood as entering into the patient's way of experiencing and as a sharing of emotional experience, particularly in the context of interpretation. It is seen as facilitating the patient's emotional contact with a side of himself being spoken about in the interpretation. Correspondingly, many analysts also think that empathy demonstrates to the patient the analyst's ability to be in inner contact without difficulty or impediment with the spoken mental contents of the patient, thus communicating the understandability and (natural) humanity of the patient's way of experiencing (for example, Emde, 1990). That helps the patient to accept the matter being talked about as part of his own humanity.

Empathy is also a way of "seeing" the patient, to see him from a viewpoint that is new to the patient, or which has not been available to him because of his judgmental self. Empathy as "seeing" the patient is thus in addition to, and connected with interpretation, one of the therapeutic factors in analysis; the patient, in addition to insight, also identifies with the analyst's way of seeing him. This seeing is also evident in the tone of the interpretation, not just in its thought content. Winnicott (1967) is one of the best known representatives of this view. Empathic perception, and the patient's identification with it, is probably also an important explanatory factor for those successful psychotherapies, in which there has been little interpretive understanding. In explicating psychoanalysts' deepest motivations, Greenson refers to the object relationship-significance of empathy in this way: "For the empathizer the ununderstood patient is a kind of lost, need-fulfilling love object. Empathy, then, is an attempt of restitution for the lost contact and communication" (1960, p. 423).

Counter-transference and complementary response

A considerable advance in the psychoanalytic writing on counter-transference took place, when counter-transference began to be considered, notwithstanding its harmful effects, a tool for the understanding of the patient's mental contents which would otherwise remain hidden (Sandler *et al.*, 1973). They present Heimann (1950) as the first to introduce the idea that the emotions evoked in the analyst by the patient may also yield useful information about the analysand. Her basic proposition was that the analyst's unconscious understands the patient's unconscious. This connection on a deep level surfaces through the emotions arising in the analyst. The analyst can use this emotional response to understand the patient. This formulation contains the idea that counter-transferential emotions can be used to reach the patient's self-experience as well as his need for an object, where only the content of the insight will reveal which aspect is being understood, that is, whether it is to do with empathy or with a complementary response. In any case, Heimann's paper introduced a new principle: the possibility for the analyst to use the emotions evoked in him by the patient in the service of understanding.

In the following, I will select from the literature on counter-transference those works that relate to the *complementary response* evoked by the analysand's need for an object. Anna Reich (1951) and Money-Kyrle (1956) saw counter-transference as a necessary and essential demonstration of the analyst's interest in, and wish to attend to, the patient's well-being. Money-Kyrle's paper also contains the idea that the analyst cannot refrain from reacting, internally, with parental attudes towards the child he recognizes in the patient. Spitz (1956) similarly wrote on the anaclitic–diatrophic relationship between analyst and patient as the deepest basis for the analytic stance, where by anaclisis he meant the patient's attitude of needing support, and by diatrophy he meant the attitude on the part of the analyst which is maintaining and nourishing. Schafer's (1959) generative empathy is evidently a similar concept, by which he refers to the empathy that focuses on and strengthens the patient's growth potential. From Winnicott (1960, p. 53) a parallel view can be found: ". . . analyst, not unlike the mother, needs to be aware of the sensitivity, which develops in him or her in response to the patient's immaturity and dependence". Loewald's notable article (1960) "On the therapeutic action of psychoanalysis" also mentions counter-transference referring to Spitz's view, above, in this article, the idea of the new object signifies the analyst's sensitivity to the patient's "developing core", as he puts it, and in relation to his need for an object. Leo Stone (1961) wrote of a need for a "physicianly" attitude on the part of the analyst meaning an explicit concern and care for the well-being of the patient. Tähkä (1979) writes,

> Reacting complementarily to another human being's needs and feelings seems to be a biologically important human propensity,

which not only helps the parental person to react appropriately to an infant and child at different developmental stages . . . and becomes especially important to medical and therapeutic professionals while they are dealing with sick and disturbed individuals.

A new developmental object

The question about how the analyst should view the complementary responses arising in him is in my opinion critical and of crucial significance. Most of the above-mentioned authors, though not all, who see the complementary response of the analyst as a necessary part of analysis, emphasize that these emotions do have to remain in the background, that they are not to be openly expressed, and that they are also not to be realized on a practical level, which would mean a counter-transferential acting out. Instead, in their sublimated form, they serve analytic work and are part of the basic requirements of working as an analyst. But analytic thinking has not stopped here, but the question has been asked, whether these complementary responses might have, in certain situations of analytic interaction, some more specific and more purposeful role to be communicated to the patient and significance in analytic technique. At this point, Loewald's (1960) concept of *the new object* and Tähkä's (1993) concept of *the new developmental object* are relevant and have provided an opportunity to take a significant step forward on this question and also in the understanding of the curative factors in psychoanalytic treatment in general.

The purpose of this selective summary of the literature on counter-transference has been to show that *the idea of the new (developmental) object has emerged* organically, though clearly as a new step, in the discussions about counter-transference. Loewald (1986, p. 186) also makes this connection quite explicit:

> If capacity for transference, from its most primitive to its most developed form, is a measure of the patient's analyzability, the capacity for countertransference is a measure of the analyst's capacity to analyze. Countertransference, in this general sense, is a technical term for the analyst's responsiveness to the patient's love–hate for the analyst. [. . .] The patient's transference to the analyst (as a new rendition of patient's original love life) [. . .] is increasingly modified by the libidinally based transactions in the analytic

encounter between patient and that special new object—the analyst.

On the other hand, in identifying and distinguishing complementary response from counter-transference made by Tähkä (1970, 1979, 1984, 1993) is an important conceptual step, which has paved his way for the concept of a new developmental object. Complementary response is, as defined above, an emotional "answer" of the analyst to the patient's growth enhancing need for an object.

Thus the theories of empathy and counter-transference on the one hand and half a century of psychoanalytic research into developmental psychology on the other have found each other in the concept of the new developmental object introduced into the psychoanalytic method of treatment. Both the psychoanalysis of children, where the developmental viewpoint is very apposite, and the treatment of severe psychic disturbances have also had a significant part to play in this development.

On the basis of the above account, there might be sufficient grounds for a view of the history of the psychoanalytic method of treatment, which sees theories of the ego and the ego's autonomy as the most significant development *from the point of view of the therapeutic effect of analysis* in the first half century of psychoanalysis. The capacity of the autonomous ego, aided by the analyst, to acknowledge its defences, its ability to see childlike transference repetitions as no longer appropriate, to draw from this realistic conclusions and to put them into practice were seen as the crux of analysis' curative effect. The latter part of the century has been, again from the point of view of the therapeutic effect of analysis, a time of growing understanding of the meaning of empathy and counter-transference (in positive sense). This has meant that the analytic interaction has been increasingly defined using object relations concepts. At the same time, the general rise of object relations theory as well as a strong strengthening of psychoanalytic developmental research has taken place. Defining the analyst's function *also* as a new developmental object as Tähkä has done, seems to arise from these foundations and represent a naturally evolving step in the development of the theory of therapeutic technique.

Tähkä (1993) defines the analyst's empathy as a search and discovery of an object, and complementary response as the experiencing of and (through the expression of understanding) responding to the patient's growth-enhancing need for an object. These two ideas represent essential steps in the development of the theory of the analytical treatment I outlined above, and are important and clarifying formulations. These definitions express the forms in which the analyst's function as a new developmental object is realized. When the analyst in his empathy searches for contact with the analysand's current emotion and quality of experience, he is then also an object searching for an other. So, both empathy and complementary response are forms of being an active object. Empathy as the searching for and discovering an other is about actively perceiving, recognizing, and coming into contact with the analysand in a way that is often new to the patient; to respond complementarily to another is to make oneself available to another in a way required for the analysand to develop psychically. An example of empathic seeking is when a patient of mine, who frequently sulked after being disappointed, said that it is so nice when I search (contact) for her.

*   *   *

The developmental direction in the psychoanalytic method of treatment outlined here is a version of the new paradigm ("two person psychology") that according to Wallerstein (2002b) has grown into a rival of current ego psychology ("one person psychology") for the leading position. The new paradigm can be viewed as adding to, not replacing the earlier paradigm. Wallerstein (2002b, p. 162) proposes Joseph Sandler (1987) and Otto Kernberg (1975, 1976, 1980) as examples of theorists who in their work have "made an effort to fit together, even creatively suffuse, ego psychology and object relations theory's apparently very different metapsychologies".

What, then, do the new formulations of empathy and the new developmental object mean in clinical theory and practice? In the analysis of neurosis, they do not replace or displace any of the main principles of the technique of classical analysis, which are the analysis of resistance, the facilitation of transference regression, and the central role of interpretation. The viewpoint of the new developmental object can be seen as an important addition that can be integrated into it. The new formulations further help to understand factors of change in psychoanalysis which are not dependent on insight. They also mark a change in the theory of interpretation and the understanding of the effect of interpretation in the analysis of neurosis, as Loewald (1960) already touched on. This change is also evident in Tähkä's (1993) developmental and object relational psychoanalytic theory, and in the idea that through interpretative work "the transference child" is replaced by the "developing child".

One of Tähkä's aims has also been to outline the entire developmental continuum of psychoanalytic treatment, in which the new developmental object gains its stage-specific expressions on different levels of structuralization.

Clinical illustration

By the following clinical vignette I try to illustrate how the developmental viewpoint and the concept of a new developmental object can take shape to complement the technical principles of classical analysis in the treatment of a neurotic person.

My focus on these sessions in her analysis does not mean that the theme of the developmental object dominates her entire analysis. This type of session quantitatively form only a small part of her analysis. However, six months before the fragment in question, there was a period of several analytic hours when her longing and effort to reach an attitude of trusting neediness in relation to her analyst was thoroughly analysed. Then, as now, the fears of rejection and loss in the way of such a trusting attitude were overcome. This is therefore a new working through of the patient's central problem.

The patient had experienced abandonment by her mother during the latter part of the first year of her life and the loss of two other mother figures (aunts) in subsequent years , until, when she was aged six, her mother returned. Additionally, she had lost her father for good through divorce at the age of five, later gaining a good stepfather. Thus she had clear developmental problems and disappointments both in the psyche's preoedipal and oedipal areas.

This vignette concentrates on a dyadic transference relationship; however, she has subsequently shown herself well able to deal with her oedipal developmental stage. The analysand is a middle-aged woman and the vignette comes from the fifth year of her analysis. The extract spans four consecutive analytic sessions.

Session 1

In the previous sessions, we had dealt with her neediness and the way she protects herself against it. The present trigger for this conversation was the fact that we had been at the same concert. She had avoided meeting and shaking hands with me in the concert hall foyer because she had wished to spare me from herself, to be invisible to me, to not be a burden. Second, she had felt it was good that she had been sitting some rows behind me, because she could see me but I couldn't see her. Had I been able to monitor her movements, she would have caused me disappointment, stress, and annoyance by fidgeting and not paying attention, and she would have distracted me. By sitting behind me she spared me from all this stress. I was somewhat shocked when I understood this. She also found it awful.

The conversation became focused on her fear that her great neediness in relation to me would become evident, would show through. She said, "You wouldn't be able to handle it, to tolerate it, it would lead to a catastrophe, it would lead to abandonment." I said to her, among other things, "You find it difficult to imagine that responding to neediness might be satisfying; that one might do it with pleasure. As a mother you do know this." She said, "I don't know anything about that." She continued by saying, "You don't know what you're talking about; my neediness is so very great." I said that a baby's neediness is also very great, but a mother can have faith in her ability to respond to it and that the neediness gradually lessens and changes form; self-sufficiency gradually increases; we can surely have confidence in this.

After a moment she began to speak of her efforts to hide completely her neediness from me by having tried to weep only with her right eye, not the left one that I could see, so that I would not be stressed, tired, or annoyed by her crying and neediness and so that she might keep me and not be abandoned. (This had echoes of the repeated childhood experiences of being abandoned.) I told her that if she felt moved, or cried, then we would know that we had reached something meaningful and touching.

Session 2

The content of the session was about the gradual understanding of the deep significance of the previous session. After her session, she had gone to buy a potted rose for work and had gazed at it and watered it with pleasure. This was analysed for almost the entire session and the conclusion drawn was this: the flower represents her, the child in her who has dared to need, whose neediness is not a flaw, but something that she wants to nurture in herself. She ended the session by saying, "This is probably true, but what has led to this?"

Session 3

The patient reported that she had pondered the question that concluded the previous session. "I thought that it may have been that I was able to hold on to what you said about it being possible to respond to neediness with pleasure." She also referred to the fact that we had discussed her crying and said, "I was granted permission to cry here." She continued (referring to a familiar expression in our conversations), that a kind of existing on opposite sides had ceased between us. "Now it feels like peace has entered our relationship." After a pause this issue was clarified, and spoken by her: "I have plucked bits of you and then at times withdrawn to be someone who is brave and can make it on her own, and then I have returned to the picking. It's been an issue about imagining that you haven't wanted to give, that's why I have been picking at you, and then when I have grown frightened that you will lose your temper, I have withdrawn into being independent, so that you would like me more again. And then I have begun the picking again, furtively."

Session 4

She reported a dream, in which she was on her way to a very trying situation (in fact a real current concern), but I accompanied her and I had my hand on her shoulder. The essential content of the session was to deal with the restlessness she felt as a result of this dream image. The dream image was understood as a new version and representation of what she had experienced during the previous Thursday session (Session 1) and to what she felt she had surrendered in relation to me. I said that it was as if doubt, not in the dream, but in this session, was rearing its head again, doubt about what she already felt she could hold on to, that is, that responding to need could be satisfying and that one could take pleasure in doing so. She said that it was probably true that with every new change and issue, like with this dream image, she needed to investigate and test whether this, too, was acceptable, could this be allowed to be, or whether something else is expected of her. This was also crucial: she felt the need to run away from the relationship expressed by the dream image because she so needed it, but was simultaneously afraid that I would withdraw my hand, something more important would take precedence, or I might tire of her.

Discussion

A new developmental object included in the intervention

I said to my patient "You find it difficult to think that responding to neediness might be satisfying; that one might want to do it with pleasure. As a mother, you surely know this." I will concentrate on examining this intervention, although my other responses during the session also supported the implicit message contained in this sentence.

First, I think it is noteworthy that the interaction on the first session happened here and now, on the level of the present unconscious (Sandler & Sandler, 1987). Childhood experiences were not dealt with in this connection.

The intervention under discussion can be viewed from the point of view of interpreting a defence. The analyst said that the patient protects herself, she finds it difficult to (dare to) see that the object could respond to neediness with pleasure. In itself, this capability to respond to another person's neediness is a characteristic of human existence; one could say that for neurotic reasons, her reality sense regarding this aspect of human relationships had been clouded. But this wasn't only about human relationships in general, but about the fact that she did not believe the object to be capable of responding to *her* neediness with pleasure.

The latter part of the intervention contained another message. Although I was speaking about her, her neediness and the problem of it, I was also referring to a general human propensity to respond to another human being's neediness, and linking this to her own experience as a mother. In this situation of transference regression this was not only a general question either; it was me who was the object of her neediness; right now it was a burning issue in her relation to me, the analyst. When I said, during this transference situation, "You find it difficult to think that responding to neediness might be satisfying; that one might do it with pleasure", she had in her grasp the conclusion that I might also have this quality, evoked in me, in her analyst, right now and in relation to her. Thus, this general human quality became available to her through me, relevant to her in the analytic actuality, *implicitly* contained in my statement. This was what she reported being able to hold on to. Loewald (1960, p. 17) states, "Through the objective analysis of transference distortions the analyst becomes available to the patient as a new object, not just potentially but actually, eliminating step by step the impediments to a new object relationship formed by the transference." The symbol for daring to engage in a new object relationship was, in this instance, in addition to the purchase and watering of the flower, the dream where I held my hand on her shoulder. In my statement about her crying I also expressed my willingness to receive her tears, to tolerate and accept that kind of search for support from her.

The double-message structure of the interpretation

From the discussion above, a double message structure can be seen in my interpretation. This is also implied in the Loewald quotation above and is an essential aspect of his thinking about interpretation in his article. The first, overt message was about her way of protecting herself. The other, covertly expressed, message was about my willingness to respond to her neediness with pleasure. In this, however, I was not just referring to that particular moment, but to the below-the-surface aspect of the analytic relationship also mentioned in the counter-transference part of this paper, within which she had already during her analysis sensed the interactive substance that had existed between us. In the intervention I referred to the aspect of our relationship, which she had not previously dared to see (or which she had newly repressed when she had seen it earlier on) and to which she did not dare to surrender herself, as much as she would have wished to. In this relived transference crisis and in its analysis she was helped to see it. So it is possible to see my intervention as an interpretation, in which I interpreted her resistance to seeing the interactive fact that had existed between us, in which I had long accepted my role as the object of her neediness and her need for support without being frightened away. I interpreted both the resistance and this interactive focus of her self-protective behaviour. The way this interpretation differs from classical analysis is that the interpretation of the self-protection was not focused on the patient's infantile instinctual wish, or in general to mental contents that existed only in the mind of the patient (one person psychology) but on the interaction in the relationship between the analyst and analysand. The thing that she was defending herself against, the "phenomenon", was an aspect of the analytic object relationship that included the analyst. She could now see my part in it and to hold on to it. When interpreting in this way, the analyst is actively experiencing the neediness of the patient and identifying with an object in himself that can be accepting of and complementary to neediness.

The interpretation and classical analytic technique

One could ask whether this kind of interpretation (which the patient experienced as an offering from the analyst) was an acting out in the counter-transference of the analyst's need to give. Was it not the kind of gratification that halts the analytic process, when here there might have been an opportunity to place the patient's self-defensiveness into the genetic context, that is, beside her childhood experiences of abandonment and disappointment? Did not the analyst forget about analytic abstinence?

The same question can also be asked in a different way: Although it seemed that the patient gained from the way that the analyst handled her neurotic transference, did not the analyst give up his analytic stance, abstinence, to provide *psychotherapy* instead; that is, merely psychotherapy, to which satisfaction to different degrees is typical even with so-called analytic elements? Was there not some kind of greater analytic triumph to be had here, immediately or in the future, if the analyst had not had difficulty distinguishing between psychoanalysis and psychotherapy? Did not the analyst here alloy the pure gold of analysis with the copper of psychotherapy? Despite the fact that my response to these questions cannot be objective, I will state some facts that support the view that the analytic process was not interrupted or disturbed, but progressed, and that in addition to this the patient seemed to achieve something analytically valuable.

1. We can assume that even before her analysis there was in existence in the patient's mind an object who could respond positively to her need and wish to lean on someone, but in a repressed state. The analytic process had strengthened this object in her and at the same time, through the interpretation of defence, had weakened and questioned her need to protect herself. She had long defended against neediness by placing in front of it a negatively responding object. But this inner conflict had now become unbearable in the transference and she was looking for a way out of the impasse. The interpretation being examined here on the one hand dealt with the defence "you find it difficult to believe", and in the subordinate clause confronted her with a complementary object available in the here and now, activated in the analyst. The needy self was recognized and an object capable of responding to it was made available. The analysand could hold on to it.

It seems, that these two aspects of the analyst's interpretation were sufficient to remove the defensive behaviour and the fear that had caused it. But in my view, it removed the fear not in the way of neurotic neediness, but in the way of surrendering to a developmentally valuable, support-seeking, needing relationship generally necessary in human existence. The interpretation was not about satisfying an infantile neurotic wish, but rather about responding to a legitimate, developmentally crucial issue: the right to be in a safe, supportive relationship with a significant object. It signified a way out of a neurotic dead end and not the reinforcement of neurosis by satisfaction. In the case of developmental needs, as Tähkä (1993) has emphasized, abstinence is not called for. En route to her workplace, she expressed this new attitude of hers in relation to the potted flower she purchased, where the flower represented her neediness and she herself by tending it represented the new attitude to her own neediness, which she had internalized from the object experience in analysis. It was in the process of becoming established as part of a new superego that could be accepting of her own neediness.

2. Was the analytic process halted by the intervention because of the gratification implied in it? The immediate reaction of the

patient, the purchase and tending of the flower, but also the dream she narrated in the fourth session, would seem to fulfil the criteria of a correct interpretation in that it seemed to move the matter forward. She did recount a dream in the fourth session, where she was on her way to a currently relevant and trying situation, but together with me and with my hand on her shoulder. In this dream she was putting in practice her changed attitude and discovery regarding her neediness in relation to me that she had made a few sessions previously. In the dream she could bring herself to believe in my willingness to be supportive of her.

What was essential in the session was the conscious coping with the deepening needy attitude expressed in the dream, and dealing with the restlessness evoked by this dream image; that is, this was the working-through of an achievement of a few sessions back. Again, the conflict between longing for the supportive relationship expressed in the dream and the anxiety about losing it, was alive in her. Thus, the conflict between self-protection and the developmentally valuable ability to seek support had been reawakened and its analysis continued on a deeper level. This is how the analytic work continued and progressed. But already in the previous session it was evident that my intervention was useful and a step forward in the analysis of the neurotic transference. In the third session described, she expressed through her metaphor of "picking" how the analysis of this issue during the previous visit had increased her self-understanding of her earlier relationship to me. I understand the terms "giving" and "picking" in her statement as referring to gains from the object, which she could experience and feel to be signs of the object's caring for her.

Adult and child in the patient

The interpretation under discussion spoke both to the adult and the child in the patient. The child, activated by the transference regression, was ready to hold on to the object experienced in the analyst responsive to neediness. To express it using Tähkä's (1993) metaphor, the developing child stepped forward and overtook the transference child fearful of neediness. The analytic process continued, and this new position, in which her adult self accepted a child's neediness in herself, helped her to better see and analyse her relationship to me. What actually took place during these sessions cannot therefore really be described (as I have understood the original ego psychological view) as her having moved from an infantile position to an adult attitude and put away childish things through the power of a rational, conscious ego. What was crucial was her movement, in the analytic relationship, from a position of a child inhibited in her neediness to the position of a needy child. At the same time, her adult analysing ego preserved its ability to cooperate and analyse these childlike positions of hers. Here the conflict is resolved on an infantile level, as the saying goes; the patient moved from a neurotic childlike attitude to a developmental childlike attitude. The adult person, as it connected with the needy, childlike self, released from the prison of neurotic self-protection, can now find such forms for its neediness which serve her adult existence. Mutual influence between the formerly repressed neediness and the adult self can begin and the ability to need can now develop. Thus the adult self becomes enriched; it was a childhood ego, after all, that had constructed this defence against neediness.

The analyst's anonymity and function as a new developmental object

It is part of analytic technique that in wording his interpretations, and generally, the analyst leaves his personality in the background. This is why we word interpretations as follows, "You find it difficult to believe that responding to neediness might be satisfying, that one might do it with pleasure." Whereas we do not say, "You find it difficult to think that I nevertheless am that kind of person, one who responds to neediness with pleasure". The reason for this reserve is that the analyst should remain anonymous, the transference relationship should be protected so that it can be analysed.

But this reserve is also desirable from the developmental point of view. In this illustration, the fact that the analyst in his *analytic function* was such that he had (and had had) been capable of being experienced as willing to respond to neediness did not remain hidden from the patient. The analyst *indirectly* revealed something about himself, *but as an analyst*. In his analytic function, when he is available to be experienced as willing to respond to the neediness in his patient in transference regression, the analyst expresses, not specifically his own personal human quality, but a general (parental) quality belonging to humankind. This quality had become current and activated in him, as a complementary response, not just in the session in question, but in the course of the analysis, in his analytic work with just this kind of patient. Thus the analyst's anonymity serves not only the analysis of transferences. It also gives the patient the chance to gain in relation to the analyst as a representative of humankind a new experience of an object. Through this experience, she will be able to reorientate herself in relation to herself and to others and to find new alternatives in her life with others. But the transference in the here and now and the analyst's complementarity did dictate (and does dictate) the fact that the patient experienced (experiences) this quality as available in the analyst and specifically relevant to her. This individual aspect is mediated through the analyst's tone and nuances of involvement.

The same holds also true for empathy (defined here as understanding of patient's self-experience), which being inevitably also the analyst's individual response, is also a general human (and parental) characteristic and which has long been considered essential for analysis without this interfering with the analyst's anonymity.

Thus, the analyst's responding to a developmental need is not about him responding to the patient as a real person with certain attitudes, but one of his functions. The introduction of a real person at such a juncture would disturb the analytic situation and the analysis of the transference. Both the patient and analyst would be transformed into real adult persons and the fundamental mode of impact of analysis would slip away. The "serious play" of analysis would be shattered. The issue is about the "developing child" emerging into view through the transference regression. This "developing child" lives on its own level in the analytic relationship and responding to it must take place not on the realistic level but on the complementary level in the analyst. Based on this, Riitta Tähkä (2000) calls this kind of relationship a developmental illusion. It is experientially real, but exists outside everyday reality, in the specific setting of the analytic relationship that enables a psychic reality containing two parties. When the patient is allowed to *discover* this object in the analyst, then the developmental level is preserved. The analyst must only take care that what is needed is available through understanding.

The structural viewpoint

The flower purchased by the analysand and her attitude towards it, and her later dream about surrendering to being supported, seems to fit a thought already expressed by Strachey (1934) that the developmental object (which Strachey called the real object) can shift and become integrated as part of the analysand's superego. As the superego is the inheritor of certain precipitates of object relationships to begin with, it is logical that it would also become the inheritor of developmental object relationship experiences arising in an analysis of neurosis. Strachey understood the effect of a transformative interpretation as the patient introjecting into his own superego another kind of superego substance from the analyst which is different in kind to his own projections. In this case that was the object approving of neediness.

Summary

The concept of a new object coined by Loewald (1960) and later significantly elaborated by Tähkä (1984, 1993) by the concept of a new developmental object in the context of his wider theory of psychoanalytic treatment, seem to have evolved organically from the concept of counter-transference as it was beginning to be understood in the 1950s, that is, as an unconscious route to the understanding of the patient's hidden experience. Complementary response (Tähkä, 1970) describes the part of the counter-transference that represents the emotion and stimulus for action awakened in the analyst by the patient's need for an object. Its awakening in the analyst illustrates his identification with the parenting he experienced during the developmental years. The activation of this response in relation to the patient is an expression of a general human capability and, therefore, the indirect communication of it to the patient through understanding does not conflict with the analyst's anonymity. The latter is, in fact, essential for the analyst's inevitably individual response (getting expression in the tone and nuances of involment) to be experienced also as an example of the object in a more general sense, thus opening prospects to life outside the analytic relationship. The same holds true for empathy.

It is important to distinguish the analyst's function as a developmental object from the acting out of parental feelings and responses. An optimal or prototypal form of such a developmental response is the verbalized understanding of a developmental need in the patient. This makes it possible for the patient to find and experience in the analyst an activated complementary object.

Note

1. An earlier version of this paper was presented at the weekend conference of the Finnish Psychoanalytic Society in Helsinki 25–26 January 2003.
2. My intention is not to question Hartmann's significant role as a developer of psychoanalytic theory, but in my efforts to trace the essential phases of the formation of psychoanalytic technique, to draw attention to the critical attitude of this important and influential theorist towards the concepts of empathy and understanding.

Acknowledgement

My thanks to Kristiina Jalas, PhD, for her translation of this chapter.

References

Breuer, J., & Freud, S. (1895d). Studies on hysteria. *S.E.*, 2: 17. London: Hogarth.

Deutsch, H. (1926) [1953]. Occult processes occuring during psychoanalysis. In: G. Devereux (Ed.), *Psychoanalysis and the Occult*. New York: International Universities Press.

Eissler, K. (1953). The effect of the structure of the ego on psychoanalytic technique. *Journal of the American Psychoanalytic Association*, 1: 104–143.

Emde, R. (1990). Mobilizing fundamental modes of development: emphatic availability and therapeutic action. *Journal of the American Psychoanalytic Association, 38*: 881–917.

Fenichel, H. (1941). *Problems of Psychoanalytic Technique.* Albany, NY: Psychoanalytic Quarterly.

Ferenczi, S. (1928) [1955]. The elasticity of psychoanalytic technique. In: *Final Contributions to Problems and Methods of Psychoanalysis.* pp. 87–102. New York: Basic Books.

Fliess, R. (1942). The metapsychology of the analyst. *Psychoanalytic Quarterly,* 11: 211–227.

Freud, A. (1936). *The Ego and the Mechanisms of Defence.* London: Hogarth Press [reprinted London: Karnac Books, 1993].

Freud, S. (1919a). Lines of advance in psycho-analytic therapy. *S.E., 17*: 159–161. London: Hogarth Press.

Freud, S. (1923b). The ego and the id. *S.E., 19*: 13–59. London: Hogarth [reprinted London, Karnac, 1993).

Freud, S. (1926d). Inhibitions, symptoms and anxiety. *S.E., 20*: 160–172. London: Hogarth Press.

Greenson, R. (1960). Empathy and its vicissitudes. *International Journal of Psycho-Analysis, 41*: 418–424.

Greenson, R. (1967). *The Technique and Practice of Psychoanalysis.* New York: International Universities Press.

Hartmann, H. (1927) [1964]. Explanation and understanding. In: *Essays on Ego Psychology* (pp. 369–403). New York: International Universities Press.

Hartmann, H. (1939) [1958]. *Ego Psychology and the Problem of Adaptation.* New York: International Universities Press.

Hartmann, H. (1964). *Essays on Ego Psychology.* New York: International Universities Press.

Heiman, P. (1950). On countertransference. *International Journal of Psycho-Analysis, 31*: 81–84.

Kernberg, O. (1975). *Borderline Conditions and Pathological Narcissism.* New York: Aronson.

Kernberg, O. (1976). *Object Relation Theory and Clinical Psychoanalysis.* New York: Aronson.

Kernberg, O. (1980). *Internal World and External Reality: Object Relations Theory Applied.* New York: Aronson.

Kohut, H. (1959). Introspection, empathy, and psychoanalysis—an examination of the relationship between modes of observation and theory. *Journal of the American Psychoanalytic Association,* 7: 459–483.

Loewald, H. (1960). On the therapeutic action of psychoanalysis. *International Journal of Psycho-Analysis, 41*: 16–33.

Loewald, H. (1986). Transference–countertransference. *Journal of the American Psychoanalytic Association, 34*: 275–288.

Money-Kyrle, R. E. (1956). Normal countertransference and its deviations. *International Journal of Psycho-Analysis, 37*: 360–366.

Reich, A. (1951). On countertransference. *International Journal of Psycho-Analysis, 32*: 25–31.

Sandler, J. (1987). *From Safety to Superego: Selected Papers*. New York: Guilford Press.

Sandler, J., & Sandler, A.-M. (1987). The past unconscious, the present unconscious, and the vicissitudes of guilt. *International Journal of Psycho-Analysis, 68*: 331–341.

Sandler, J., Dare, C. & Holder, A. (1973). *The Patient and the Analyst*. London, Maresfield reprints.

Sandler, J., Holder, A., Dare, C., & Dreher, A. U. (1997). *Freud's Models of the Mind*. London, Karnac.

Schafer, R. (1959). Generative empathy in the treatment situation. *Psychoanalytic Quarterly, 28*: 342–373.

Sharpe, E. F. (1930).The technique of psychoanalysis. In: *Collected Papers on Psychoanalysis*. London: Hogarth Press, 1950.

Spitz, R. (1956). On countertransference. *Journal of the American Psychoanalytic Association, 4*: 256–265.

Stone, L. (1961). *The Psychoanalytic Situation:An Examination of its Developmental and Essential Nature*. New York: International Universities Press.

Strachey, J. (1934). The nature of the therapeutic action in psychoanalysis. *International Journal of Psycho-Analysis, 15*: 127–159.

Tähkä, R. (2000). Illusion and reality in the psychoanalytic relationship. *The Scandinavian Psychoanalytic Review, 23*: 65–88.

Tähkä, V. (1970). *Psykoterapian perusteet.*(Basic principles of psychotherapy.) Porvoo & Helsinki: Werner Södeström.

Tähkä, V. (1979).Psychotherapy as a phase-specific interaction: towards the general psychoanalytic theory of psychotherapy. *The Scandinavian Psychoanalytic Review, 2*: 113–132.

Tähkä, V. (1984). Psychoanalytic treatment as a developmental continuum: Considerations on disturbed structuralization and its phase-specific encounter. *The Scandinavian Psychoanalytic Review, 7*: 133–159.

Tähkä, V. (1993). *Mind and Its Treatment*. Madison, CT: International Universities Press.

Wallerstein, R. S. (2002a). The trajectory of psychoanalysis: A prognostication. *International Journal of Psycho-Analysis, 83*: 1247–1267.

Wallerstein, R. S. (2002b). The growth and transformation of American ego psychology. *Journal of the American Psychoanalytic Association, 50*(1): 135–169.

Winnicott, D. (1960) [1987]. The Theory of the parent -infant relationship. *International Journal of Psycho-Analysis,* 41:585–595. Reprinted in *The Maturational Processes and the Facilitating Environment.* London: Hogarth Press 1987.

Winnicott, D. (1967). Mirror-role of the mother and family in child development. In: P. Lomas, (Ed.), *The Predicament of the Family: A Psychoanalytic Symposium.* London: Hogarth Press and the Institute of Psychoanalysis [reprinted in *Playing and Reality.* Penguin Books, 1971].

CHAPTER SEVENTEEN

When mother wasn't there to be left

From functional to developmental object: a case report[1]

Aira Laine

Man and woman are born of woman:
before all else we are our mother's child.
Yet all our desires seem designed to deny this face,
so full of conflicts and reminiscent of our primitive
dependence.
The myth of Genesis seems to express this desire to free
ourselves
from our mother: man is born of God, an idealized paternal
figure,
a projection of lost omnipotence. Woman is born from
man's body.
If this myth expresses the victory of man over his mother
and over woman,
who thereby becomes his own child, it also provides a
certain solution for woman inasmuch as she also is her
mother's daughter:
she chooses to belong to man, to be created *for* him and not
for herself, to be a part of him—Adam's rib—rather than to
prolong her "attachment" to her mother.

Janine Chasseguet-Smirgel, 1985

Beginning of the treatment

A middle-aged woman, I call her Anja, entered my office with her ten-year-old daughter, her only child. She wanted to start psychoanalysis proposed by her internist because of the high blood pressure she had had for many years and for which she had been medicated. Five years before she had also had an abortion because of it. She related her symptoms, which she had managed to keep secret from everyone, even her own family. She was not able to walk alone in the city, nor to use the bus or to go to any public places, such as theatres. That is why her daughter was waiting for her in the waiting room, although the child did not know the real reason for this. Moving around alone Anja felt dizzy, her neck became stiff, her eyes painful, and she could not see. She was afraid of losing consciousness. She did not dare to swim, although she had loved swimming. In her workplace she could walk only through the underground corridor to another building. The symptoms were very severe and they threatened her ability to work. She had consulted a psychiatrist and got drugs which didn´t help. The only symptom which her husband and parents knew about was her high blood pressure and it was, she told them, the reason for the treatment. For economic reasons Anja wanted to start twice a week psychotherapy, the intensity of psychoanalysis was incomprehensible and scary to her.

When treatment began Anja was thirty-six years old, the eldest of five children, each of them born at two year intervals. During the second World War there was a war also between Finland and Sovjet Union. Anja's father had been in this war for the first five years of her life. Her mother had a daughter ten years older than Anja, who had been born of an extramarital relationship before the marriage and whom mother's parents had taken care of.

Anja did not look neurotic or inhibited, she was cheerful, had a good sense of humour, was in a way an easy-going person. She had a responsible office job where she was very successful.

The phase of psychotherapy

From the beginning the central theme appeared to be Anja's great worry about her daughter. For instance, if she were a few minutes late Anja went in panic looking for her and forced her husband to come with her, too. She considered her own behaviour neurotic but was unable to control it. She told me that her own mother had always been with her in every situation, even in adulthood when she was applying for a job or when she was pregnant and visited the child health centre. She remembered having been afraid of her mother's and her younger brother's death for her whole life. Ten years ago her mother had had lung cancer, blood had come many times to her mouth but it had not made Anja worried which was very surprising to me and I wondered to myself how disturbed she really was. Later I got to know that mother had been seriously ill after the birth of the brother when Anja was two years old. The threat of losing mother had been absolutely unbearable and it must have been denied even as an adult, when mother was seriously ill again. Anja said very sincerely: "I can't think of death because it would mean that I or somebody else would die." This thought was like a fact for her. When it was time for her to pay for the first time for her treatment she said that she has no money and asked to pay later. I reminded her about our agreement to pay during the month's last session and felt that her request was due to something else rather than lack of money. She paid on time with the money borrowed from her mother.

During the psychotherapy I felt it was impossible to get a real contact with the patient's problems. We talked about important matters but they were always forgotten immediately. I felt as if I were on a building site where materials were lost every night before any real construction work had even been started. After two years' treatment Anja, however, was able to finish her blood pressure medication and could travel by bus. We both realized that it was not yet time to end her treatment although she could not get financial support from the communal health care any more. Now I proposed psychoanalysis again and, by charging less, made it economically possible for her. Psychologically the more intensive relationship with me was no longer too threatening for her.

The beginning of the analysis

The change was remarkable: Anja filled her analytical sessions with excited, endless talk. I felt myself breathless when listening to her. Anja, her mother and daughter were similar in her mind to three sisters. It was very hard to know whom she was talking about, all three seemed to be so merged together. She said: "When my daughter has her period I feel I have mine, too." Clarification and differentiation began to take place when I, little by little, made the patient slow down, reflect and feel the sensations of her own body. My nearly "standing" question was: What and where do you feel in your body? She found an important thought and said: "When I am excited I have no head and when I'm pleased with myself, the lower part of my body disappears." She had feelings of breaking into pieces, as though she only had a head and legs or she was losing herself. Masturbation helped with her deep anxiety. During menses she would rush to the hospital because she was sure she was bleeding to death.

Anja had already had a lot of dreams during the therapy. I was very often in them in my own person and the manifest content was often homosexual. She never associated to homosexuality and I decided to wait for her initiative. I felt that to be more active would destroy and damage her analysis. I take a vignette describing the phase in which the change happened. She had been in analysis for six months. In one session Anja had been talking about a female patient who came before her: "There is something odd about her, she has no outdoor clothes, she can't be a patient. I can't say what I'm thinking."

Anja comes late to the next session, so that she will not see the same woman. She is sorry to be late but avoids analysing it.

I : "What kind of feelings did you have yesterday after the session?"
A : "I felt furious the whole evening."
I : "You came late, you could not see the person you were talking about."
A : "I guessed you would say that. I thought about it when coming here. It became too big of an issue.——I had a dream: I was lying here in bed, it was messy, you were sitting. I was afraid of you, you were peculiar . . . I wished for a dream, I could talk about. I was jealous in some way yesterday."
I : "Bed?"
A : "Strange, the dreams about you are always like that."
I : "You have sometimes said that you are afraid that there is something strange in you, now I'm strange."

A : "That woman made me feel that way." [The atmosphere is extremely intense.]

I : "You thought that I have a homosexual relationship with her."

A : "Yes, I did but I could not say it out loud."

She began to tell about sexual play with girl-friends as a child and she felt relieved. She reflected how awfully difficult it had been for her to separate her from mother. "If I can see my mother, she will stay alive," she said. She called her mother every day and met her many times a week.

When she married she and her husband stayed at her parents' home and mother did all the cooking. Then they moved to the house of her husband's parents where they still live, although the parents are dead. When Anja's daughter was five her nanny died suddenly; at the same time Anja had an abortion. She felt that her whole life changed.

Anja's deep dependence on mother had been obvious all the time, but she was not conscious of it at all and could not accept any of my interpretations concerning the matter. After the session described briefly in the vignette she got real emotional contact with this dependence and the breaks in the analysis began to mean something to her. Before, she had always wanted to finish her analysis in connection with breaks without finding any reason for it. Now she said: "I would rather finish at once than tolerate repeated separations."

In her workplace my patient had an affair with the man of the same age as her youngest brother; they shared nothing else together, only intercourse which happened in different, peculiar places; often they were in danger of being seen by others. This relationship had started after the abortion and the nanny's death. Often after the week's last session Anja had intercourse with the man; during her session she was very excited and anxious. She quarrelled with her husband and made him blame me in many ways during the weekends. Then she felt she was badly treated and had the right to do whatever she liked.

Although the analysis had now lasted for two years and the whole treatment four years, I still had the feeling that we always started from the beginning, there was only the present time, as if the same person would have come to her very first session over and over again. There was no continuity in the patient's mind, she was repeating things as though they were new. Just at the end of the session she could say: " Oh, I have told you this before." She perceived my presence better if I was silent. When I tried to say something, she often spoke at the same time. I was desperate, everything seemed to be lost.

The change in the analysis

My pregnancy changed essentially the relationship in the analysis. It made it concrete, that we were two separate persons and I did not exist only for Anja. Anja had several dreams related to my pregnancy and I could see that unconsciously she knew about it, but my maternity dress made her doubt. "If you were pregnant, it would be the end ... it was surely the end when the others were born," she said laughingly, remembering her childhood. During her school years her best friend became pregnant and left school. They had promised each other to be always together. Now the relationship was broken. Following this Anja had also left her school and travelled to take care of her half-sister's new-born baby. The teachers had been very surprised and asked her to come back to school but Anja didn't. The parents had let her do as she liked.

At last Anja asked directly about my pregnancy and of course I answered. The answer was like a blow. "Why did you do this?" she cried very painfully. After the session she took relaxing drugs. She was not able to walk in the forest with her husband any more, all her old symptoms came back, and she had many pregnancy symptoms, too. She wanted passionately to merge with her lover. She was in a rage with me and despised me: "Only stupid women become pregnant." She was suspicious about me as an analyst. I had been like a saint to her; now I became a woman who had a sexual relationship with a man. She wondered repeatedly if her symptoms had anything to do with my pregnancy. However, she found a continuity in the analysis; the sessions became connected with each other and her ability to work with me became much better. She felt that her analysis benefitted from my pregnancy, although it was so painful to bear. Anja began to talk about her abortion and to mourn it. She was sorry that her husband also had actively wanted the abortion to be done. Her blood pressure was not the only reason for the abortion, as she had told me before. My maternity leave seemed to be endless and she wanted to change everything in her life. She became vegetarian.

A vignette from the first session after the delivery break:

A : [continues smiling] "I have not been thinking of you but I have had many dreams about you. I have been walking around our house like a small child, not daring to go far away. I have eaten half a tablet of a relaxing drug every day."

I : "I have been absent but you have had the drug breast all the time." A : [triumphantly] "My mother breast-fed me for two years at the same time as my brother." I was surprised, she had never talked about this before. She could remember the breast-feeding and how she used to ask mother to give her "yam-yam", too, and mother accepted it. She had been breast-fed for four years. Now I began to understand the atmosphere in the analysis better; the timelessness and the feeling that everything is vanishing. Anja described her feelings during several sessions and wondered why she so often felt she was in the beginning of her analysis, why analytic sessions were not connected with each other in her mind, and why she thought so little about her analysis between the sessions. I proposed, that every session is like a breast-feeding for her and she went on immediately: "I get my stomach full, during the weekends it is more difficult when we have a longer break." The moment was very moving for both of us. After the session Anja had cried very bitterly in the rest room of my office and described her feelings in the next session: "The toilet was much smaller than before and I was much bigger. I realized that I have always been looking for that breast (she used another word common with children) but in reality I can't get it any more." So actually she had felt herself as a small child, now she had a feeling of really growing up.

Three and a half months later it was revealed that after the interpretation of the analysis as breast-feeding, Anja had regularly taken a half-tablet of a relaxing drug in the toilet of my office after every session and hidden it from me. I had noticed that somebody was drinking water there regularly and guessed that it was Anja. I felt angry and disappointed when I heard about the medication. I said: "With the medication you comfort yourself but it is also a laxative, a revenge on me. You want to get everything out of yourself that you have taken in during the session."

She stopped taking medication and she had many dreams where she cared for a baby much better than I. At this time I was really breast-feeding my baby and many times during other patients' sessions my breasts began to leak, but not with Anja. Her symptoms eased up again. She was able to have walks in the forest and she described her feelings: "Always before I have been the owner of the forest, bigger than the forest, now I am smaller. It felt so good to realize that something was around me, something surrounded me."

According to Anja her mother had always given her what she wanted. Now Anja—who was very good at cooking—wanted to use mother's pan but mother refused, she needed it herself. Her mother's refusal was a shock for her daughter and very difficult to accept. Anja noticed now the real size of her mother, who was a small woman, much shorter than Anja herself. I have to confess: her mother had been a big woman in my mind, too. I had never before asked about her size as I did now. Until now only mother's psychic size, so to speak, had been meaningful.

Now we had more freedom to analyse her peculiar sexual relation with her "lover". It seemed to be more a relation to the penis than to the man: most important for Anja was not intercourse but to be able to get the penis whenever she wanted, to have control over it. I connected this with her breast-feeding: it had been irregular during the last two years but it was allowed when she wanted it. Anja could now see that she used the man as she had used her mother. After understanding this, she was now, for the first time, able to reject the man. She could feel safe without this relationship and she was ashamed and felt guilty. She got into closer contact with her anxiety and chaotic body image. She said to me: "You are not able to help me, you are a woman, no woman can help another woman." She was angry with me because I did not get anxious. One night she had a revealing dream: she had borrowed her lover's penis but she had to give it back when the time was over. She felt that it was safe to have a penis, it meant: to be closed, not open in the way that a woman's genitals are. The erect penis represented for her complete control. By controlling the penis she had a feeling of being able to control her own body and its mysterious sensations inside, too. I reminded her about her symptoms, her stiff neck and painful, immobile eyes. Her whole body had been like an erect penis protecting her from falling into pieces. Little by little she could see her "lover" as a whole man, who had a sad history. It seemed to me that the man first of all needed Anja to admire his penis and to support his masculinity in a phallic–narcissistic sense. They were both very important as functional objects to each other. Later the man wanted to give up this affair and he moved with his family to another town.

Everything had to happen very concretely in Anja's life for it to become conscious and integrated. It had been quite evident to me that she was not able to be alone; every time she got ill she went to her parents. She had always some "rational " reasons for this in her mind: cleaning or something like that to help her parents, who were about seventy years old.

One day Anja's professional union began a strike, which lasted some three weeks. First she visited her parents every day to help them in many ways. Before the strike ended, she had cleaned the whole house. She could not find a rational reason to go there any more and now she had to stay home alone for the first time during her analysis. When she came to her session on the same day she was in a panic. I said to her: "You have been alone at home but not away from this world, where we both are". Little by little we could work through her fear that to be alone is to be dead; then she could begin to take care of her garden and home although she was alone there.

She also became more interested in her father, in what kind of a person he really was. When she was at school, father had helped her with mathematics. Her actual work now included rather a lot of mathematics. She remembered how afraid she had been when father visited home during the war and how strange he was for her as a five-year-old when the war was finished. Anja had a dream: her father came close to her; mother came and said, "Why didn't you tell me?". She associated: "I have tried to keep father without gender, sex, and meaning; at the same time I have missed him." During the same session she remembered having seen the parents' sexual act. She had gone to their bed between them and woken up during the act. She had pretended to sleep but had trembled with fear.

The end of the analysis

Anja herself proposed the date of ending a year beforehand. During the last year her mother was diagnosed as having stomach cancer and was operated on. Now Anja could face the reality, she said "Despite the operation the cancer will still grow." She took care of her mother. After the operation mother was quite well and still well at the end of the analysis.

The atmosphere during the sessions in general could be put into words: "It can't be true." Anja could not believe that she was actually ending her analysis. She expressed her wish: "If I had money enough I would go on so long that I would want to finish, finishing would feel only pleasant." I said, "Perhaps your mother tried to make weaning pleasant. Perhaps, too, she could not bear the feeling of being rejected, separation is always separation." Anja told me that before her analysis she did not know what missing meant. Now she had begun to remember her childhood town and miss it, the town had become valuable; before she had been ashamed of coming from such a small town.

Anja was disappointed that the analysis had not made her a person who does not need anybody, she was only a regular woman. She began to reduce her weight. She wanted to show me she was able to do it.

I take one of her many dreams, which were of great help for the analytic work during the last year. During the previous session Anja had been furious with me, when I had connected her feelings of having been mocked with the feeling of being an outsider in the relationship between mother and father. She said: "I'll never say a good word about you, never praise you." The next night she had the following dream:

"It was the last analytic session; you were gladly chatting and said you would organize a competition at my job concerning psychoanalysis . . . Your husband shovelled shit into a bag for your flowers; you were sitting with your legs spread, without underpants on, and I was sitting facing you, I didn't know where to look."

Her associations: "The last session, what will be after it? Will I see you ever . . . All the women at my work place are competitors . . . your husband has despicable work, he has less training than you . . . I'm satisfied that it's so, the same situation as I have with my husband . . .

legs spread . . . I saw everything. My daughter didn't want to go to the sauna with her classmates yesterday, I said to her: 'Don't be a shy girl, you still have to go to the doctor, and to take your underpants off'. [She stopped to think of her relationship to her daughter, how she would like to see her]—"To be that doctor," I said.

Anja remembered what had happened during her analysis; she had nearly repeated with her daughter the situation which she had had with her mother; a doctor had to take a urine specimen while mother was in the same room. She had also experienced her mother talking about her (Anja's) intimate matters publicly and scornfully.

She experienced different somatic symptoms and she remembered how she had continuously wondered and doubted during my pregnancy if the symptoms were caused by it. Now she understood that her symptoms were connected with finishing, but she didn't want to admit it.

During the last sessions, Anja thought about her analysis as follows:

"In the beginning I didn't consider you as a human being, you were such a machine." I said, referring to one of her first dreams, "I was a juice machine." "Yes, but your pregnancy changed the situation. Afterwards, I realized how awfully anxious I was then for the whole summer . . . the separation then, a separation now. The feeling is different, I'm not so anxious but I don't feel good either. But I believe I can manage. You have taken away from me the ability to forget and to deceive myself. I can't do it any more. I felt dizzy, near to fainting, when I tried to deny my feelings. Always before when I ought to have struggled, I made other persons do it. I have felt that I never get anything because everything already belongs to me. Other people, especially my brothers and sister, have been balloons to me which I have been exploding; now they are real persons."

Anja had wished her husband would come to pick her up from her last session but she didn't ask him because she felt it was important to leave walking on her own two feet. She thanked me with roses and gave me a hug.

Only four months later I read in the newspaper that her mother had died. It made me very sad; she had died too soon after the end of Anja's analysis, I felt, but Anja didn't contact me as I anticipated. After a year I received a postcard from abroad; she greeted me and thanked me for her analysis. The card made it evident that she now dared to travel by plane.

Four years later she asked for an appointment. "The lover " had returned and the affair had begun again, but now the man wanted to end it. Anja was in a rage and did not know how to cope with it. Now I got to know that her mother had died of a heart attack, not cancer, and that Anja had had an abortion after mother's death. She thought she was too old (forty-three) to have a baby. Together we could realize with sorrow how similar the situation had been with the nanny's death. The daughter's nanny had been like a mother for Anja. We talked about the hate and feelings of loneliness that her own mother's death had roused in her. We met for some sessions and she hoped that I could again reduce my fee so that she would be able to re-enter analysis, but I did not agree. She became angry with me and she would have liked to hit me. We could discuss it and I was sure that my refusal helped her: she was not in need of help, she could manage herself and see the reality. Later, this proved to be true.

Considerations

I have described, in a very condensed form, what I considered to be the central part of my thoughts about the mother–daughter relationship in Anja's analysis. Mentally she had not achieved the phase that one two-year-old girl expressed by telling her mother gladly: "I can speak so that you can't hear it!" In other words, this little girl had become conscious that she could think without her mother knowing her thoughts. In Anja's mind the magic contact with mother had never ended. All through her early development she had unconsciously experienced intense bodily sensations connected with breast-feeding and was stimulated by it. This over-stimulation was threatning; her own bodily feelings became too excited and were out of her control. By denying and keeping them out of her consciousness she tried to keep herself together. Perhaps for this reason her body image was undifferentiated and chaotic, but I don't think that the long breast-feeding was the only reason for this. Maybe it was only one example of how her mother was unable to be left. The affects had lost their important role in the integration, because the barrier of self-regulation had been broken.

She suffered from feelings of breaking into pieces and panic states. Swimming raised the fear of losing herself. Masturbation helped with deep anxiety. According to Joyce McDougall (1995) masturbation is a bridge between mind and body.

Because of the war Anja's father had been missing as a protector of the mother–child unit and relationship in the way Robert Furman describes in his paper "The father–child relationship" (1983). The circumstances were very special; her father was continuously in danger, and I don't believe that her mother was able to sympathize with Anja's feelings concerning him. The birth of the brother and mother's serious illness must have been extremely traumatic in this context. Maybe, in Anja's unconscious, mother had made father disappear and Anja was afraid that mother would leave her as she had left her first daughter. Her aggression must have been totally denied; in the analysis it was revealed in forgetting, not having guilty feelings and denying any kind of lack. Anja tried to cope with her enormous anxiety by being a baby and perhaps by giving up her autonomy. When she took half a tablet, was she perhaps giving the other part to her brother? Mother, for her own reasons, could not support Anja's autonomy either. According to Erna Furman (1994, 1997) a mother transforms her narcissistic investment of her child into object investment; she loses her child as a part of herself and begins to love her as a separate person. Her mother had given her first daughter, Anja's ten-years-older half-sister, to her parents. I don't know the details, but I'm sure that her mother suffered from severe guilt feelings for having abandoned her child. Perhaps in a way she tried to repair her own past by giving everything to her next daughter, and maybe for the same reason, when Anja later had left her school and travelled to care for her half-sister's baby, mother's reaction had seemed to be so minor. In a way Anja did it on behalf of her mother. We have to remember, too, that the outer circumstances were exceptional because of the war, and lack of food and safety. The same conclusion that Erna Furman has arrived at in her excellent papers about motherhood Joyce McDougall (1995) has expressed by saying that when we are speaking of a child's separation anxiety, we in fact talk about a mother's own separation anxiety.

Father had returned from the war when Anja was in her oedipal phase. He was now between Anja and mother. The whole important dyadic relationship with father had been lost, which made the reunion with him unbearable. According to Tähkä:

> The individual character of these dyads, interposed between the child's functional and oedipal relations with his parents, has so far been largely neglected, as has been their importance for the nature of the child's ensuing mental developments."

He continues, saying that the dyadic ideal images

> will preserve the models for nonambivalently positive relations to the parents throughout the oedipal turmoils, contributing to motivate the preliminary experiental abandoment of the oedipal parents, as well as providing paragons for the child's relations to his parents during latency [Tähkä 1993, pp. 404–405]

As a man—different from mother—father aroused fear in Anja, the kind of fear, that she could remember even as an adult. She tried to keep father without a gender, but if we think of Anja's relationship with her "lover", it resembled to some degree a child's sexual play full of primitive curiosity. I think that her excited curiosity also made the father figure more dangerous. To find father as a real, whole person became possible after the analysis of the intense, oral longing for mother and the dependence on her. We can also speculate how much Anja in her peculiar sexual affair was repeating something which she herself had experienced of her parents' sexual life during the war.

During the analysis Anja was freed of her severe symptoms. Her deep anxiety and panic feelings disappeared when the somatic sensations and inner images were integrated. In the beginning I was worried about how weak and broken Anja's perception of inside and outside was, but it was proved that the core existed; this could be seen for instance in her ability to keep her symptoms secret and her very good ability to do analytic work, especially after the weaning interpretation. However, Anja had not been able to breast-feed her own daughter; perhaps the threat of merging had been too intense. My pregnancy had a great influence on the process of the analysis as did my approach and ability to understand its meanings. My pregnancy, for Anja, was a repetition of her past. Anja's "homosexuality" expressed how much she was still missing her mother.

In the beginning I referred to Janine Chasseguet–Smirgel's famous thoughts. They express the most essential points: our help-lessness and our primitive dependence on mother and how we have tried to solve conflicts about these in our culture. Winnicott (1986, pp. 183–194) writes that if we don't confess our complete dependence on the woman, we all, women and men, feel fear of the woman. The awkward fact remains, for men and women, that each was once dependent on woman and somehow a hatred of this has to be transformed into a kind of gratitude if full maturity of the personality is to be reached."

Anja's disturbance level was perhaps mainly neurotic but she had also many symptoms originating from the functional phase of development (Tähkä, 1993 p. 401). During the first years of the treatment I was for her a functional object, "a juice machine", according to her own words, who was able to soothe her. My pres-ence was most important but no progress took place (*ibid.*, p. 75). During my pregnancy I became a separate person, "developmental object", for my patient. The working alliance became a therapeutic alliance and we were able to progress (*ibid.*, pp. 229–230). By combining Erna Furman's (2000) deep exploring on motherhood and Veikko Tähkä's (1993) theory about functional and develop-mental objects, we can better understand what was the process for the patient and her analyst during the treatment.

Note

1   John Hadden, Jr., M.D. Memorial Lecture 28 April, 2000. The first version published in *Child Analysis*, Volume 12, pp. 93–109, 2001. Reprinted by permission, Cleveland Center for Research in Child Development.

References

Chasseguet-Smirgel, J. (1964) [1970]. Feminine guilt and the Oedipus Complex. In: J. Chasseguet-Smirgel, (Ed.), *Female Sexuality: New Psychoanalytic Views*, pp. 133–134. Ann Arbor: Michigan University Press [reprinted London: Karnac, 1985].

Furman, E. (1982). Mothers have to be there to be left. *Psychoanalytic Study of the Child*, 37: 15–28.

Furman, E. (1994). Early aspects of mothering: what makes it so hard to be there to be left. *Journal of Child Psychotherapy*, 20(2): 149–164.

Furman, E. (1997). On motherhood. *Child Analysis*, 8: 126–149.

Furman, E. (2001). *On Being and Having a Mother*. Madison, CT: International Universities Press.

Furman, R. A. (1983). The father–child relationship. Paper presented at The 1983 Workshop of the Cleveland Center for Research in Child Development.

McDougall, J. (1995). *The Many Faces of Eros*. London and New York: Norton.

Tähkä, V. (1993). *Mind and Its Treatment. A Psychoanalytic Approach*. Madison, CT: International Universities Press.

Winnicott, D. W. (1986). This feminism. In: C. Winnicott, R. Shepherd, & M. Davis (Eds.), *Home Is Where We Start From*, pp. 183–194. New York: Norton.

SCIENTIFIC BIBLIOGRAPHY: VEIKKO TÄHKÄ

Books

The Alcoholic Personality, Volume 13 (1966). Helsinki: The Finnish Foundation for Alcohol Studies.

Psykoterapian perusteet (Basic Principles of Psychotherapy) (1970) (sixth edn. 1993, in Finnish). Porvoo-Helsinki: WSOY.

Psykoanalytisk psykoterapi (Psykoterapian perusteet) (1983). Danish edition (transl. R. Vaisanen). Copenhagen: Centrum.

Psykoanalytisk psykoterapi (Psykoteraplan perusteet) (1987). Swedish edition (transl. M. Parland). Stockholm: Natur och Kultur.

Psuhhoteraapia alused psuhhoanaluutilise teooria pohjal (Psykoterapian perusteet) (1999). Estonian edition. Helsinki: WSOY; Tartu: Tallinn.

Psichoterapijas pagrindai remiantis psichoanalizes teorija (Psykoterapian perusteet) (1999). Lithuanian edition (transl. R. Augis, L. Kovarskis, S. Meskauskiene, V. Pocius, & A. Vicinaite). Vilna: UAB "Errata".

Potilas–lääkärisuhde (The Patient–Doctor Relationship) (1977) (3rd edn. 1987, in Finnish). Helsinki: Suomen Lääkäriliitto.

The Patient–Doctor Relationship (Potilas–lääkärisuhde) (1984). English edition (transl. C. Gronlund). Sydney: Adis Health Press.

0 relacionamento medico–paciente (Potilas–lääkäririsuhde) (1987). Portuguese edition. Porto Alegre: Editora Artes Medicas sul Ltda.

Psykoanalyysin ja psykoterapian suuntauksia (*Directions in Psychoanalysis and Psychotherapy*) (1978) Eds. V. Tähkä & Y. Alanen. Espoo: Weilin & Göös.

Mind and Its Treatment: A Psychoanalytic Approach (1993). Madison, CT: International Universities Press.

Mielen rakentuminen ja psykoanalyyttinen hoitaminen (*Mind and Its Treatment*) (1996). Finnish edition (transl. V. Tähkä). Juva: WSOY.

Psihikai ee lechenie (*Mind and Its Treatment*) (2001). Russian edition (Ed. M. Romackevitch, transl. V. Starovoitov). Moscow: Akademicheskii proekt.

Papers and book chapters

1952

Alemmuudentunnosta (On inferiority feelings). *Lapsi ja nuoriso, 11*: 9–12.

1953

(With Siurala, M.) Gastric and duodenal ulcers in patients of the hospital of the central prison of Helsinki. A statistical study. *Annales Medicinae Internae Fennica, 42*: 240–248.

(With Westling, A.) The first information on sexual matters. A statistical study. *International Journal of Sexology, 6*: 197–203.

1954

Juoppouden psykodynaamisesta etiologiasta (On the psychodynamic etiology of alcoholism). *Alkoholipolitiikka, 6*: 1–8.

1958

(With Westling, A.) Kastraatiouhkauksista ja penikseen kohdistuvista pienuusfantasioista (On so-called castration threats and inferiority fantasies concerning size of penis). *Duodecim, 74*: 449–457.

1959

On psychotherapeutic interpretation. *Acta Psychiatrica Neurologica Scandinavica, 34*: 242–247.

1960

(With Alanen, Y.) Alkoholin väärinkäytön psykodynamiikasta erään tapauksen valossa (On the psychodynamics of alcohol addiction in the light of one case). *Duodecim, 17*: 43–56.

(With Alanen, Y.) Skitsofrenian somaattisesta- ja perinnöllisyys-tutkimuksesta (On somatic and genetic studies in schizophrenia). *Duodecim, 76*: 95–112.

(With Alanen, Y.) Skitsofrenian psykodynaamisesta tutkimuksesta (On psychodynamic studies in schizophrenia). *Duodecim, 76*: 113–131.

1961

(With Alanen, Y.) Skitsofrenian somaattisista seka ryhmä- ja yhteisö-terapeuttisista hoitokeinoista (On somatic methods, group psycho-therapeutic methods and allied measures in treatment of schizophrenia. *Duodecim, 77*: 254–268.

(With Alanen, Y.) Skitsofrenian psykoterapiasta (On the psychotherapy of schizophrenia). *Duodecim, 77*: 269–280.

1963

Alkoholismin psykodynamiikasta (On the psychodynamics of alcoholism). *Duodecim, 79*: 748–758.

1965

Eräs ns. terapeuttinen yhteisö Yhdysvalloissa (A so-called therapeutic community in the United States). *Sosiaalilääketieteen Aikakausilehti, 3*: 34–39.

Psykoterapeuttisia näkökohtia yleislääkärin työssä (Psychotherapeutic aspects in general practice). *Suomen Lääkärilehti, 20*: 2039–2045.

Psykoterapia eri oireyhtymissä (Psychotherapy in different psychiatric syndromes). *Duodecim, 81*: 1190–1199.

1966

Lääkäri–potilassuhteesta (On the doctor–patient relationship). *Suommen Lääkärilehti, 21*: 1624–1630.

1967

Syistä ja syyllisistä (On causes and the guilty). *Duodecim, 83*: 257–260.

Psykoterapiasta ja sen eri muodoista (On psychotherapy and its techniques). *Suomen Lääkärilehti*, 22: 2331–2339.

1968

Acting-out ja sen käsittely (Acting out and its management).*Duodecim*, 84: 17–25.
Alkoholistin persoonallisuudesta (On alcoholic personality). *Sosiaalilääketieteen Aikakausilehti*, 6: 17–25.

1969

Psykoterapiasta, lääkäripulasta ja koulutuskysymyksistä (On psychotherapy, shortage of physicians and problems of education). *Sairaala*, 1: 17–22.
Lääkäri ja psykoterapia (Physician and psychotherapy). *Suomen Lääkärilehti*, 24: 1857–1863.
Aggressiivisuudesta (On aggression): *Duodecim*, 85: 1205–1213.
Psykoterapiakoulutus Suomessa (Psychotherapeutic training in Finland). *Mielenterveys*, 9: 62–66.
Psykoterapian osuudesta terveydenhuollon palveluksissa (The share of psychotherapy in the health care services). *Mielenterveys*, 9: 56–61.

1970

(With Aalberg, V.) Psykoterapiakoulutus Pohjoismaissa (Psychotherapeutic training in the Nordic countries). *Sosiaalilääketieteen Aikakausilehti*, 25: 183–189.
(With Holmström, R.) On the effects of the abandoning of the use of uniforms on patients in a psychiatric hospital ward. *Psychiatria Fennica*, 1: 91–99
(With Holmström, R.) On the effects of the abandoning of the use of uniforms on the staff of a psychiatric hospital ward. *Psychiatria Fennica*, 1: 100–109
Lääketieteen identiteettikriisistä (On the identity crisis of the medical science). *Medisiinari*, 34: 15–20.
Ahdistuneisuus psykodynamiikasta (On the psychodynamics of anxiety). *Orion's Psychiatric Symposium in Helsinki 18–19 April 1969*, pp. 52–59.
(With Hirvas, J., Holmström, R., & Tuovinen, M.) Coping with an exceptional reality situation. How chronic respirator patients have

adapted to the regulation of their lives by a mechanical contrivance. *Reports of the Psychiatric Clinic of the Helsinki University Central Hospital, 10.*

Psykoterapian opetuksesta psykiatrikoulutuksessa (On teaching psychotherapy in the psychiatric education). *Suomen Lääkärilehti, 25:* 1701–1708.

(With Achte, K., & Rechardt, E.) Psykoanalyyttisia näkökohtia saunasta ja saunomisesta (Psychoanalytic aspects of sauna and bathing). *Suomen Lääkärilehti, 25:* 1878–1888.

Vielä psykoterapian opetuksesta psykiatrikoulutuksessa (Additional aspects of teaching psychotherapy in the training of psychiatrists). *Suomen Lääkärilehti, 25:* 2064–2066.

Om de psykoterapeutiska utbildningsmöjligheterna i Finland (On the possibilities of psychotherapeutic training in Finland). *Nordisk Psykiatrisk Tidsskrift, 24:* 87–91.

1971

(With Holmström, R.) Virkapuvusta luopumisen vaikutuksesta psykiatrisen osaston potilaisiin (Reactions of the patients to abandoning uniforms in a psychiatric ward). *Sairaanhoitaja, 46:* 8–11.

(With Holmström, R.) Virkapuvuista luopumisen vaikutuksesta psykiatrisen osaston henkilökuntaan (Reactions of the staff to abandoning uniforms in psychiatric ward). *Sairaanhoitaja, 47:* 60–63.

(With Rechardt, E., & Achte, K.) Psychoanalytic aspects of the Finnish sauna bath. *Psychiatria Fennica, 2:* 63–72.

1973

Potilas–lääkärisuhteeseen vaikuttavista psykologisista tekijöistä (On the psychological factors affecting the patient–doctor relationship). *Suomen Lääkärilehti, 28:* 2355–2368.

(With Hägglund, T.-B.) Psykoterapia ja lääkärintodistukset (Psychotherapy and the medical certificates). *Suomen Lääkärilehti, 28:* 2681–2686.

Poliklinikka Toivola—psykoterapeuttinen tutkimus-, kuntoutus- ja koulutuslaitos (The Toivola clinic—an institute for psychotherapeutic research, treatment and training). *Suomen Lääkärilehti, 28:* 2991–2995.

Parantavan suhteen prognoosi (Prognosis of the curative relationship). *Suomen Lääkärilehti, 28:* 3116–3118.

1974

Lääkärikoulutuksen tavoiteohjelmista hoitotulosten parantamiseksi (On improving the programmes of medical training) *Suomen Lääkärilehti, 29*: 269–276.
What is psychotherapy? *Psychiatria Fennica, 5*: 163–170.
Mourning work and working through. *Psychiatria Fennica, 5*: 171–180.

1975

Ten years of organized psychoanalysis in Finland. *Psychiatria Fennica, 6*: 373–382.

1976

Om psykoterapins kurativa faktorer (On the curative factors of psychotherapy). *Nordisk Psykiatrisk Tidsskrift, 30*: 220–227.
On the curative factors of psychotherapy. *Acta Psychiatrica Scandinavica Supplementum, 265*: 41–42.

1978

Hartmann ja psykoanalyyttinen ego-psykologia (Hartmann and the psychoanalytic ego psychology). In: Y. Alanen & V. Tähkä (Eds.), *Psykoanalyysin ja psykoterapian suuntauksia (Directions of Psychoanalysis and Psychotherapy)* (pp. 44–67). Espoo: Weilin-Göös.
Psykoterapian hoidollisesti vaikuttavista tekijöistä (On the therapeutically effective factors of psychotherapy). In: Y. Alanen & V. Tähkä (Eds.), *Psykoanalyysin ja psykoterapian suuntauksia (Directions of Psychoanalysis and Psychotherapy)* (pp. 132–139). Espoo: Weilin-Göös.
Psykodynaamisen tutkimuksen asema mielenterveystutkimuksessa (The position of psychodynamic research in the mental health research). *Suomen Lääkärilehti, 33*: 1043–1046.
On some narcissistic aspects of self-destructive behavior and their influence on its predictability, *Proceedings of the IX International Congress on Suicide Prevention and Crisis Intervention*, Helsinki 20–23 June 1978, pp. 250–254.
On some narcissistic aspects of self-destructive behavior and their influence on its predictability. Psychopathology of direct and indirect self-destruction. *Psychiatria Fennica Supplementum*, pp. 59–62.

On sociotherapeutic measures on a psychiatric ward. In: G. V. Morozov (Ed.), *Current Problems in Psychiatry* (pp. 161–166). Moscow.

1979

(With Boss, M., & Salminen, H.). On differences between phenom-enologic and psychoanalytic approaches to psychotherapy—some comments to Prof. Boss's case presentation. Medard Boss, *Psychoanalysis and Daseinanalysis. Reports of Psychiatria Fennica*, 34: 57–64.

Sairaus biologis-psykososiaalisena ongelmana (Illness as a biologic psychosocial problem). *Suomen Lääkärilehti*, 34: 180–186.

Sjukdom som ett biologiskt-psykosocialt problem (Illness as a biologic psychosocial problem). *Finska Läkarsällskapets Handlingar*, 139: 23–32.

Voiko syöpä syntyä surusta ja stressistä? (Can cancer originate from sorrow and stress?). *Syöpä-Cancer*, 5: 2–3.

Sosioterapeuttisten toimenpiteiden teoriasta ja käytännöstä (On the theory and practice of sociotherapeutic measures). *Reports of Psychiatria Fennica*, 32: 48–60.

Psychotherapy as phase-specific interaction: towards a general psychoanalytic theory of psychotherapy. *Scandinavian Psychoanalytic Review*, 2: 113–132.

(With Achte, K., Alanen, Y., Anttinen, E., Arajärvi, T., Niskanen, P., & Tienari, P.) Lapsen vuoden vetoomus: Luo lapselle yhdessa hyvä elämä (Appeal of the children's year: Let's create together a good life for the child). *Suomen Lääkärilehti*, 31: 2552–2553,

1980

Patient–läkar-relationen 1: Vilka faktorer påverkar kontakten mellan patient och läkare? (Patient–doctor relationship 1: Factors influencing the interaction). *Nordisk Medicin*, 95: 21–25.

Patient–läkar-relationen 2: Den medicinska intervjun, kroppsundersökning och information (Patient–doctor relationship 2: Medical interview, physical examination and information for the patient). *Nordisk Medicin*, 95: 57–61.

Patient–läkar-relationen 3: Vård och behandling (Patient–doctor relationship 3: Care and treatment). *Nordisk Medicin*, 95: 86–92.

Psykoterapian merkitys terveydenhuollossa (The importance of psychotherapy in the general health care). *Psykologia*, 15: 327–338.

Vuorovaikutus yksilöpsykoterapiassa (Interaction in individual psychotherapy). *Publications of the Academy of Finland*, 18: 5–15.

1981

Persoonallisuus työvälineenä: mielenterveystyöntekijän henkilökohtaisista varusteista (Personality as working instrument: on the mental worker's personal aquipment). In: K. Achtè & J. Suominen (Eds.), Psykiatria 1979. *Publication in Honor of Toivo Pihkanen*, pp. 328–339, *Psychiatria Fennica*.

Psykoanlyyttisia näkökohtia sosiaalisesta ahdistuksesta ja sosiaalisista peloista (Psychoanalytic considerations of social anxiety and social fears). In: K. Achtè & A. Pakaslahti (Eds.), *Sosiaaliset pelot (Social Fears)* (pp. 91–110). Helsinki: Psykiatrian tutkimussäätiö.

Psychotherapie als phasenspezifische Interaktion (Psychotherapy as phase-specific interaction). *Jahrbuch der Psychoanalyse, 13*: 115–139.

The importance of psychotherapy in health care. *Psychiatria Fennica, 1981: 12*: 11–23.

1982

Fasspecifica aspekter i psykoterapi (Phase-specific aspects in psychotherapy). *Nordisk Psykiatrisk Tidsskrift. Psykiatr.Tidsskr., 36*: 105–113.

Sairausregressio parantamisen palveluksessa (Illness regression in the service of healing). *Publication in Honor of Erik Anttinen* (pp. 291–299). Helsinki: Societas pro Psychiatrica Fennica.

Potilasinformaatio potilas–lääkärisuhteessa (Informing the patient in the patient–doctor relationship). *Potilasinformaation käsikirja (Handbook of Patient Information II)* (pp. 40–76). Helsinki: Recallmed.

1983

Regressiivisista ilmiöistä ruumiillisesti sairaiden potilaiden hoitosuhteessa (On regressive phenomena in the treatment relationship with somatically ill patients). In: H. Jokela, L. Mensola, B. Z. Taajama & L. Taajama (Eds.), *Akuutti psykiatria (Acute Psychiatry)* (pp. 85–98). Helsinki: Recallmed.

Suomen psykiatriyhdistyksen psykoterapiatoimikunnan historia (The history of the psychotherapy section of the Finnish Psychiatric Association). In: T. Achtè, J. Suominen & T. Tamminen (Eds.), *Seitsemän vuosikymmentä suomalaista psykiatriaa (Seven decades of Finnish psychiatry)* (pp. 64–70). Helsinki: Suomen Psykiatriyhdistys ry.

Yliopistopsykiatrian kehitys Kuopiossa (The Development of University Psychiatry in Kuopio). In: T. Achtè, J. Suominen & T. Tamminen (Eds.), *Seisemän vuosikymmentä suomalaista psykiatriaa (Seven Decades of Finnish Psychiatry)* (pp. 32–35). Helsinki: Suomen Psykiatriyhdistys ry.

Psykiatrian suhteista arvoihin (Psychiatry and the values). *Suomen Psykiatriyhdistys seitsemänkymmentä vuotta 12.5.1983 (The Finnish Psychiatric Association 70 years 12. 5.1983)* (pp. 32–35). Helsinki: Suomen Psykiatriyhdistys ry.

1984

Hoitomyönteisyys ja potilas–lääkärisuhde (Compliance and the patient–doctor relationship). In: *Compliance—hoitomyönteisyys?* (pp. 14–20). Helsinki: Recallmed.

Personligheten som arbetsredskap. Om mentalvårdsarbetarens personliga utrustning (Personality as working instrument). *Nordisk Psykiatrisk Tidsskrift, 38*: 151–159.

Miten opettaa lääkärinä olemista (How to teach being a doctor). *Suomen Lääkärilehti, 39*: 818–823.

Dealing with object loss. *Scandinavian Psychoanalytic Review, 7*: 13–33.

Om psykiatrins relation till värden (Psychiatry and the values). *Nordisk Psykiatrisk Tidsskrift, 38*: 347–351.

Psychoanalytic treatment as a developmental continuum: considerations of disturbed structuralization and its phase-specific encounter. *Scandinavian Psychoanalytic Review, 7*: 133–159.

1985

De kliniska lärarna har nyckelrollen i undervisningen om att vara läkare (The clinical instructors play the key role in the instruction concerning the practice of medicine). *Nordisk Medicin, 100*: 236–238.

1987

On the early formation of the mind I: Differentiation. *International Journal of Psycho-Analysis, 68*: 229–250.

Menetysten psyykkisestä käsittelystä (On the mental management of losses). *Suomen Lääkärilehti, 33*: 3273–3278.

1988

On the early formation of the mind II: From differentiation to self and object constancy. *Psychoanalytic Study of the Child*, 43: 101–134.

1990

(With Viinamäki, H., & Koskela, K.) Interaction in health education. *International Journal of Social Psychiatry*, 36: 99–110.

1991

(With Viinamäki, H., & Koskela, K.) Unconscious factors in health education. *XIV World Congress on Health Education, Helsinki*. Abstract number 936.

1992

Menetyksen psyykkisestä käsittelystä (Mental dealing with experiences of loss). In: E. Roos, V. Manninen & J. Välimäki (Eds.), *Mielen ulottuvuudet* (*Dimensions of the Mind*) (pp. 31–49). Helsinki: Yliopistopaino.

1994

Depressioalttiuden merkityksestä ja psykodynamiikasta (Development and psychodynamics of the susceptibility to depression). *Duodecim*, 110: 267–276.

1997

Psykoanalyyttinen psykoterapia nykypäivän lääketieteessä (Psychoanalytic psychotherapy in the present day medicine) *Suomen Lääkärilehti*, 52: 2093–2099.

Muistelua ja ajatuksia Suomen Psykoanalyyttisen Yhdistyksen 25-vuotisjuhlapäivänä (Memoirs and thoughts on the Finnish Psychoanalytical Society's 25-year anniversary celebration) In: A. Laine, H. Parland & E. Roos (Eds.), *Psykoanalyysin uranuurtajat Suomessa* (*Finnish Pioneers of Psychoanalysis*) (pp. 53–70). Kemijärvi: Lapin Painotuote.

Veikko Tähkän puhe 70-vuotisjuhlassaan (Veikko Tähkä's talk in his 70th year celebration) In: A. Laine, H. Parland, & E. Roos (Eds.), *Psykoanalyysin uranuurtajat Suomessa* (*Finnish Pioneers of Psychoanalysis*) (pp. 211–214). Kemijärvi: Lapin Painotuote.

2001

Ihmismielen arvorakenteiden kehityksestä (Development of the psychic value structures) In: E. Roos, V. Manninen, & J. Välimäki (Eds.), *Rakkaus, toive, todellisuus* (*Love, Wish, Reality*) (pp. 14–39). Helsinki: Yliopistopaino.

INDEX

Abelin, E., 185, 197
Adler, 58, 60
affects/affect theory, 38, 42, 45,
    63–64, 121–124, 165, 170, 240,
    242–243, 246–247, 312
ageing, 34, 36, 46
    and death, 36, 39, 46
    patients, 33–34, 37–40, 42–45
    process, 30, 45, 48,
    psychoanalyst, 44–50
Alexander, F., 4, 6, 22
Araham, K., 33–34, 49, 51
Arlow, J., 123, 140
Ast, 120, 123, 129, 136, 138–139 141

Balint, M., 6, 35, 51–52
Benjamin, J., 60, 71
Benvenuto, B., 65, 71
Beres, D., 123, 140
Bergmann, M. S., 55–57, 59, 61–63,
    66–67, 72
Bibring, E., 4
Bion, W. R., 68, 199, 215

Bjork, S., 30
Blos, P., 49, 181, 194, 197
Blum, H. P., 60, 72
Böhm, 112, 115
Bollas, C., 188, 197
borderline (patient/state), 6, 8–12,
    14, 18–21, 24, 112, 115, 119–120,
    122, 129, 134, 145, 154–155,
    203
Bowlby, J., 6, 35, 52
Breuer, J., 1, 107, 277, 297
Britton, R., 189, 197
Bruschweiter-Stern, 111, 116,
    275–276
Bryan, D., 33–34, 49, 51
Burgner, M., 186, 192, 197
Busch, F., 64

Campell, D., 192, 197
Chaplin, C., 255–258
Chasseguet-Smirgel, J., 59–60, 72,
    244, 247, 301, 315
Clement, C., 65, 72

counter-transference, 283, 290–291,
    296
and complementary response,
    281–282, 284
and empathy, 279–280, 284
complications, 169
hazard, 168
impulses, 140
object, 16
reactions, 154
Curtius, E. R., 233–234

Damasio, A. R., 239, 242–243,
    247–248
Dare, C., , 278, 281, 299
Davids, M. F., 189, 197
Descartes, R., 235–240, 243–248
Deutsch, H., 279, 280, 297
Dicks, H. V., 24, 26
Dreher, A. U., 278, 299
Drewermann, E., 221, 223
dual drive theory, 63–64
dyad/dyadic relationship, 35, 66,
    163, 176–177, 179, 181–182, 184–
    186, 189–190, 192, 195, 287, 314

ego psychology, 5–6, 24, 61, 70,
    278–280, 285
ego-ideal, 15, 37–38, 43
Eissler, K. R., 2, 23–24, 26, 146, 156,
    279, 297
Emde, R., 281, 298
Enckell, H., 247–248, 254, 258, 261,
    272, 276
Enckell, M., 225,
English, A. C., 73, 98
English, H. B., 73, 98
Erikson, E. H., 35–36, 52, 97–98
erotic/eroticism/erotism/, 45, 62,
    64–65, 77, 128–129, 158–159,
    161–163, 167–173, 218–220, 228
Escalona, S., 35, 52

Fairbairn, W. R. D., 6, 35, 52, 63
fantasy/phantasy, 19, 40, 42, 45–46,
    78–81, 83–84, 87–89, 91–96, 98,

119, 121–140, 146–147, 154, 159,
    163–167, 173, 175, 179, 187, 200,
    203–204, 212, 255
father's/analyst's penis, 123, 126,
    133, 138, 165, 188, 257
father/father–child relationship,
    123–124, 128, 130–133, 135, 145,
    149, 150–152, 155–156, 165, 167,
    172, 175–197, 209–210, 212, 244,
    253, 286, 302, 309–310, 313–314
analyst/father, 127, 131
identification with, 134, 165, 184,
    188, 190
oedipal, 133, 135–138
victimizing/traumatizing,
    124–126
–man, 181–184, 190, 192–193, 195
Federn, E., 252, 258
Fenichel, H., 280, 298
Fenichel, O., 34, 36, 52, 121, 140
Ferenczi, S., 57–58, 62, 72, 280, 298
Finnish Psychoanalytical Society, 7,
    29, 51, 297, 326
Fliess, R., 280, 298
Folch, P. 199
Folch, T. E., 199
Fonagy, P., 112–113, 115, 180–181,
    185–186, 189, 197–198
Freud, A., 4–5, 35, 52, 67, 278, 298
Freud, S., 1–4, 8–9, 14, 19, 22–23, 26,
    31–34, 42, 52, 55–66, 70–71, 73,
    76–78, 80, 82, 90, 98–99,
    101–109, 114–117, 119, 121–122,
    140, 146–147, 156–157, 164, 173,
    196–197, 201–202, 213, 215, 233,
    240–241, 244–246, 248, 251–254,
    256–258, 261–264, 274–275,
    277–278, 280, 297–298
Fromm, E., 60, 63, 72
Fromm-Reichmann, F., 4, 6, 23, 26
functional object(s)/relatedness, 15,
    309, 315
Furman, E., 313, 315–316

Gadamer, H.-G., 261, 263–264, 268,
    270, 272, 274, 276

Galenson, 163, 173
Gammelgaard, J., 244, 248
Gedo, J. E., 5, 9, 13, 25–26
genital/genitalia/pregenital, 40,
    133, 163–165, 167, 188, 257–258,
    308
Gill, M. M., 4, 6, 26
Gittelson, M., 62, 66
Glover, E., 2, 26
Goldberg, A., 9, 13, 25–26, 112
Gray, P., 64
Green, A., 108, 116, 253, 258
Greenacre, P., 35, 52
Greenson, R., 5, 280–281, 298
Grunberger, B., 59–60
guilt, 36, 46, 128, 131, 165, 189, 203,
    208, 230, 253, 308, 313

Habermas, J., 7, 261–264, 274, 276
Hägglund, T.-B., 191, 197
Hägglund, V., 191, 197
Halgrimsson, O., 256, 258
Hardin, H. T., 252, 258
Harrison, A., 111, 116, 275–276
Hartmann, H., 5, 11, 35, 52, 61,
    278–279, 297–298, 322
Heidgger, M., 261
Heimann, P., 35, 53, 281–282, 298
Helmholtz, H. von, 101–109, 114,
    116
heterosexual/homosexual/
    monosexual, 158–159, 161,
    163–170, 173, 228, 304–305,
    314
Hoffer, W., 242, 248
Holder, A., 278, 281, 299
Horney, K., 57, 60, 63, 67, 72

identification(s), 15, 18, 59, 106, 120,
    134, 140, 147, 154, 165, 177,
    182–185, 190, 192–194, 242, 280,
    296
Ikonen, P., 86, 99, 191, 197, 217
incest/incestuous, 124, 128, 132,
    203
Inderbitzen, L. B., 123, 140

Innes-Smith, J., 254, 258
internalization(s), 15, 21, 25, 75, 82,
    93, 161, 184, 186, 189
International Psychoanalytical
    Association (IPA), 2, 29, 47, 68
introjection(s), 15, 17–18, 150,
    159–161, 296
Isaacs, S., 35, 53

Jacobson, E., 15, 35, 52, 60
Jacobson, E., 35, 52, 60
Jaques, E., 36–37, 52
Jones, E., 2, 27
Jones, M., 24
Joseph, B., 202, 215
Jung, C. G., 57, 59, 62

Kant, I., 101–105, 116, 220
Kaplan, B., 125, 141
Kennedy, R., 65, 71
Kernberg, O. F., 5–6, 10–11, 15, 55,
    60, 63–64, 66, 70, 72, 285, 298
Kestenberg, J., 188, 198
Khan, M. M. R., 35, 38, 52
King, P., 29, 52–53, 72
Kjellqvist, 114
Klauber, J., 75–78, 99
Klein, M., 6, 35–36, 53, 58, 60–62, 67
Klockars, L., 175, 182, 198
Knight, R. P., 4–5, 7, 24, 27
Kohut, H., 5–6, 10–11, 15, 63, 68,
    110, 116, 280, 298

Lacan, J., 60, 65–66, 110, 116,
    180–181, 189, 198
Laine, A., 30, 53, 301
Lehtonen, J., 235, 241, 248
Leroy, M., 244–246
Levy, S. T., 123, 140
Lewin, B. D. 241, 248
life-cycle, 32–34, 36, 38, 41–43,
    45–47, 49–50
Lipps, T., 104, 116
Loewald, H. W., 4, 16, 21, 78–80, 96,
    99, 113, 115–116, 280, 282–283,
    286, 290, 296, 299

Longfellow, H. W., 29, 51, 53
Lyons-Ruth, K., 111, 116, 275–276

Mahler, M., 6, 11, 15, 58, 181, 198,
    240, 248
Main, T. F., 37, 53
Makari, G. J., 101–103, 105–107, 116
Marcuse, H., 60
Marx, K., 60, 263
McDougall, J., 157, 161, 173, 181,
    198, 257–258, 313, 316
McGuire, W., 59, 72
Meltzer, D., 200, 215
menopause, 32
metapsychology, 14, 162
Meyer, A., 4, 24
Milner, M., 44, 53
Modell, A. H., 82, 86–88, 99
Money-Kyrle, R. A., 35, 53
Moore, G. E., 238, 248
Morgan, A., 111, 116, 275–276
mother–infant/child relationship,
    58, 62–63, 74–75, 82, 87, 91, 95,
    110–111, 113–114, 120, 130, 135,
    159–163, 172, 175–177, 179–184,
    189, 242, 252–253, 301–315
mother–whore, 191
mother–woman/wife–woman,
    178–179, 191, 195
mourning, 19, 43, 95, 140, 164

Nahum, J., 111, 116, 275–276
narcissistic (disorder/state), 6, 10,
    25, 37–39, 41, 110, 115, 122,
    129–130, 134, 146, 161, 163–165,
    181, 188, 257, 309, 313
Neubauer, P. B., 49
Nietzsche, F. W., 263
Nunberg, H., 252, 258

object(s), 16–19, 25, 35–38, 43–44, 73,
    75, 90–94, 103–105, 107, 110,
    125, 132, 145, 148–149, 157, 178,
    182, 186, 205, 207, 213, 232,
    262–263, 266–268, 272, 277, 282,
    285, 292–293, 297, 309

addictive, 160–161
analyst as an, 113, 140, 264–265,
    268, 272–273, 284, 289–291,
    294–296, 315
and sexual aim/choice, 157,
    159–160, 168–170, 219–220
bad, 91, 150
cathexes, 38
destroyed/neglected, 208
developmental/new
    developmental, 17–18, 21–22,
    82, 86–87, 89, 94, 97, 120,
    265–266, 272, 283–286, 289, 294,
    296–297, 301, 315
good, 86, 94
identification, 190, 192–193,
    280
-images, 89, 92, 121–122, 124
investment, 313
-libido/libidinal, 37, 83
loss(es), 124
love, 184–185, 190, 217, 219,
    221–222
mother-, 242, 246
of idealization, 183–184, 195
partial/total, 201
-related child, 147
relation(s)/ship(s)/relatedness,
    16, 21, 24, 35, 63–64, 74–75, 78,
    91, 110, 123–124, 134, 138–139,
    147, 161, 184, 187, 189, 195, 201,
    240, 264, 279, 281, 284–285,
    290–291, 296
transitional, 81, 160–161
world, 74, 98, 150
oedipal, 88, 123, 177, 179
areas of the psyche, 286
conflicts/issues/turmoil, 56,
    62–63, 125, 134–136, 194–195,
    314
constellation, 58, 164
crisis, 163–164
development/pre-development
    phases, 58, 66, 192–194, 287,
    313
fantasy, 123–125

father, 126, 133, 138
junction, 184, 187–188, 196
love, 191
object(s), 15, 19
parents (relationship with, 19,
    177, 314
–phallic phase, 163
relationship, 187–188, 314
situation, 66, 179, 186, 191, 203
solutions, 257
son, 190–191
struggle, 130
transference, 126
triangle, 189
triumph, 128
Oedipus, 51, 133, 178, 191
complex, 257
omnipotence/omnipotent, 37,
    74–75, 91–92, 94, 151,
    181–182–183, 190, 193–194, 210,
    232–233, 255, 301

Parland, H., 53
penis, 129, 135–139. 171, 178, 188,
    308–309
detachable, clay, 125–126, 129
envy, 60
good/bad, 126
lost/castrated, 136–137
–man, 189
super-, 138
phallic
desire, 178
defence, 191
–narcissistic, 188, 309
pleasure, 191
stage, 192
phallicism, 191–192
Piaget, J., 185, 198, 241
Pine, F., 115–116, 198, 248
primal scene, 122, 131, 163, 168, 170,
    187, 309
Proust, M., 227–230, 233
psychoanalysis, 1–8, 12–14, 19–20,
    22–25, 31–33, 43, 45–47, 49–50,
    76, 92, 101, 109, 111, 115, 123,

125, 253–254, 256, 262–264, 266,
    271, 277–278, 284, 286, 302–303,
    310
and analytic trainng, 254
and early development, 113
and empathy, 279–280
and Marxism, 60
and natural science, 279
and psychotherapy, 291
and religion, 59
and symbol/metaphor, 275–276
and the value of people, 223
birth of, 101
classical, 3, 19, 123, 251
clinical aim/goal of, 107–108,
    255
conceptual space of, 251–258
dissidence in, 55–71
French, 108
hermeneutics and, 261–262, 274
of children, 284
sexual theory and, 161
therapeutic action of, 282
therapeutic tool of, 121
psychotherapy (psychoanalytic), 1,
    3, 5–8, 13–14, 20, 23–24, 32, 71,
    81, 112, 291, 302–303
psychotic (patient/state), 4, 7–12,
    14, 17–21, 25–26, 45, 84, 115,
    120–121, 130, 134, 166–167,
    170–171, 229, 253
puberty/pre-puberty (and adoles-
    cence), 32, 34, 41, 43, 149, 156

Rangell, L., 4, 47, 49, 253, 258
Rank, 57–58, 62
Rapaport, D., 35, 53
Rechardt, E., 30, 86, 101, 107, 111,
    116, 321
Reich, A., 282, 299
Reich, W., 57, 60
Rickman, J., 35, 53
Ricoeur, P., 7, 261–264, 269–271,
    274–276
Riviere, J., 35, 53
Roiphe, 163, 173

Roos, E., 53
Rosenfeld, D., 23, 27, 121, 140, 189, 198
Rosenfeld, H. A., 23, 27, 121, 140

Salonen, S., 242, 249, 251, 253, 259
Sander, L., 111, 116, 275–276
Sandler, A.-M., 143, 146, 156, 200, 215, 289
Sandler, J., 146, 156, 200, 215, 278, 281, 285, 289, 299
Schafer, R., 262, 280, 282, 299
schizophrenic, 17
Schleiermacher, F., 261
Segal, H., 36, 50, 53, 64, 72
self-ideal, 15, 95
self–object/relatedness/
    differentiation, 15, 98, 140, 143, 147–148, 150, 155, 162, 184, 240, 273–274
separation anxiety, 15, 128, 313
sexual abuse, 62, 171
sexual/sexuality/sexualizing/
    neosexuality, 25, 31, 37, 39–41, 62–63, 71, 145, 156–157–173, 181–182, 187–191, 194, 196, 219–220, 228, 256–257, 277, 305–306, 308–309, 314
shame/shameful, 40, 86, 92–94, 113–114, 149, 155, 188, 191, 204, 253, 308, 310
Sharpe, E., 201, 215, 280, 299
sibling(s), 40, 56, 123–124, 130, 150–151
Sirola, R., 182, 198
Sjovall, T., 29–30
Spitz, R. A., 35, 53–54, 241, 247, 249, 282, 299
Steiner, R., 67, 72, 262, 276
Stern, D., 110–112, 115–116, 186, 195, 240–241, 249, 275–276
Stoller, R., 171, 173, 181, 198
Stone, L., 4, 25, 27, 281, 299
Strachey, A., 33–34, 49, 51
Strachey, J., 32, 54, 108, 296, 299

Symington, N., 76, 99
Tähkä, R., 73, 267–268, 274, 276, 295, 299
Tähkä, V., 1, 3, 5, 7–10, 12–17, 19–23, 25–27, 29–30, 51, 71–72, 82–85, 87, 89–90, 95, 99, 112–113, 115–116, 119–120, 125, 134, 141, 143, 150, 154–156, 176, 180–182, 184, 186, 198, 240, 249, 256, 259, 264–266, 276, 279–280, 282–286, 292–293, 295–296, 299, 314–318, 322, 327
Taine, H., 104, 116
Target, 180–181, 185–186, 189, 197–198
theory of development, 14, 16
Tonick, E., 111, 116, 275–276
transference(s), 9, 11, 21, 24, 40, 42–43, 49, 62, 64–65, 68–69, 71, 76–77, 85–86, 88, 91, 101, 106–107, 133, 151, 202–203, 254–256, 265, 267, 283, 287, 290–291, 294–295
    analysis, 65, 295
    and counter-transference, 65–66, 162
      special problems of, 45–46
    and erotic feelings, 129
    and memory, 109, 111–114
    and the theory of dreams, 107–108, 214
    as metaphor, 272
    child, 16, 85–86, 90, 286, 293
    dependent/containing, 87
    drama of, 79, 214
    expectations, 95
    figure(s), 43
    iconic/projective, 86
    illusion/fantasy, 76–82, 84–85, 88, 90, 93–95, 97, 267, 274
    images/manifestations, 120, 147, 154, 267
    interpretation of, 108
    issues, 128
    love, 76–77, 80

neurosis, 1, 8–9, 17, 19, 42, 79–81, 87, 127, 130, 132, 291, 293
    object, 83, 113
    reflections, 137, 256, 258
    regression, 285, 289, 293, 295
    solution, 92
    the role of, 111–112
    wish, 83–86, 89
triad/triadic relationship, 66, 176–177, 182, 185–187, 189, 192, 195
Tyson, P., 240, 249
Tyson, R. L., 240, 249

vagina, 131–133, 165, 188
    dentata, 132–133
    –woman, 189
Välimäki, J., 277
Vangaard, T., 29

Viderman, S., 254, 259
Volkan, V. D., 119–121, 123, 129, 141

Wallerstein, R. S., 1, 3–5, 25, 27–28, 256, 259, 279, 285, 300
Werner, H., 125, 141
White, E., 233–234
Winnicott, D. W., 6, 15, 29, 35, 38, 51, 54, 58, 74–75, 80–82, 84, 89, 94, 99, 159–160, 241–242, 246, 249, 252–253, 259, 281–282, 300, 315–316
Wolff, P. H., 241, 249
Wride, F., 29
Wright, H. von, 238–239
Wundt, W., 104–105, 117

Zachrisson, A., 189, 198
Zetzel, E., 5